ABOUT THE AUTHOR

Gaby Naher is the author of two novels, *The Underwharf* and *Bathing in Light*, and of the acclaimed memoir *The Truth About My Fathers*. She is also a Tibet activist and a director of the Australia Tibet Council, an NGO that campaigns for the basic rights of the Tibetan people.

Gaby lives in Sydney with her husband and daughter.

Also by Gaby Naher

The Underwharf

Bathing in Light

The Truth About My Fathers

Praise for *Wrestling the Dragon*:

'In a world desperate for spiritual leadership, the Karmapa's escape over the Himalayas in 1999 created headline news.

'Gaby Naher has entwined Tibetan history, Indian politics, religious intrigue and her own pilgrimage to explain the Karmapa's ongoing quest for freedom.

'This is a riveting story of a courageous young Tibetan lama, tracked by China, gagged by India and yet full of promise for the world.'

Senator Bob Brown

GABY NAHER

WRESTLING THE DRAGON

IN SEARCH OF THE BOY LAMA WHO DEFIED CHINA

V

VINTAGE

A Vintage Book
Published by
Random House Australia Pty Ltd
20 Alfred Street, Milsons Point, NSW 2061
http://www.randomhouse.com.au

Sydney New York Toronto
London Auckland Johannesburg

National Library of Australia
Cataloguing-in-Publication Entry

    Naher, Gaby, 1967- .
    Wrestling the dragon : in search of the boy lama who defied
    China.

    ISBN 1 74051 279 0.

    1. Dalai Lamas. 2. Buddhism and state - China - Tibet. 3.
    Communism and Buddhism - Tibet. 4. Tibet (China) - History
    - 1951- . I. Title.

951.506092

Cover and internal design by Nanette Backhouse, Saso Design
Cover photograph of Karmapa © Angus McDonald;
cover photograph of Tibetan scene © Galen Rowell APL/Corbis;
back cover dragon image courtesy of the Norbulingka Institute
Typeset by Midland Typesetters, Maryborough, Victoria
Printed and bound by Griffin Press, Netley, South Australia

10 9 8 7 6 5 4 3 2 1

LIST OF ILLUSTRATIONS

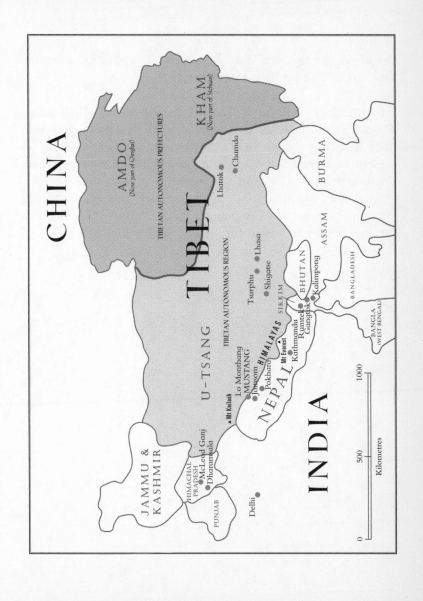

On being questioned about his purpose, Peter Matthiessen, in his book *The Snow Leopard*, writes:

'I shrugged, uncomfortable. To say I was interested in blue sheep or snow leopards, or even in remote lamaseries, was no answer to his question, though all of that was true; to say I was making a pilgrimage seemed fatuous and vague, though in some sense that was true as well. And so I admitted that I did not know. How could I say that I wished to penetrate the secrets of the mountains in search of something still unknown that, like the yeti, might well be missed for the very fact of searching?'

AUTHOR'S NOTE

Those readers who come to this book with some prior knowledge of Tibet's XVIIth Karmapa will be aware that there is more than one claimant for the title. They may even know that according to some in the Karmapa's Karma Kagyu school, there are two rival 'candidates'. The reader should therefore know from the outset that this book tells the story of the young man given the name Ogyen Trinley Dorje at his enthronement in 1992. He is the one called Karmapa by the majority of the Kagyu school, by most Tibetans, and by the Dalai Lama. While I will give an account of the controversy surrounding the claim to the title, this book does not attempt to decide the validity of those claims. Who am I, an *inji* or Westerner, to pronounce on such things?

I would also like to acknowledge some key sources at the outset: Michele Martin's fine book, *Music in the Sky: The Life, Art and Teachings of the 17th Karmapa,* on which I have relied for certain details about the Karmapa's childhood and his escape from Tibet; Tsering Shakya's outstanding book, *Dragon in the Land of Snows, A History of Modern Tibet Since 1947;* and the beautiful *Karmapa, the Sacred Prophecy* published by Kagyu Thubten Chöling. Without these resources I would not have been able to write this book.

While I work in a voluntary capacity as one of the directors of the Australia Tibet Council, and am currently chair of its Board, the views expressed in this book are my own.

To protect the privacy of those who shared their stories with me, some names have been changed. While I have relied on the scholarship and expertise of many friends and colleagues, all errors are my own.

DECEMBER 1999
JANUARY 2000
ORIGINS OF THE KARMAPA

December 1999

On 27 December 1999, the Karmapa announced to his monk and lay fraternity at Tsurphu Monastery, near Lhasa, that he was entering a strict twenty-one-day retreat. This was the trigger that moved the escape plan into its final phase. The four-wheel-drive vehicle that would transport the party was brought to the monastery and those who would be travelling with the Karmapa started to spin the tales that would give their absence, at least initially, a legitimate appearance.

At Tsurphu, Lama Nyima, the Karmapa's tutor who normally stayed in his master's quarters by night and served him by day, would remain to make the various devotional noises that would normally be associated with the Karmapa's retreat. Lama Nyima knew that he was putting his life at risk, but if his master reached freedom then this would be an acceptable price to pay. The cook, Thubten, would come and go, bringing his master's meals and taking away the empty bowls afterwards, and all would appear perfectly regular. Lama Tsultrim and the driver, Dargye, had already received permission to travel away from the monastery in the vehicle they'd been preparing for the last few days.

The journey would take at least seven days. While it was likely that they would be driving off-road, over difficult terrain, they knew, also, that they would have to walk. The departure time was confirmed in code over the telephone. The party had decided upon ten-thirty pm, when the monks who were guarding the monastery that night would be absorbed in some particularly gripping television. What's more, those on the security shift – some of whom were known to be Chinese sympathisers – would be unlikely to venture outside in the biting cold of that winter's night.

In his own room, the Karmapa was making his final preparations to leave all he knew and loved. He had written a letter of explanation, stating that he was leaving so he could receive the *dharma* (Buddhist teachings) from his teachers, as he had requested many times. In it, he also promised that he would be returning to Tibet and asserted that he was not turning against the country, or the Chinese. Alongside his own letter, which would be widely misquoted by the Chinese, he left a letter from the Dalai Lama in which the Tibetan leader had specifically asked the young Karmapa to 'serve the teachings in Tibet'. In the tradition of so many other great lamas who had fled Tibet before him, the Karmapa changed into lay clothing for his escape journey, wearing a scarf, hat and glasses to make his disguise all the more convincing.

This journey was a far cry from the Karmapa's other trip west in 1992, when he was a young *tulku* being taken to Tsurphu for his enthronement. It was, however, every bit as significant.

JANUARY 2000

One of the most senior Tibetan religious figures, the XVIIth Karmapa, Ugyen Trinley Dorje, has left Tibet, arriving in Dharamsala in India two days ago, according to an official spokesperson for the Tibetan government in exile. The 14-year-old boy, head of one of the four major schools of Tibetan Buddhism and the first Tibetan Buddhist reincarnation to be recognised by both the Dalai Lama and the Chinese authorities, is reported to have arrived at the seat of the exile government and home to the Dalai Lama at 10.30 on the morning of 5 January. According to his followers in the West his arrival followed a seven-day journey on foot from his monastery in Tibet.

A *Xinhua* report, acknowledging that the Karmapa has left his monastery in Tibet, said that he left behind a letter which stated that he had gone abroad to collect 'the musical instruments of the Buddhist mass' and the 'black hats' used by previous Karmapas. The report, dated 7 January, also quoted the Karmapa as saying in his letter that his actions did not mean that he intended to 'betray the state, the nation, the monastery or the leadership'.

Tibet Information Network, 7 January 2000[1]

The Chinese government was obviously thunder-struck at the escape of the young man who was, until last week, its key trophy lama. Whatever it was that impelled the young 17th Karmapa to risk his life in his week-long trek to India, picking up a hat and some musical instruments, however significant the objects, is unlikely to be the whole story. When the government decided to publish the note it said the Karmapa had left, it only succeeded in making itself more ridiculous.

The Karmapa, the government spokesman insisted, had meant no disloyalty towards the Chinese State. Never mind that he had left illegally after a dazz-lingly successful act of deception and turned up on the doorstep of the Dalai Lama, Beijing's arch-enemy, routinely described by the Chinese government as a 'religious fraud' and 'traitor to the motherland'. What mattered, apparently, was that the Karmapa had meant no harm by it.

The Guardian, 10 January 2000[2]

ORIGINS OF THE KARMAPA

Many in the West know one thing only about Tibetan Buddhism, and that is the name of its leader and figurehead, the Dalai Lama. Some know that he is the fourteenth in a line of incarnations, but many Westerners – including those with particularly close knowl-edge of Tibet's history – might struggle to define the nature of reincarnation. At times, I find I am one of them, yet some understanding of the concept of reincarnation is as important to grasping the Karmapa's story as a familiarity with contemporary Tibetan history. Consequently, I take any opportunity to discuss reincarnation with believers and sceptics alike. Some may doubt my credentials to write of Tibet and its Karmapa because of this uncertainty. I like to think, however, that my constant questioning on the subject enables me to present the Karmapa's story in a manner that is accessible to all, not just to Buddhists.

The XVIIth Karmapa is believed to possess the same consciousness as all of the previous Karmapas. According to Tibetan Buddhism, when each sentient being dies, its consciousness returns to the earth in another living being. It is only the most enlightened beings, however, who actually choose where and when their consciousness will return to earth. The Karmapa is one of these enlightened beings, as is the Dalai Lama. Not only does he actively choose his rebirth, but the knowledge of all of his predecessors is reborn in the new being. Thus the notion of lineage is not merely an issue of the continuation of a name or a title – as it is in the West – but of a whole body of wisdom and learning.

Buddhism itself originated in India more than 2500 years ago with a young man named Siddhartha. He meditated until he attained enlightenment and became 'the one who is awake', known as Buddha. His teachings spread to many of India's neighbours over the course of centuries. Buddhism was introduced to Tibet in the seventh century by King Songsten Gampo and is the primary religion of contemporary Tibetans. Buddhist teachings – *dharma* – are passed across generations from an enlightened master to his most promising student in a method known as 'transmission'.

The Dalai Lama incarnations have served as Tibetan leaders since his Gelug school of Buddhism gained precedence over the Kagyu school in the seventeenth century. The other schools are the Nyingma and the Sakya, but even as Tibet's temporal leader the Dalai Lama does not have religious authority over the other three schools. The XVIth Karmapa, although technically the leader of one of the four major sub-schools within the Kagyu school (the Karma Kagyu), was far and away the highest profile leader within that school because of his personality and charisma. The XVIIth Karmapa seems to have inherited this profile as well.

The oldest school of Tibetan Buddhism, the Nyingma, was founded in the eighth century at the invitation of King Trisong Detsen. The school's head, Penor Rinpoche, currently lives in exile in Bylakuppe, southern India.

The Sakya school dates back to the eleventh century. Its head, Sakya Trizin, lives in Rajpur, northern India.

The Dalai Lama's school, the Gelug, was founded in the fourteenth century by a student of the IVth Karmapa, Je Tsongkhapa. This, the youngest and largest of the Tibetan Buddhist schools, advocates strict adherence to monastic discipline and scholarship as the basis for religious practice.

The XVIIth Karmapa is leader of the Karma Kagyu school, which has its roots in tenth-century India with the enlightened teacher, Tilopa. Before Tilopa (988–1069) gained enlightenment, he spent twelve years meditating in a charnel ground and another six working for a prostitute by night and pressing oil from sesame seeds by day. The Karma Kagyu lineage is distinguished by secret meditation instructions that are passed orally from master to student. The unbroken succession of these teachings is known as The Golden Rosary.

Tilopa passed his teachings to the scholar Naropa (1016–1100), who in turn passed them to Marpa the Translator (1012–1097). Marpa subsequently passed the teachings to Milarepa (1052–1135) and from Milarepa they went to Gampopa (1079–1135). It was one of Gampopa's students who would go on to become the first Karmapa.

PART ONE

25 SEPTEMBER 2003
LINEAGE: THE FIRST KARMAPA
THE BOY LAMA: LOGA
TIBET

25 September 2003

I am sitting in an aeroplane on the tarmac at Sydney's Kingsford-Smith Airport and tears are pooling in the corners of my eyes. Every book I've ever written has opened with a flight and this one is no different. Never before, however, have I felt quite so compromised about leaving home. Never before have all my powers of reason and logic nagged at me so keenly . . . What am I doing? Ever since the first enthusiastic reaction to the proposal I'd written for a book on Tibet's XVIIth Karmapa, a proposal that had flowed from me effortlessly as though it had come to me in a dream, I had started asking myself what possibly could have possessed me. What's this young man to me? How did I ever let the idea of him get under my skin?

In January, before I mentally embarked on this journey, I'd sit at my desk, looking westward. On a clear day, I could see Sydney's Blue Mountains – out there on the horizon, beyond the red tiled roofs – but it was not their canyonesque majesty for which I hankered. The mother of a one-year-old child, what I craved was something far less familiar than this wilderness region on my own city's fringe. I dreamed of something more remote. I dreamed of the Himalayas, rich in stories that seem to me to span worlds, not just cultures.

Since my daughter was born, I have felt both blessed and trapped. I have known moments of absolute joy and moments of utter despair. I have felt both liberated from earthly dross, yet utterly shackled to it. Isla is a bright, alert, smiling child with tight, ash-blonde curls. At her first Christmas, she was so astounded by her new world that she kept her little eyes open for thirteen consecutive hours, instead of for the single hour that baby books advised was appropriate for an infant of her age. Even more than a year later, the world remained so exciting to her that sleep was impossible anywhere but in her own bed, at home. And I, the mother at home at my desk while she slept, or out in the park or library with her while she was awake, frittered away days and hours of my precious writing time, dreaming of other worlds, looking beyond domesticity towards other horizons. I lived in abject terror of losing my *self* in mothering.

I was between books – the publicity finished for the memoir I had published six months earlier – and I was ruminating over what might come next. I dismissed the long-coveted plan of a book on the mysterious disappearance of a Swiss anthropologist, on the basis that its research would involve travel in both the remote highlands of Borneo and in Switzerland. I could not picture Isla, with her lily-white skin and mosquito allergy, in Borneo. Nor did I think my writerly budget could accommodate a second book researched in Switzerland; my last book, the family memoir, had taken me on a father quest that encompassed Switzerland, Ireland and Canada. Nonetheless, I continued to speculate on the anthropologist's story and what its writing would involve.

In what I thought of as my third job – that is, in addition to being a mother and a writer – I was, and still am, one of the directors of an Australian non-government organisation, the Australia Tibet Council. It campaigns to achieve United Nations Resolution 1723 of 1961, calling for 'the cessation of practices which deprive the Tibetan people of their fundamental human rights and freedoms, including their right to self-determination'. As such, my head was already daily in the Himalayan region, in that I read most everything that was published on Tibet and the Tibetan diaspora.

When I got to my computer one January morning, once our part-time nanny had Isla giggling in delight across the hallway, I read what would, for me, prove to be a very fateful feature story. A Tibetan news service had posted an article that had just appeared in the *Sunday Times Magazine* in London. It was entitled 'A God in Exile' and was about a young man whose story I was already vaguely familiar with: Tibet's XVIIth Karmapa.

> There's a rumour that he [the Karmapa] is about to appear on his balcony, and a crowd of devotees is gathering outside his home, perched high in the foothills

of the Himalayas. There are, among others, Tibetan schoolgirls carrying devotional white scarves waiting to catch a glimpse of him, several policeman and a couple of government intelligence officials. A few feet away, one man is armed with an AK-47. The authorities are there not only to protect him and make sure his followers don't get too close, but also to keep him under lock and key.

Ugyen Trinley Dorje is the 17th incarnation of the Karmapa, leader of one of Tibet's four main schools of Buddhism, the influential Karma Kagyu. He occupies a unique position: since his recognition as the 17th Karmapa in 1992, his legitimacy has been acknowledged not only by the Dalai Lama, but also by China. He is the first incarnate lama to be officially recognised by Beijing since 1959, perhaps in deference to historical tradition – previous Karmapas had been gurus to the emperors of China. The Dalai Lama, the focus of all Tibetan groups, is now 67, and when he dies Ugyen will most likely become one of the most influential spiritual and political figures in the world, with a following of millions. Which makes him, if you like, a kind of deity-in-waiting.

He is . . . a religious leader for the 21st century. He may be a 10th-level Bodhisattva – one at the threshold of enlightenment who works for the benefit of all beings – but he's also pretty proficient on a PlayStation. The senior monks say he beats them every time, skillfully downing virtual planes and crashing cars with gusto. 'I really enjoy rap music, though I don't understand the words yet,' Ugyen says. Then he pauses. 'I also enjoy some Chinese instrumental music. Music is meant to make you happy, but I sometimes find I can't listen to it, because it makes me sad.' He finds in poetry and painting a freedom that is missing from his real life. And in a distinct tone of wistfulness, he says: 'The westerners I've met have lots of freedom; I find them to be very open-minded and easy-going.'

'A God in Exile' by Kate Saunders, Sunday Times Magazine, 5 January 2003

By the time I had finished reading the piece, I had decided what I would be doing with the next two years of my life. I had decided that Ogyen Trinley Dorje, the XVIIth Karmapa, was the one whose personal story would bring Tibet's struggle to a whole new generation of readers. I also knew I had to write of him quickly, while he was still a young man, poised to leave his mark. I was, I admit, intrigued by the prospect that this handsome young lama – born in a nomad's tent in Tibet's east and hand-fed by the occupying Chinese – might go on to lead the Tibetans once the Dalai Lama could no longer do so himself. I cannot recall ever having made such a rash decision . . .

Now, as the aeroplane's jets fire up and I am hurtled down the runway, the tears start to roll down my cheeks. When we ascend from the tarmac, I feel a stab of near-physical pain. I first experienced something like this at Isla's birth; I had imagined that she and I would maintain our intimate physical contact for days after her birth but, only moments after she was born, the midwives took her away from me because she was not breathing.

Isla is now eighteen months old and to date we have been separated only once, and then just for a single night. I'm no full-time mother; indeed, I've continued my work as a writer since my daughter was five weeks old, but I have always known that she was just down the hallway. As I sat at my desk in my study, part of me remained attuned to the unfolding of each moment of her day. I knew whether she'd slept, whether she'd eaten and, most importantly, had been able to hear her laughter and squeals of delight, as she played somewhere just nearby.

Yet, since my pregnancy with Isla, as much as I dreamed of mothering her, I dreamed of books that would take me from her. The rainforests of Borneo, the high valleys of Tibet, and, finally, the Indian Himalayas. I struggle to be a mother, struggle to be a writer, and struggle hardest to be both.

And so here I sit, watching the detail of the city in which I live with my daughter and husband blur as the plane ascends. Here I sit, clutching pages of notes on a young Tibetan lama, the Karmapa. At home in my study there are two signed contracts for a book that I have proposed to write on the Karmapa, on the young Ogyen Trinley Dorje.

LINEAGE: THE FIRST KARMAPA

The XVIIth Karmapa traces his direct lineage back to 1110, when Dusum Khyenpa (1110–1193) was born in Kham, in eastern Tibet. He would become known as the first Karmapa. As a child, educated by his parents who were accomplished Buddhist practitioners, Dusum Khyenpa mastered the ability of leaving imprints of his hands and feet in solid rock. He became a monk at sixteen and met his teacher, Gampopa, when he was thirty. After his teacher's death, Dusum Khyenpa promised that he would live until eighty-four, so he could teach *dharma* and help all sentient beings. He had already attained enlightenment by the age of fifty and his name, which means 'Knower of the Past, Present and Future', reflects that state. He is credited with miracles such as restoring sight to the blind, curing sickness and ending wars.

On Dusum Khyenpa's head appeared a mystical crown that would materialise magically over the head of each Karmapa, on into the future. The hat, said to have been made from hair offered by 1,300,000 *dakinis* (or goddesses), had been fashioned centuries earlier but only appeared in Tibet, for the first time, upon Dusum Khyenpa's head. This mystical hat, called the Vajra crown, crown apparently is visible only to those 'who have the capacity to see it', such as particularly enlightened practitioners. The black hat to which the Chinese government referred when Ogyen Trinley Dorje fled Tibet in 1999 is a replica of this sacred, mythical original.

Dusum Khyenpa was accomplished in meditation and in the other practices that had been transmitted to him by his teachers. He established a number of monasteries in his lifetime, the most notable of which was Tsurphu, in the Tölung Valley northwest of Lhasa. Tsurphu went on to become the seat, or head monastery, of the Karma Kagyu school, of which the XVIIth Karmapa is now the leader.

One of Buddhism's most fundamental tenets holds that one's soul or consciousness returns to inhabit another newborn living being. Of particular significance to Tibetan Buddhists, Dusum Khyenpa was the first in the history of enlightened Buddhist masters to intentionally reincarnate as a particular master. In a letter that is known as 'the Sealed Words of the Last Testament', Dusum Khynpa predicted exactly where his consciousness would reawaken. Almost every successive Karmapa has predicted where, when and to which parents he would reincarnate. These details, recorded in similar documents, are usually given to one of the Karmapa's closest devotees for safekeeping with instructions about an auspicious time for reading the text.

As he predicted, Dusum Khyenpa died aged eighty-four. His heart and tongue, representing his realisation and pure speech, were said to have been found intact in the ashes of his funeral pyre, along with pieces of his bone that appeared in the shape of buddhas. This would not be the last time that such notable remains were found in a Karmapa's funeral pyre.

THE BOY LAMA: LOGA

When she bore her husband their sixth daughter, Loga experienced a mixture of acute joy and anguish. Her child's tiny, red face – eyes closed tight but mouth latched greedily to her mother's breast – stirred Loga deeply. Her exhausted body hummed with a fierce, protective love. Yet she had longed for a boy, for a second boy who, in the future, would work beside her husband, Karma Döndrub. Her eldest child and only boy, Yeshe

Rabsel, had been promised to a monastery at birth, as was the custom, but even now, at twenty-one, he spent most of his time at home, helping his father tend the family's eighty-odd beasts. Daughter after daughter had come after Yeshe Rabsel, until they numbered five in total, and now here was the sixth.

And so, with her sixth daughter lying there in her arms, barely dry after the birth and sucking on her mother's breast with vigour, Loga started imagining the next child, who would certainly be a boy. Quietly, almost beneath her breath, she chanted for something in the future that only the buddhas could bring her. Indeed, she and her husband had already sought blessings for another boy far and wide. One *rinpoche* (precious one, a high incarnate lama) had sent her husband from their home in Kham, in eastern Tibet, on a pilgrimage to the Jokhang Temple, Tibet's holiest shrine, in Lhasa. He had also told Loga and her husband that in order to conceive a boy, they must 'Help those in need every day, feed the fish in the river and the birds and stray dogs, and say the prayer of refuge 111,000 times.'[3] Loga's mother, who lived with them, was saying 1000 prayers per day. By the time she reached 50,000, her daughter was pregnant. As it transpired, this child born at the beginning of the 1980s was yet another girl.

When Loga left their yak-hair tent briefly, the day of her sixth daughter's birth, the intense cobalt blue of the sky made her gasp involuntarily. A sky like this was not in the slightest bit unusual, but Loga rejoiced in it all the same. From inside, she could hear one of her daughters singing to the tightly swaddled newborn and she reminded herself, again, why girls were, in fact, a blessing. On the rolling grassland nearby, another of her daughters sat, watching over the lambs and calves that were too small to go to the high pasture with the adult beasts.

When Karma Döndrub returned that evening to their tent, with the cold hanging on his clothes and in his hair, the expression on his face revealed so much to Loga. As always, his first reaction to the sight of his wife holding a newborn to her breast was one of sheer relief; his beloved Loga had brought another child into the world and, thanks to Chenrezig, the *bodhisattva* of compassion, she and the infant were safe. Next came the look of hope, anticipating almost without asking, 'A son, my wife, you have borne me a son.' And finally came the recognition that he was the father of a sixth daughter – a sixth – and the slow, slow smile of pleasure and pride.

Only a few months later, at Loga's urging, she and her husband undertook the day's journey by horse to their local monastery at Lhatok. With her infant daughter strapped to her chest inside her sheepskin coat, they would seek the prayers and blessings of Karlek Monastery's revered master, Lama Amdo Palden. It was Loga who had instigated the visit; her husband would not dream of putting his wife through another pregnancy when the child at her breast still demanded so very much of her. Loga, however, could not let it rest – this desire to give her husband another son who would live with them and work beside his father should their eldest son, Yeshe Rabsel, ever truly be called to Khampa Gar Monastery.

The approach to the monastery triggered conflicting feelings in Loga each and every time. Much of the once glorious building still lay in ruins and this cut her to the core. The damage had been wrought during the terrifying years of the Cultural Revolution when, for a decade dating from 1966, Tibetan religion and culture had been so brutally targeted by the Chinese authorities. Some Tibetan monasteries had been damaged by China's People's Liberation Army (PLA) even before then. Loga sometimes found it difficult to believe that, once again, she and her people were free to practise their faith publicly. There was some pleasure and a very small amount of pride in the fact that donations from her own family had helped Amdo Palden restore parts of the monastery. Loga was reminded again of the deep respect their lama, who had spent some twenty-five years in prison since China's occupation of Tibet, was accorded in her sprawling nomadic community. It was the sheer power of respect for him, as much as devotion to the *dharma*, that had made those in her community give so much towards the rebuilding.

As the couple was ushered in to see the master, only the child swaddled at her mother's breast made her feelings known. Upon entering the darkened room, lit only by a few butter lamps, the infant sobbed as though her very life was being taken from her. As quickly as she started this terrible commotion, Loga had quietened her again, but mother and baby exchanged a look that seemed to Loga to say so much. 'From this moment, we are giving ourselves over to destiny', and so they were. For in asking of the master, she knew that one must be prepared to give.

Amdo Palden listened to the woman speak, her head lowered in respect so he could not see the tears that glistened in her eyes. She was slight and sinewy, her skin drawn tight across her red cheeks and deeply lined around her eyes – a worker. Karma Döndrub remained all but silent; somehow it was his wife who could find the right words in such situations. The master muttered his prayers and sat, rocking back and forth on his cushioned seat in silence as though contemplating some profound problem. Finally, he made his grave pronouncement. He would pray for them to bring a boy into the world. They, however, and others in their family, must recite prayers, also. The boy child would be born safely, the master stressed with certainty. Loga heard her sharp intake of breath, easily audible in the silent room. The lama's words corresponded with a curious sensation inside her, as though the idea of a baby was already taking hold there.

Amdo Palden interrupted Karma Döndrub's words of thanks. When the child is four, he told them, Loga and Karma Döndrub must bring him to the monastery, into lama's care.

The nomad couple, their youngest child whimpering softly now, backed from the room repeating their thanks, their heads bowed low in deference to their master's status. During the long ride home over high terrain and through mountain streams, not a single word passed between the pair. Loga was certain of one thing only – that somehow her life was no longer her own.

TIBET

I confess that I feel surprised when I encounter people who know nothing of twentieth-century Tibetan history. To my mind, not knowing that Tibet was invaded by the People's Republic of China (PRC) more than fifty years ago is akin to being wholly unaware of the Holocaust. While there are some notable similarities between the story of Europe's Jews and the Tibetans during the last century, there is one fundamental difference. Western nations united to condemn Nazi Germany's treatment of Europe's Jews, yet most of these same nations, and some from the East, as well, consciously chose inaction when the PLA first entered Tibet then clashed with its troops in May 1950.

The history of China's occupation of Tibet has been told and retold by historians and journalists alike, and I shall not attempt to do so again in any detail here. I am no historian and cannot claim impartiality. The XVIIth Karmapa's story and that of the XVIth, however, have been shaped by this history and their tales, therefore, cannot be told without it.

Historian Tsering Shakya refers to a 'denial of history' that blights the majority of published accounts of the Sino-Tibetan conflict. This, he says, has occurred because, 'Neither the Tibetans nor Chinese want to allow any complexities to intrude on their firmly held beliefs'.[4] The history of the Sino-Tibetan conflict is regularly told as though it is two utterly different stories, depending on the writer's allegiance. According to one party, Tibet's last fifty years is a glorious tale of peaceful liberation, while for the other it's a saga of bloodshed, military occupation and colonisation.

The XIVth Dalai Lama's own account of Tibet's history, *My Land and My People*, dates the amalgamation of early Tibetan tribes into a nation at approximately 127 BC, more than 2000 years ago. The first Tibetan king, Nya-Tri-Tsenpo, was succeeded by no fewer than forty generations of kings. Historian Warren Smith asserts that any ethnic similarity as a result of ancient kinship between Chinese and Tibetans in millennia past would have all but vanished as a result of adaptation to radically different environments and the two people's history of conflict.[5]

From 1912, and for a number of other periods preceding that date, Tibet claimed independence. Communist China, however, seems to have forgotten that on a number of occasions Chinese emperors accepted Tibet's independence. While other nations had enjoyed direct relationships with the Tibetan government, even Britain, which had established trade and diplomatic ties with Tibet during her occupation of India, was unwilling to categorically disagree with the mighty PRC over Tibet. Tibet's historical relationship with China has been described in a number of ways including that of priest and patron, suzerain and sovereign, and, quite simply, as a Chinese state. In the middle of the twentieth century, China would claim absolute ownership over Tibet, proclaiming her to be part of the 'glorious motherland', part of China itself.

26 SEPTEMBER 2003
LINEAGE: THE SECOND KARMAPA
THE BOY LAMA: DREAMS AND OMENS
TIBET: CHINA INVADES

26 SEPTEMBER 2003

It's my first time in India but my head is full of Tibet. For the last eight months, I've immersed myself in things Tibetan. I've perused every obscure work on Tibetan history to which I could find reference on the internet and have sent the librarians at the State Library of New South Wales scurrying for books that have not seen daylight in decades. I read so much Tibetan history in such a short period that when my eyes closed in tiredness and my head nodded forward I would jolt awake, imagining I could smell butter tea and burning juniper, or the pungent, bovine odour of a great beast of burden.

To friends and colleagues' questions about why I, a novelist, had chosen such a topic for my next book, I fudged awkward responses. I am not even a practising Buddhist. I'd mutter to them about wanting to retell the Tibet story from a contemporary perspective. The Karmapa's short life, I would insist, had seemed like the perfect vehicle. As time passed, though, I began to realise that I hoped for more from the Karmapa than just a good story . . .

True to my own themes, I've come to realise that I have set myself on a hero quest. In my own mind, I find it difficult to separate the Dalai Lama's flight from Tibet from that of the XVIIth Karmapa. Both men, albeit forty years apart, were poised to become the most powerful Tibetans in communist-ruled Tibet. Both rejected this compromising option, choosing to cross the Himalayas into the 'free world' – India – where both believed they could better serve their faith and their people.

Since I've been researching the story of the XVIIth Karmapa, I have read again and again that Tibetans and Westerners alike see the young man as some sort of heir to the Dalai Lama. What could this mean? If the Karmapa were to be named an heir to the Dalai Lama, surely it could only be in some nominal capacity. Both technically and traditionally, the next person to take the Dalai Lama's place in Tibetan society can only be the reincarnation of the XIVth Dalai Lama.

While the Dalai Lama introduced the first democratic election of a head of state in 2001, declaring himself spiritual leader, not temporal leader to his people, in the hearts of most Tibetans he remains their leader in every sense of the word. And as there are no nations who dare to defy the mighty China and recognise the Tibetan Government-in-Exile, it is the Dalai Lama who travels the world speaking to foreign leaders (in his capacity as Tibet's spiritual leader), rather than the newly elected prime minister. If Tibet remains an occupied country, beyond the lifetime of this Dalai Lama, Tibetans will undoubtedly still need a respected, charismatic religious figure to remind the world of their existence. As I prepare to meet the young Karmapa, I cannot deny that I long to know whether he could possibly be the public face of Tibet's future.

I cannot sleep in my dingy Delhi hotel room so I climb onto one of the beds, push aside thick curtains and open a high, frosted window to see outside. It's pre-dawn and the buildings in the neighbourhood are visible to me only as silhouettes against the inky sky. I'm three floors up and look out across rooftops and stairways that form an Escheresque maze in the darkness. Across the lane, atop a low building, two people are out walking beneath the night sky. I imagine them as lovers strolling in their exquisite, tropical roof garden. I know Delhi not at all.

The grey of early morning dispels my romantic illusions. From the same window, the nearby buildings look concrete and unfinished. In the lane below my window, men sleep on *charpoys*, simple wooden-framed beds, scratching, yawning, stretching – oblivious. A guttural moan prompts me to lean from my window; I chuckle at the sight of a dazzlingly white cow with a massive hump on its neck and a collar of marigolds. It lies on a bed of sacking more comfortable than any other sleeping place in the vicinity.

I have two days in Delhi. On my first day, I will be alone and will try to see as much of India's history in the city as possible; a steep task for anyone, let alone the newly arrived and dazed first-timer. On my second day, an Australian friend will arrive and we'll wander the city's streets together. These two days are my small concession to 'seeing India' before I head for the home of the exile Tibetans in the northwest.

First stop on my brief tour of Delhi – before I get down to the business of 'seeing India' – is Tibet House Museum. There I inquire after books on the XVIIth Karmapa. Upstairs in the museum proper, a Tibetan monk in maroon robes fills ceremonial lamps with oil and we take turns bowing at each other. The only sound within is that of the monk's bare feet, shuffling on the polished cement floor; the human throng that is Delhi seems of a different world.

LINEAGE: THE SECOND KARMAPA

The IInd Karmapa, Karma Pakshi (1203–1283), was a child prodigy who could read and write perfectly by the age of six and spent a significant part of his early life in meditative retreat. According to some sources, Karma Pakshi is credited with introducing to Tibetans the now globally recognisable chant, '*Om mani padme hung*', known as the mantra of compassion. Like his predecessor, Dusum Khyenpa, he too was responsible for a very significant first for Tibetan Buddhism.

Karma Pakshi would only need to read a text once to know it completely. Despite this aptitude, he and his successors were formally educated in the teachings of the lineage by the lineage holder to whom the teachings had been entrusted during the Karmapa's previous incarnation. In other circumstances, this process might be described as Chinese whispers.

Karma Pakshi travelled to China at the invitation of Kublai Khan, Genghis Khan's grandson. While at the Khan's court, it was widely reported that he performed spectacular miracles. Marco Polo referred to the lamas as enchanters, claiming they could make glasses of wine and milk rise to the Great Khan's lips without the glass ever being touched.

As the result of a perceived slight by Karma Pakshi against the newly enthroned Kublai Khan, the emperor ordered his arrest.

Despite sending great numbers of men to capture him, all Kublai's efforts were thwarted. One battalion of 37,000 men is said to have been paralysed on the spot by the Karmapa, who later pitied and released his would-be captors. The troops then seized him, wrapped him in a cloth and bound him, but it is said his body was like a rainbow with no substance.[6] The troops forced the Karmapa to drink poison, but instead of killing him it caused blinding rays of light to stream from his body. When they pushed him off a mountain, he simply glided back to earth, and when they tried to burn him, water poured from his body. When Kublai Khan ordered that the Karmapa be incarcerated with no provisions, heavenly beings came to provide him with food and drink. Chastened after going to such lengths with no results, Kublai Khan became Karma Pakshi's devoted student.

On his return to Tibet, Karma Pakshi had a vast statue of Buddha constructed at Tsurphu Monastery. It was said to have stood more than fifteen metres tall. When the statue was finished, however, it rested at a displeasing tilt. Karma Pakshi, it is reported, stood before the Buddha and adopted the same tilt himself, before slowly straightening to the vertical. At the same time, the statue straightened itself.

THE BOY LAMA:
DREAMS AND OMENS

From here to the north [in] the east of [the land of] snow
Is a country where divine thunder spontaneously blazes.
[In] a beautiful nomad's place with the sign of a cow,
The method is Döndrub and the wisdom is Lolaga.
[Born in] the year of the one used for the earth
[With] the miraculous, far-reaching sound of the
   white one:
[This] is the one known as Karmapa.[7]

An extract from the English translation of the
XVIth Karmapa's prediction letter

In the letter he wrote about his rebirth, the XVIth Karmapa tells his disciples that he will be reborn in eastern Tibet, which he refers to as 'the east of snow'. He explains that he will be born in the Lhatok region, the word literally meaning 'divine thunder' and that the place will be a nomad community called Bagor, whose name includes the Tibetan word for cow. The 'method' referred to denotes the father, Döndrub, and the 'wisdom' denotes the mother, Lolaga. In fact, the Karmapa's mother is known by her family and community as Loga, the shortened form of Lolaga. The 'year of the one used for the earth' refers to the year of the Wood Ox in the Tibetan calendar and the 'white one' is the conch shell.[8]

Just as the lama promised them, Loga soon fell pregnant once again as she finished giving her own milk to her youngest daughter. It was 1984. Normally she would convey this news to her husband with unreserved joy but this time was different. Something made Loga hold back, as though what she had to tell Karma Döndrub was incomprehensible. After meditating for some time at the family altar, before the images that included the XVIth Karmapa, Loga finally approached her husband with the news. Loga's mother, who had always believed her daughter would be of great service to Buddhism, was already reciting her prayers diligently in anticipation of a grandson.

At times in the early stages of the pregnancy, during which Loga experienced not the briefest moment of sickness or weakness, she found herself imagining that she was carrying another girl and would, therefore, not have to part with the child. When she caught herself in such thinking she chided herself as though she'd engaged in profane thoughts. Loga had always believed that she was as devoted to her *dharma* as she was to her children, to her husband, to her very life, but at this moment during her eighth pregnancy she started to doubt it. Somehow the longing for this child – her baby boy – was all the more intense because Loga knew he was destined to leave her.

When the omens started appearing to her, however, Loga forced herself to begin the process of letting go of the child inside her. This one was not hers, she kept telling herself, not hers.

Each new sign caused Loga as much pain as it did wonder. These visits and dreams lent an air of unreality and otherworldliness to the ordinary, daily tasks of churning the butter, tending the live-stock and weaving.

The first of the omens took the form of an adult sparrow hawk, a bird so wild and shy that humans rarely see it at close proximity. The next was a cuckoo, whose song had the feeling of a divine gift; even Loga, who was already mourning the loss of her child, experienced it. Never before had she felt so torn between wonder and dread. Another bird came to visit in Loga's dreams; this time, by way of three cranes. One of them offered her the gift of a bowl of yogurt and another carried a letter around its neck. The crane told Loga that this was a letter of recognition for her son but that she should not speak of it to anyone else.

Yeshe Rabsel, Loga's eldest child, also had an unusual dream while staying at Khampa Gar Monastery. In it, he had been walking by a wide river and coming towards him, among a group of lamas, was Lama Amdo Palden. They were clearly searching for something. During the course of their search they found conch shells – the sound of which is associated with the Buddha's teachings – but when they blew on them the shells were silent. Yeshe Rabsel found a conch shell and this one, when he blew into it, made a deep, powerful sound. The lamas told him that this is what they had been looking for and asked him for it. Lama Amdo Palden then announced that Yeshe Rabsel's mother had given birth to a fine child. Upon waking, Yeshe Rabsel remembered his dream quite clearly. As it transpired, it coincided with the birth of his brother. It was 26 June 1985.[9]

Although Loga, despite herself, was reluctant to give this child she was carrying to the world, the birth was swift and near painless. Her effort in childbirth had never been so minimal. Instead of the cries of a newborn emanating from the tent, the air was filled, once again, with exquisite birdsong. Perched atop the tent, in clear view, was another beautiful, unafraid cuckoo.

Mother and child had three days of respite, with only their immediate family for company. Loga would look back and cherish these days of normalcy, this semblance of something akin to the simple birth of an ordinary child.

On the third day, the seventy-odd families in the Bagor community, near Lhatok, heard the sound of a conch shell but could not identify its source. It was almost as though the music were being produced by the sky itself. Then, adding to the celestial orchestra, came the clash of cymbals and the buzzing of reed horns. Loga's children searched both in and outside their tent for the strange humming sound.

Loga barely noticed the stir the celestial music was causing, so enchanted was she by her second son. His eyes already hypnotised those who gazed upon them, one eye quite clearly of a different shape and size to the other. Just as she was thinking that nothing about him could surprise her, the baby pulled away from her breast and looked her in the eye.

'Ama,' he said loudly, using the Tibetan word for mother.[10]

Once again, from the tent's roof, came the song of the cuckoo. This strange new reality made the dreams that Loga had experienced seem almost ordinary. She, unlike the others in her family, was not surprised by any of these occurrences, even by the strangeness of a child born only three days ago addressing his mother quite clearly. All Loga could think was, 'Let him stay with me for as long as possible . . .'

TIBET: CHINA INVADES

When the XIIIth Dalai Lama expressed interest in joining the League of Nations in the 1920s, the idea was rejected by the *Kashag* (government) for fear of the consequences of having to open the country to foreigners. Although a handful of Western missionaries had visited Tibet since the eighteenth century, and although several hundred English soldiers reached Lhasa in 1905 and different groups of Chinese had come and gone, Tibet remained largely closed to foreigners. This is how the Tibetan leaders liked it. It was, alas, not until China's invasion in 1950 that Tibet attempted in vain to join the United Nations (UN).

On the eve of the communist victory in China in mid-1949, both the ruling nationalist Chinese government and the government of India had their own trade missions in Lhasa. The existence of these missions meant different things to different parties. China took her own presence there to signify that the Tibetans had accepted her sovereignty. The *Kashag*, however, had asserted that having a British mission in Lhasa (which subsequently became the Indian mission upon India's independence), as well as that of the Chinese, was proof of Tibet's independence. Maintaining her own international relations with her two large neighbours meant that, as far as Tibetans were concerned, Tibet was independent at that moment in its history just as she had been on and off throughout her history. Indeed, Britain's hold over India and her contribution towards maintaining Tibet's status as a neutral buffer zone between China and India had been crucial to Tibet's recent independence. The Chinese communists would later make anti-imperialist propaganda of the fact that independent India's representative in Lhasa was the Englishman who had also been the last British representative in Tibet.

In July 1949, fearing communist infiltration of the Chinese mission in Lhasa, the *Kashag* expelled all Chinese connected with the Nationalist Chinese government. This action was dubbed the 'anti-communist incident' and it prompted the communist government to suggest somewhat zealously that 'imperialists' and their 'running dogs' aimed to turn Tibet into a colony.[11] It is China, however, who became Tibet's coloniser. Well before the PRC was established on 1 October 1949, the Chinese communists openly expressed their intention to 'liberate' Tibet.

The *Kashag*, in conjunction with Tathag Rinpoche, prepared to defend Tibet. (Tathag Rinpoche was Tibet's regent, who would act as head of state until the fifteen-year-old Dalai Lama reached his majority at eighteen.) They reorganised the government, invigorated and bolstered the army, and negotiated for the supply of arms and ammunition from the Indian government, some of which was granted to them. The Tibetans also established a radio station in Lhasa in order to counter the communists' propaganda about Tibet. On 31 January 1950, Radio Lhasa declared that Tibet had been 'independent since 1912 when the Manchu garrison had been driven out'.

In December 1949, the *Kashag* had asked the British government to support Tibet's admission into the UN. The Tibetans did not receive this crucial lifeline because in Britain's assessment Tibet's application was certain to be blocked by the Russian and Chinese nationalist representatives at the UN. The United States initially shared a similar view, preferring to leave Tibet's fate in the hands of the British and the Indian government. Britain eventually deemed that the matter of Tibet should be solely India's affair; quite simply, her interest in the land of snows had waned.[12]

The Tibetans strived to establish ties with anti-communist America; in August 1950, officials in Washington, now frustrated with the inaction of the Indian government, promised Tibet assistance in procuring weapons should she choose to resist communist aggression. Tangible US support, however, was contingent upon Tibet actually declaring her intention to resist the communists. Caught between a rock and a hard place, India wished to perpetuate Tibet's existence as a buffer state between herself and China, but was reluctant to provoke the communists.[13]

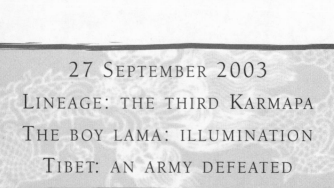

27 SEPTEMBER 2003
LINEAGE: THE THIRD KARMAPA
THE BOY LAMA: ILLUMINATION
TIBET: AN ARMY DEFEATED

27 SEPTEMBER 2003

The Indian history I glean as I roam Delhi, I try to apply to the Tibetans' story. I am in Delhi for the first time in my life and I am only going through the motions of playing the good tourist. In reality, I am barely present. There is a distance between me and my surroundings. Every small child I see on the street, either walking in her prettily pressed blouse to school or thrusting her grubby hand towards me, takes me home to Isla.

My driver and guide, an eighteen-year-old Nepali boy who is in Delhi merely to earn money for his poor rural family, watches me with uncanny knowing. 'You are sad,' he announces. 'You miss your daughter.'

I look away from him, out at the Red Fort that is a blur of clay through my window, so he will not see the misery on my face. How did I come to be this reluctant traveller, so torn by my responsibilities?

In 1990, five years after the birth of the Tibetan boy who would be recognised as the XVIIth Karmapa, I was working as a book publicist in London. At twenty-three I was very Australian – a mixture of self-deprecation and bravado, both in my element at the heart of the British publishing industry in London's Bedford Square, and yet an outsider at the same time.

The firm at which I worked published two of my then 'greats': Angela Carter and Toni Morrison. Despite the long hours and the dubious privilege of working under Virago's founder, the Australian Carmen Callil, I felt I'd found my place in the world. Had I not been out of favour with Carmen at the time I may never have bothered to wander across the square when a friend mentioned a job vacancy at another publishing house.

I had decided in advance that this was not a job I wanted; the company's stars, John le Carré and Stephen King, were not part of my reading world, but something pushed me to go through with the interview, regardless. Over at Hodder & Stoughton, I chatted with the ebullient publicity director, wondering how to politely convey my disinterest. She started to recount a list of forthcoming titles and among them was the Dalai Lama's auto-biography. I'm not sure that it even had a title at the time.

'I want the job!' I interjected, surprising us both with my sudden animation. And yes, I was surprised. Although I knew the Dalai Lama had been awarded the Nobel Peace Prize the pre-vious year, I was no Tibetophile. Indeed, I was largely oblivious to 'the Tibet struggle'. My interest in the Dalai Lama sprang, I think, from some childhood notion of Tibet as a land of snow and mountains, not unlike the Switzerland of my forebears, but so much more exotic. I was already intrigued by the stories of Alexandra David-Neel, the first Western woman to reach Lhasa, albeit disguised as a Tibetan lama, early last century. In the books she published about her travels in Tibet, she reinforced my sense of the country's inherent magic and mystery. Until I started to read about the life of the XIVth Dalai Lama, Tibet had remained for me a far-flung realm in which mysteries endured, staunchly defying scientific explanation.

It was autumn in London and I had spent six months arrang-ing a press conference for the Dalai Lama. It would mark the launch of his autobiography, *Freedom in Exile*. During those months, I worked closely with the Dalai Lama's representative in London, the indomitable yet diminutive Mrs Kesang Takla, and received a couple of phone calls from irate officials at the Chinese Embassy asking me exactly what I thought I was doing. In trying to arrange a venue for the press conference, which we needed to hold near Heathrow Airport as the Dalai Lama would be in transit between Delhi and New York, one of our meetings was brought to an abrupt halt at the orders of the hotel manager. The company was in the process of opening the first foreign-owned hotel in Lhasa.

As a publicist, I was in an enviable position. Having only recently been awarded the Nobel Peace Prize, the Dalai Lama was in seriously high demand among the nation's press corps. Invitations to the press conference were limited and journalists on the nation's broadsheets vied to win the coveted prize of the single, one-on-one print interview. In the days prior to the press conference, my anxiety, and that of my colleagues, was diminished by our negotiations with courier companies over the transport of an enormous 'blow-up Dalai Lama' between central London and Heathrow. This was the exponentially enlarged version of the book's jacket that would act as a backdrop to the stage from which the Dalai Lama would address the press.

It was impossible not to be infected by the excitement surrounding the Dalai Lama's flash visit, but part of me feared that the man himself would not meet expectations – my own expectations. As a child I remember being told, time and time again as my parents entertained senior figures from the Catholic Church in Australia, that this priest or that bishop was a 'holy man'. I had been impressed by only one of them, a former army chaplain whose party trick was to remove his false leg.

How, I wondered, would the Tibetan leader make me feel? Did it matter?

On the morning of the press conference, three of my colleagues including the book's publisher, John Curtis, editor, Alex Norman, and I formed a guard of honour at the Heathrow hotel. We all held the *khatags*, the long white silk scarves the Tibetans use to greet honoured guests, that we would present to the Dalai Lama. I'd been coached on the protocols of being in the Dalai Lama's presence but was certain I'd commit the faux pas of accidentally touching him, or of forgetting that my own head must always be lower than his.

My first impression of the Dalai Lama, as he strode through a private side entrance of the hotel, was that he was robust. If I were English, I might have called him strapping. Although nothing I'd read about the Dalai Lama had suggested it, somehow I expected him to be slight, more ascetic than farmer. Little passed between us at that moment of greeting – some polite words and a bow that felt oddly natural to me. My job, after all, was not to stand and feel transported but to herd journalists from A to B, to ensure that they understood the ground rules, to see that everything ran to schedule; in other words, to hold everything together.

I ushered *The Sunday Times*' Bryan Appleyard – the chosen

journalist – into the Dalai Lama's suite for the prized exclusive interview. As we travelled in the lift and walked the hotel's corridors, I feared that we'd made a great mistake. He had been chosen for the paper's circulation and for our belief that he had not, in his writing, declared himself pro-China. Appleyard came across as a mixture of nonchalance and cynicism, clearly not expecting to be affected by his meeting with Tibet's leader. An hour later, perhaps more as I'm sure the interview was extended beyond the agreed time, a transformed man left the Dalai Lama's suite. Appleyard's whole body language had altered, and as we retraced our footsteps through the hotel I caught him beaming.

The room in which the press conference would be held was already filled to the gunnels with journalists and photographers, vying for a decent vantagepoint near the stage on which the Dalai Lama would appear. The atmosphere seemed to crackle with tension; the journalists were all too aware of their very limited access to this recent Nobel Prize-winner and so-called god king. I, having spoken briefly with the Dalai Lama and having heard him speak to others, feared that his broken English might leave the media pack confused and annoyed. My anxiety, on this point, was utterly unfounded. From the moment the maroon-robed Dalai Lama strode onto the stage, he held those gathered in a state of respectful, bemused awe. Even from where I stood at the back of the packed room, I was deeply moved when the Dalai Lama spoke of having compassion for the communist Chinese, for those who had inflicted so much bloodshed on his fellow Tibetans.

More than a decade later, from all the noise of the day one thing stays with me more profoundly than the image of a journalist's wonder. I'd been so busy within the hotel that I had not realised what was taking place outside. In the hotel's grounds and on the side access road, Tibetans were gathering. These were Tibetan refugees who had travelled from their homes in exile across the United Kingdom. We had not scheduled a public event nor an audience with the community as there simply was not time – I think the Dalai Lama had been able to give us only six hours – but still they came.

By the time the Dalai Lama was ready to leave with his entourage in the cavalcade of black limousines, Tibetans lined the road that led from the hotel to the motorway. As the Dalai Lama's limousine drove by, the Tibetans raised their *khatags* to him and chanted their prayers. Even before the procession of black cars had left our sight, some of the Tibetans were wailing, others crying, and a couple of the women had fallen to the ground in distress. I looked on, stricken. For a moment it was as though I'd had a vivid glimpse of a people's history, into the agony of a life of exile. In that moment, some kernel of resolve hardened in my chest – I would take on some of the Tibetans' struggle. There was no choice in this for me.

Afterwards, my boss sent me home early. In reality, I was probably so overwrought and dazed that I would have been of little real use to anyone sitting at my desk. It was a cool, clear London day and as soon as I returned to my Brixton home I changed my clothes and left again, cycling northwest up to Battersea Park. Despite the chaos of the day and the noise of all those people and all those questions, I felt profoundly still. For a moment, I felt as though my life had been inexplicably simplified.

LINEAGE: THE THIRD KARMAPA

The IIIrd Karmapa, Rangjung Dorje (1284–1339), was born in Tingri, western Tibet, just as the moon was rising. He is reported to have announced, immediately after birth, that: 'It is a waxing moon.' When he was five, Rangjung Dorje was taken by his parents to meet the Karma Kagyu lineage holder and he is reported to have climbed onto the teacher's throne and declared himself the lama. By the age of seven, he had been ordained and enthroned at Tsurphu Monastery. Another report has him producing a black crown from nowhere.

A particularly devoted scholar, Rangjung Dorje was not satisfied until he had learned and mastered all the Buddhist teachings that had been brought to Tibet from India. He is reported to have been able to spontaneously read books and receive teachings in his dreams. He became a student and subsequent master of medicine. When he was thirty-five, Rangjung Dorje revised the Tibetan system of astrology as a result of a vision he received during the *Kalachakra* teachings. (The *Kalachakra* is one of the most important Tibetan Buddhist initiation rituals and is conducted before a public audience over the course of three days. In it, the magnificent sand painting called a *mandala* is prepared.) The third Karmapa's astrological system is still used in Tibet today; from it, Tibetans derive the dates for the commencement of any major undertaking.

Rangjung Dorje travelled to China at the invitation of the last of the Mongol emperors, where he taught and established temples and monasteries. The Karmapa presided over the enthronement of new Chinese emperor Toghon Temur and gave him a longevity elixir that would see him become the longest living Mongol emperor of China.

The IIIrd Karmapa died at the Chinese court and, on the night of his death, palace guards, courtiers and the emperor clearly saw his likeness in the moon.

THE BOY LAMA: ILLUMINATION

Loga's child seemed to emanate light.[14] From around three months after the boy's birth, there was more than the glow of health about the infant. Indeed, some nights the inside of the family's tent was gently illuminated by a light that seemed to come from their tightly swaddled child's face. Loga was the only one to find this phenomenon in any way ordinary, although the younger girls soon learned that if they sat beside their brother there was better light in which to complete their indoor chores. To Karma Döndrub and Yeshe Rabsel, who had a stronger sense of the family's standing in the community, the baby's illumination seemed to confirm the child's status as utterly extraordinary.

Loga and Karma Döndrub took their baby to Lama Amdo Palden for naming. The lama, however, advised that the child was a *tulku* – a high incarnation – and should therefore be named later, when his true identity was revealed to them.

Not long after the child's birth, Loga had sent one of her daughters to the river to fetch water and, upon her return, the girl reported a strange encounter with a magpie. The bird had apparently given her a name for the new baby. It was Apo Gaga, 'the one who makes us very happy'. In the absence of a name bestowed on him, the boy would be known as Apo Gaga for the next seven years.

With his serious expression and his dark, knowing eyes, the sisters vied with each other to look after him, to see that he was given the nicest pieces of food and the freshest milk. Soon Apo Gaga was no longer their baby; Loga conceived again and bore her husband a third son with almost as much ease as she'd borne him their second.

One night, one of their yaks escaped from her tether and made off on a wonderful adventure. Karma Döndrub, only recently having returned from the high pastures himself and still recovering with some tea from the cold and from his exertion, sent two of his daughters out after it. Yaks are neither small nor agile, so it was not too difficult for the two girls to locate the creature on the path ahead of them, making for greener pastures on the slopes above. The sisters captured the docile beast and started leading it down the mountain towards home.

They knew the path well, having walked it many times before and did not actually need to see where they were going, which was fortunate on this overcast night with neither stars nor moon in the sky. Ahead of them down the path a light appeared, hovering, and they called out to Yeshe Rabsel to announce that they had found the escapee and were bringing her home. Their brother did not make a sound and the girls assumed he was playing a trick on them. The light continued to hover at the same height and always at the same distance before them. After walking for some minutes, they were certain that this was no torch and shrugged off the goosebumps that had started to form on their skin. They were not afraid; no, not these two. They had already come to accept that their lives had been touched by another realm. The floating light was of some use to them and therefore clearly benevolent.[15]

Apo Gaga was certainly not like other small children in his region. He possessed more concentration than others of his age and was just as happy to sit quietly as to run freely with his siblings. Indeed, at times his energies seemed to be focused on things of a higher order.

One day, Apo Gaga spent some time carefully constructing a great building from clay and a host of smaller outbuildings. His dark eyes gleamed with concentration and he seemed to be chanting mantras to himself beneath his breath. Whenever his siblings tried to distract him with other games, he'd shoo them away, not unkindly, and continue his labours.

'There,' he announced to his baby brother, who was cooing happily on a sheepskin nearby. 'The monastery is finished. We are both lamas.'

When his sisters returned to try to distract him again, they found him chanting intently, conducting pretend religious ceremonies. This became one of his favourite games and, when the mood took him, he would extend 'lamahoods' to his brother and sisters as well. Sometimes he made impromptu cymbals out of two stones and made a great racket with them.

Loga would look on in both delight and concern at the care her son took with the animals and insects around him. No living creature could be harmed in the boy's presence. In addition, Apo Gaga reserved his deepest affections for a young goat, born shortly before him. The young boy saw the animal as special because it had three ears, not two. One of them, smaller than the other two, appeared just behind one of the goat's regular-sized ears. Apo Gaga and the goat often took off into the mountains together, the small boy perched elegantly on the creature's back.

The young boy quickly acquired a reputation in the district, with stories of his qualities, his character and of the good omens surrounding his birth reaching many interested parties. Lamas from a number of the monasteries in the region made inquiries about the boy's future, and asked for him to be sent to them one day. However, it was to Karlek Monastery, and Lama Amdo Palden, that the boy had been promised. From the age of about four, the serious, young Apo Gaga would spend between a week and ten days at a time at the monastery before returning to his family.

Amdo Palden practised in the Kagyu tradition and was himself a *thogden*: a master of diverse meditative techniques who never cut his hair. At Karlek Monastery, a small throne was built for the young Apo Gaga in the shrine room beside Amdo Palden's. Although none of them yet knew the young boy's identity, the monks and their master were certain that he was an important and high incarnation and happily honoured him as such.

While he was at home, Apo Gaga started to make claims about his identity. One day, Loga had churned some butter and went to offer the first of it at the family altar and to the images of the two high lamas. When the boy asked his mother to whom she was offering the butter, she told him it was to 'the deities'. The boy went on to gesture towards the picture of the XVIth Karmapa, telling his mother, 'If you're offering it to him, that's me and I'll have it.'[16] Loga outwardly discouraged this talk and chided her son affectionately. Not only did it show a lack of humility but it made her all the more certain of her son's destiny, far, far from her.

When Apo Gaga was seven, for no apparent reason he started insisting that his family move from the house in which they spent the winter months to the summer pasture earlier than usual. As their son had never made such a request before and knowing that he was somehow important, they acceded to his demand. They gathered their belongings and herded their live-stock to Bagor, the 'place with the sign of the cow' from the XVIth Karmapa's prediction letter.

TIBET: DEFEATED

The first fighting between bands of Tibetans and the Chinese troops took place in May 1950, in Kham, the same region in eastern Tibet in which the XVIIth Karmapa would be born thirty-five years later. By October, the PLA threatened to take the regional capital, Chamdo. The now infamous story has it that when Ngabo Ngawang Jigme, Governor of Kham, tried by radio to gain advice and reinforcements from Lhasa, he was told by an official, mindful only of protocol, that the *Kashag* could not be disturbed as it was at a picnic. Unable to contact the *Kashag*, therefore without Lhasa's knowledge, Ngabo surrendered to the PLA on 19 October and Tibetan troops began handing over their arms.

Explaining China's motivation for invading Tibet, Chinese Premier Zhou Enlai said, 'The PLA is determined to march westward to liberate the Tibetan people and defend the frontiers of China. We are willing to undertake peaceful negotiations to bring about this step which is necessary for the security of our Motherland. The patriots in Tibet have expressed and welcomed this and we hope that the local authorities in Tibet will not hesitate to bring about a peaceful solution to the question.'[17]

In reality, there were only very few Tibetans who felt any affection for China, or who saw her as the glorious motherland. When Zhou Enlai talked of 'liberating' the Tibetans, he meant that the PLA would free the Tibetan peasants from what the communists regarded as their feudal existence. What the Chinese premier did not mention in his speech about China's occupation of Tibet is that the Chinese word for Tibet means 'treasure house in the west'. The PRC sought not only militaristic control of her neighbour, but also to plunder Tibet's wealth of natural resources.

The military defeat had been relatively swift and it was certainly definitive. The resistance to China's invasion was now all but at an end; the Tibetan Army had comprised only 8500 officers and men. There seemed little choice but for the *Kashag* to negotiate with the PRC and respond to China's demands that had long since been laid upon the table that Tibet was to be considered part of China, that China was to be responsible for Tibet's defence, and that she would deal with all of Tibet's international relations, including foreign trade.[18]

A compromise to the PRC's demands was eventually reached among the members of the *Kashag*, but when the proposed response was put to the Dalai Lama he requested that the state oracle or medium be consulted. The oracle, who put himself into a trance so he could communicate with Tibet's protector divinity, Dorje Drakden, announced that the demands should not be accepted and subsequently declared that the young Dalai Lama should assume his powers as head of state immediately. Tibet had been jointly ruled by the *Kashag* and by different regents since the death of the XIIIth Dalai Lama in 1933. With what he described as trepidation, the XIVth Dalai Lama, Tenzin Gyatso, accepted. On 17 November 1950, a ceremony was held at the Potala Palace to mark the beginning of his leadership. He was only sixteen years of age.

With 40,000 Chinese troops poised to enter Lhasa in January 1951, the Dalai Lama and the *Kashag* fled to safety in Dromo, Tibet's southernmost outpost between Sikkim and Bhutan, more than 300 kilometres or fourteen days' journey away. Many others had fled before them and wealthy Tibetans had long since been sending their assets elsewhere for safekeeping. With the Korean War in full swing, international attention was also elsewhere. The Dalai Lama and the *Kashag* had decided that it was essential that they be close to the border should the situation with the Chinese deteriorate. That way they could more easily seek asylum in India. The young Dalai Lama felt excitement over making the journey to Dromo, in that it gave him the opportunity to see something of his country. He was, he wrote in *Freedom from Exile*, particularly pleased that he would be disguised as a layman. Those Tibetans who knew he was leaving Lhasa, however, greatly distressed over his departure.[19]

The Tibetans saw no other hope but to ask the UN directly to intervene on their behalf to request that the PLA withdraw from Tibetan territory. Neither Tibet nor the PRC was a UN member nation. Indeed, officials at the UN Secretary-General's office were so ignorant of Tibet's situation that they were prepared to dismiss the appeal as 'a communication from a nongovernmental organisation'. It fell upon the British delegation to explain Tibet's situation; even so, the only course of action taken was for the appeal to be distributed informally to the delegates on the Security Council.

The three countries most likely to come to Tibet's aid, at the very least by way of supporting her request to the United Nations that they intervene to get the PLA to withdraw from Tibet, procrastinated and ultimately did nothing. Britain continued to insist that the matter should be handled by India. The US, for the time being, agreed. For a myriad of reasons, not least being the commonly held belief that the PRC could not be persuaded to withdraw from Tibet, as well as India's own fear of the PRC, India chose not to act. Her inaction meant that the Commonwealth delegation did not intervene either.

When it appeared that all doors had been firmly closed to Tibet at the UN, the Chairman of the El Salvadorian delegation requested that 'the invasion of Tibet by foreign forces' be tabled on the agenda for the General Assembly and he drafted an accompanying resolution. The British delegate, however, argued successfully that discussion of the matter be postponed. As the war in Korea developed, the Tibetans' request lost any sense of urgency it might once have had. All that remained for the Tibetans was to attempt a negotiated settlement with the PRC.

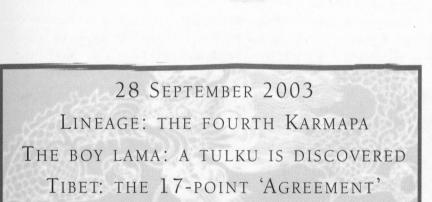

28 September 2003
Lineage: the fourth Karmapa
The boy lama: a tulku is discovered
Tibet: the 17-point 'Agreement'

28 SEPTEMBER 2003

It's dawn on the Jhelum Express and, when I peer through the train's window, I cannot tell whether the air outside is brightly hazy or whether the glass has simply not been washed for a decade. I decide that it's a combination of both and stare in fascination at the bustle of Jalandhar Station on the Punjab plains. Everywhere are women, children, the elderly and men, men, men. Some are waiting beside vast piles of baggage; some await their train with nothing but a tin canister of *chai*. Others appear simply to live on the station's platforms, clearly not going anywhere. India is as absorbing as it is diverse and has started to distract me from my mission; I have only two weeks in which to meet and know the Karmapa.

My destination is Dharamsala, former British garrison and Indian hill station, present-day home of His Holiness, the Dalai Lama, the Tibetan government-in-exile and of the XVIIth Karmapa. There, sprawling across forested slopes towards the town of McLeod Ganj, up above on a craggy ridge, live about 7000 exiled Tibetans. Some of them engage in government work, some are so recently arrived from Tibet that they are simply in recovery, while others are in business of various sorts, content to live out their days near their deity and leader, the Dalai Lama. Dharamsala is more than 500 kilometres from Delhi and the journey, by train and taxi, can take more than twelve hours.

From within the train's air-conditioned compartment, this all appears costume drama and I nearly applaud when a tall, arresting man strides into scene, his wife and child following in his wake. The man's skin is very dark and he has a long, pointy beard only slightly tinged with grey. Atop his head is an immaculate white turban and he wears a *salwar kameez*, a flowing white tunic that reaches his knees; below it is a pair of tight, white cotton trousers. On his feet – oh, vision splendid! – is what from a distance of about ten metres appears to be a pair of shiny, white snakeskin loafers. Before I can excavate my camera from the depths of my bag, he and his small entourage have gone and the train is inching its way from the station.

The Jhelum Express departs New Delhi Station late at night and has crossed most of the Punjab by dawn. In the light of early morning it snakes its way north, up towards the Himalayas and the state of Himachal Pradesh, before veering west towards Jammu and Kashmir, and Jhelum, just across the Pakistani border. I have always had a yearning for Kashmir, but Pathankot, below Himachal Pradesh, may be the closest I'll ever get. Kashmir has been the scene of two wars between India and Pakistan (1948 and 1965) and it's estimated that some 30,000 Kashmiris have been killed in the fighting. The area remains unstable. My Lonely Planet guide to the region advises strongly against travelling there until all the militant groups have confirmed that tourists are not targets.

On this part of my journey I am accompanied by a friend, former colleague, former publisher and now, like me, a writer chasing a story in the Himalayas. I imagine that passages from both of our books might sound spookily similar, although our paths will diverge once we reach Dharamsala. It's not as though my friend Sophie and I are travelling into uncharted territory: so many other writers before us – along with Westerners on all manner of quests – have made this very journey.

At Pathankot Station, Sophie and I hire a battered taxi to take us from the plains of the Punjab and up into the verdant foothills of the Himalayas. Along the road, monkeys sit, scratching, gawking, as we, in turn, shift in our seats and gawk back.

Our route up to McLeod Ganj takes us past the picturesque church, St John in the Wilderness, which dates back to 1852. There is a fine stone certainty about the church and the graveyard that surrounds it, a defiant permanence that is at odds with the reality of the English mission in India. Could the British, who once went to such lengths in endeavouring to establish Christianity here, ever have imagined that the country would one day be returned to its rightful owners? I cannot help but wonder whether the Chinese can possibly imagine this of Tibet . . .

The taxi leaves us at the top of a steep rocky path that we must negotiate wearing our heavy backpacks, taking care not to tread on one of the enormous slugs that bask there in the sun. Entering our hotel, Chonor House, at the foot of the path, feels like stepping into the mind's Tibet.[20] In the foyer, a magnificent carpet showing green valleys and yaks is the softest thing I've seen since arriving in India. Tibetan women in their *chubas* – long pinafore dresses with silk blouses underneath – greet us warmly. 'Welcome Miss Gaby,' they say to us both. Each of the hotel's rooms is adorned with themed murals. Mine is the Lhamo Opera room, decorated in deep reds and with so many characters from Tibetan opera on the walls that I, at all times, feel I have an audience.

Chonor House, with its gardens overlooking the Dalai Lama's temple, is a whimsical gesture to a place we Tibetophiles long for, but will never know, even should we travel to Tibet itself.

LINEAGE: THE FOURTH KARMAPA

Rolpe Dorje (1340–1383), the IVth Karmapa, is said to have chanted '*Om mani padme hung*', quite audibly, while in his mother's womb, and practised yogic exercises in utero that were said to have shaken his mother's body. Rolpe Dorje repeated the mantra the moment he was born and was only three when he announced that he was the Karmapa.

The young *tulku*'s parents took him to Lhasa and, en route, he greeted people everywhere, recounting to them details of their own lives that such a small child could have no logical way of knowing, and reminding them of the gifts they'd given him in his previous incarnation. Rolpe Dorje displayed the seemingly normal Karmapa attributes of spontaneous reading and receiving significant teachings in his dreams. The Chinese emperor who had been enthroned by Rolpe Dorje's predecessor invited him to China where he spent three years teaching and establishing monasteries. Notably, Rolpe Dorje ordained a child from the Tsongkha region of Tibet and predicted that he would go on to play a significant role in Tibetan Buddhism; this child later became Tsongkhapa and founded the Dalai Lama's own Gelug school of Buddhism.

The IVth Karmapa was a poet and something of an artist. When one of his students had a dream about an enormous *thangka* (scroll painting) of Buddha, the Karmapa was able to map the Buddha's outline from the back of his horse, the hoof-prints clearly defining the image. The finished *thangka* was the product of 500 workers who laboured over it for a year. When Rolpe Dorje was cremated, it is said that divine flowers fell from the sky and the earth trembled six times.

THE BOY LAMA:
A TULKU IS DISCOVERED

The party dispatched from Tsurphu Monastery seeking the reincarnation of the XVIIth Karmapa left Lhasa on 12 May 1992. For the first time in history, the Chinese-controlled government of the Tibet Autonomous Region (TAR) had officially given its permission to invite the young Karmapa to Tsurphu. The Chinese government had established the TAR in 1965, which comprised only part of the vast area inhabited by Tibetans. The autonomy referred to in its title was largely nominal. The government would go on to endorse the Karmapa's enthronement. This approval was seen by the Tibetans as both prudent and necessary, in the wake of the Cultural Revolution that had made religion illegal. Much negotiating had taken place before arriving at this seemingly auspicious result that appeared to confirm that the government really had granted the Tibetans freedom to practise their religion.

For the first time in many years, the Chinese government and senior members from the community of exiled Tibetans had collaborated successfully. The government also provided some material assistance to the search party, such as the use of vehicles, and all of this amounted to an historic first. Never before had the secular Communist Party of China been involved in the installation of a high *tulku*. The Chinese referred to these incarnate lamas as 'living buddhas'.

As was customary on such expeditions, the search party would not disclose its purpose as it journeyed east from Lhasa. After some days' travel, and as the group approached Bagor, the region of the prediction letter, it was necessary for the three monks and their assistants to leave their cars and continue by horse, so rugged was the terrain. The region in which they believed their *tulku* would be found was blanketed in deep snow.

When, eventually, the three monks of the search party arrived at Karlek Monastery in Lhatok, they made a carefully worded inquiry. It was 18 May and the monastery's steward greeted them with some suspicion. One of the monks asked the steward for directions to Bagor, but the man would not give them without knowing their purpose in the area. The monks announced that they were carrying letters from India for Lolaga. The steward responded with instant recognition, commenting in passing that this must be Loga, the wife of Karma Döndrub. He went on to tell them that one of the family's sons happened to be staying there at the monastery.

Exchanging glances of excitement, the monks struggled to conceal their emotions from the curious steward. Everything was fitting into place: not just one but both the parents' names from the prediction letter corresponded with the names the steward had mentioned. The letter had stated that the method, or father, was Döndrub, and the wisdom, or mother, was Lolaga.

Yeshe Rabsel was brought to meet the monks, who told him that his brother was a *tulku* from their monastery. The Karmapa's name was not spoken, but plans were made for the party to visit Yeshe Rabsel's home.

Yeshe Rabsel left the monastery to return to his family and announce the exciting news. A search party from Tsurphu Monastery, he informed them, would be coming imminently to find the reincarnation of a *tulku*. Apo Gaga, apparently, started dancing with joy. That very morning, before his brother's arrival, he had already started gathering together his few belongings, ready to attach to his goat's back. He had told his mother gaily that it was time for him to go to his monastery.

While Karma Döndrub and Yeshe Rabsel beamed proudly at each other, Loga turned away briefly so that none of her family would see that her eyes were wetter than usual. She looked up to the dazzling blue sky, flecked white here and there with the vaguest suggestion of cloud. 'It is not as though I have not been awaiting this moment for the last seven years,' she told herself, before turning back to her family to start making the sensible suggestions for which she was known. They must have a tent for the visitors, Loga insisted, and some sheepskins for them to recline on. All the children threw themselves into this activity with uncharacteristic zeal, although Apo Gaga clearly saw his role as directing the proceedings. He behaved as though only he could possibly know what the visitors required. His family members, naturally, humoured him.

The searchers from Tsurphu arrived at Bagor on 21 May. The young boy they were seeking had assumed a much more serious mantle than he'd worn the day before, and kept something of a distance from the visitors. As the twenty-first was not an auspicious date, the monks agreed to hold off speaking to the family in any depth until the following day.

When the monks officially entered the family's tent on 22 May, Loga offered them tea and fine food. It was only once Karma Döndrub and Loga starting telling their son's story – all of it in chronological order – that they saw the weight of all those small omens and auspices amount to something very substantial. The search party clearly saw the substance of the story themselves, and of the boy before them, as well. With no doubts in their mind about the boy's identity, the monks from Tsurphu handed Karma Döndrub the XVIth Karmapa's letter of prediction.

A photograph was taken of the young *tulku*'s father reading the prediction letter. Later, when it was developed, the man appeared to radiate white light.[21]

As for Loga, she stood back and simply watched her son while she still could.

When the search party left the family and travelled to Karlek Monastery on 24 May, the blue sky put on a show for them. Around the sun appeared three smaller suns. Throughout the region, others reported seeing this curious phenomenon.

By 27 May, the searchers had returned, jubilant, to Lhasa to inform the authorities of the success of the mission and to make preparations to bring the *tulku* from his home and enthrone him. At Tsurphu, the next day, the news was announced publicly: 'The reincarnation of the glorious Karmapa has been born.'

TIBET: THE 17-POINT 'AGREEMENT'

On 23 May 1951, a Tibetan delegation in Beijing for negotiations with the PRC signed 'The Agreement of the Central People's Government and the Local Government of Tibet on Measures for the Peaceful Liberation of Tibet'. It was to become known as the 17-Point Agreement and would be broken by the Chinese so many times that it would have as little worth as the paper on which it was written. It claimed that Tibet had always been part of 'the motherland' (specifically over the previous hundred years), but that over the past century the 'local government' had failed to oppose 'imperialist deceptions and provocations'. The imperialists to whom the Chinese referred were the British, whose army had entered Tibet in 1905 but did not stay. The British had, however, established a trade mission there and up until China's occupation had treated Tibet as a sovereign nation. The agreement went on to promise Tibetans regional autonomy; claimed that the existing political system, including the status of the Dalai Lama, would remain in place; and vowed religious freedom would be upheld.

In fact, the Tibetan delegation had no authority from the *Kashag* to sign such an agreement. The Dalai Lama, at the monastery in which he was staying in Dromo, listened in horror to the announcement on Radio Peking heralding the agreement.

The delegation's leader, Ngabo Ngawang Jigme, had no power to sign on the Dalai Lama's behalf, only to negotiate. The fact that the Dalai Lama had the seals of state with him in the south confirmed that no final decision would be made without him. He assumed, correctly, that the former Governor of Kham had been coerced.[22] Rather than repudiate the agreement outright, even though its terms were odious to the Dalai Lama and the *Kashag* the Tibetan leader waited to hear his delegation's account.

What followed is something of a cat-and-mouse game between Tibetan and American representatives. By now, America had decided to support Tibet covertly in some way, careful to keep India in ignorance as Prime Minister Nehru felt that US involvement might result in a Cold War erupting in the Himalayas. The thrust of America's overtures was that she would not publicly commit to helping Tibet until the Dalai Lama had himself publicly rejected the 17-Point Agreement and declared his opposition to communist rule in Tibet. The Tibetans, for their part, were unwilling to publicly oppose the PRC without prior guarantee of American allegiance. Perhaps a significant issue in the Dalai Lama's reluctance to accept the US as Tibet's staunch ally lay in the fact that all US correspondence to him came in the form of unsigned letters on blank paper – for security reasons.

After a nine-month absence, the Dalai Lama returned to Lhasa in August, having decided that the only option, for the present, was to try to work with the Chinese.

On 20 October 1951, the *Kashag* and the Dalai Lama – by now returned to Lhasa – publicly accepted the 17-Point Agreement. It has been argued that the Tibetans' act of formal acceptance of Chinese sovereignty at this moment – despite the fact that the agreement was accepted under such duress – severely compromised both its legal and moral case for Tibetan independence, and that by signing the 17-Point Agreement Tibet eliminated her claim to independent statehood.[23]

Tibet's independence, for the twentieth century, had come to an end.

29 September 2003
LINEAGE: THE FIFTH KARMAPA
THE BOY LAMA: TO TSURPHU
TIBET: LHASA UNDER OCCUPATION

29 SEPTEMBER 2003

I am a hundred per cent Westerner in the East and spend my first morning in Dharamsala in my hotel room working the phones. And it really is hard work because for each person I speak to I must make many attempts beforehand. Mobile phone numbers are constantly unavailable because of congestion on the lines and I leave messages for people that never seem to be delivered. All the while, I watch the clock ticking, my brief time in India slipping away.

It is not that the people with whom I've been corresponding do not wish to see me, but they simply don't share my own sense of urgency. Indeed, I am to meet with some of the most senior people in the exile government, and speak on the telephone, a number of times, with the Dalai Lama's private secretary.

I have been given all the best contacts, not because of my credentials as a writer but because I have metamorphosed from a publishing worker to a Tibet activist. That resolve I felt after the Dalai Lama's press conference did, eventually, amount to something.

At first, my commitment remained merely a passionate interest and a willingness to take to the streets of London and join others in demanding a Free Tibet. It was not until some years after my return to Australia that I finally felt I could make the time to volunteer for a non-government organisation, the Australia Tibet Council, that campaigned for the Tibetans' rights. My small commitment – that of helping with the organisation's magazine – grew into volunteering in the office one afternoon a week, until eventually I joined the board. By now, the time of my visit to India thirteen years after my first contact with Tibetans and meeting with the Dalai Lama, I have been a director of Australia's largest Tibet support group for more than three years.

I eventually succeed in reaching the Karmapa's private secretary by telephone after some months of exchanging polite emails. Despite the encouraging words in Lama Phuntsok's emails to me, his reluctance to make a time or date to meet has been driving me crazy. Is it my paranoia or does he sound surprised to hear my voice? It's as though I am a completely unannounced visitor. He will come to meet me at the guesthouse down in the Kangra Valley to which I plan to move tomorrow. We do not make a time; instead, he mentions 'the afternoon' somewhat vaguely. It is not his sanity I question, but my own . . .

LINEAGE: THE FIFTH KARMAPA

The great Vth Karmapa, Deshin Shekpa (1384–1415), was born in southern Tibet. While he was in utero, his parents, who were advanced tantric practitioners, heard him reciting the Sanskrit alphabet and chanting mantras. It is reported that so many auspicious signs appeared during his mother's pregnancy that the local people gathered to make offerings to the child as soon as he was born. The baby apparently sat upright after his birth and announced, 'I am the Karmapa. *Om mani padme hung hri*.'

The Chinese emperor at the time, Yung Lo, had a vision of the Karmapa as Chenrezig, the *bodhisattva* of compassion, and subsequently invited him to China. While at the Ming court, the Karmapa is described in Chinese records as having been responsible for one hundred days of miracles. It is also reported that he prevented the Chinese invasion of Tibet a number of times by persuading the emperor, who was intent on imposing a single religious system over the land, of the value of different systems for different peoples.

The Karmapa became Yung Lo's guru and teacher. The emperor, making great progress with his practice, had a vision of the Vajra crown (in the form of a black hat) atop the Karmapa's head. This is the mystic black crown of Chenrezig that rests on the heads of all the Karmapas. Wishing for others to gain liberation from a vision of the crown, the emperor had a replica made and presented it to Deshin Shekpa, requesting that he wear it on special occasions. This event marks the origins of the Karmapa's Vajra Crown ceremony.

The ceremony that evolved, and that was practised up until the time of the XVIth Karmapa, entails the Karmapa initially wearing another hat while he prays and calls upon members of his lineage to give their blessings. The moment at which the Karmapa finally dons the Vajra is the point at which blessings transfer to the gathered assembly.

Deshin Shekpa made an important prediction. He claimed that troubles for his lineage were likely to arise 'after the XVIth in the rosary of Karmapa [and] before the XVIIth'. His prediction proved accurate.

The Vth Karmapa died young, at thirty-one years of age. Fully formed images of different buddhas and rainbow-coloured relics were found in the ashes of his funeral pyre.

THE BOY LAMA: TO TSURPHU

The boy the Tibetans would soon enthrone as the XVIIth Karmapa had changed somewhat since the lamas' visit. His habitual seriousness had only intensified, but with that had also come a more intense pleasure in the play that remained to him. More than anything else, during this last short period at home, Apo Gaga spent time in the mountains with his goat. It was as though he simply could not get enough of his remaining freedom or of Kham's wide, cobalt-blue skies.

One day, Apo Gaga came riding down to his family's tent, perched on his goat's back, calling for his little brother, Tsewang. When the three-year-old appeared, the elder boy took him by the hand and told him that together they had some important work to do. Apo Gaga led his brother some distance from the tent to the site of a once fertile spring that had run dry. In the past, it had been a well-used source of water for his family but its present barrenness meant that his mother, or one of his sisters, now had to carry water a longer distance. This situation had troubled the six-year-old Apo Gaga for some time now.

From inside his *chupa*, the elder boy produced a tiny juniper sapling that he had taken from another spot where the sacred trees were in abundance. The two boys found flat stones and used them to dig a good-sized hole for the plant, then placed it in the ground gently, together covering its fragile roots with soil and tamping it down around the narrow stalk. The two of them travelled between the stream and the dry spring to pour water on the sapling, Apo Gaga continuously speaking the Seven-Line Prayer to Tibet's founder, Guru Rinpoche, almost without pausing to take breath. He made his young brother promise to continue watering the plant in his absence, stressing that its survival was crucial to the family's well-being.

Many months later, when one of Apo Gaga's sisters happened to pass the site of the dried spring, she stopped short at the appearance of the tree that seemed to have grown so quickly from nothing. Beside the tree the spring, once again, had started to flow. When the girl scooped the cool, clear liquid into her mouth, it had more the taste of nectar than water. The spring, apparently, would ultimately prove crucial to the survival of the small community. When other water sources handy to the summer grazing lands failed, it continued to flow. Without it, the pastures would have been of little use to the people of Bagor. In summer the area appears barren, with Apo Gaga's tiny juniper a testament to hope and faith on the denuded slopes. When Loga was a girl, the area had been heavily forested and she had simply to collect fallen sticks for her family's fuel. Four decades after Chinese occupation, the only fuel available to them came from their family's yaks.[24]

Loga, for her part, took special care in preparing her son for departure, although when she allowed herself the opportunity to reflect she could see that this was for her own benefit more than for his. The boy had very few possessions and Loga suspected that they would quickly be replaced by more of the beautiful brocades and precious items of which she'd already seen a sample at the time the lamas visited. Nonetheless, the preparation of the boy's possessions made Loga feel she still had a role to play. As for preparing the boy in any other way, emotionally for instance, this was clearly unnecessary. He seemed to know exactly what awaited him and often seemed hard pressed to contain his delight at the prospect of the journey before him.

While the entire family would together travel the relatively short distance to Karlek Monastery, only Apo Gaga's parents, his two brothers and the youngest of his sisters, Mönlam, would travel all the way to Tsurphu with him. The journey would take at least seven days and Loga and Karma Döndrub were not certain about the length of time they would be gone. While Loga had no qualms about leaving her daughters within the tight-knit nomad community of Bagor, she had all manner of concerns for her son's well-being at Tsurphu Monastery, west of Lhasa.

Loga busied herself with preparing all that the family would need for their travels and tried not to fret over the threadbare nature of the clothes in which they would travel. They were, after all, content to be nomads, country folk, and they did not hanker after the finery of the lamas or city dwellers. Karma Döndrub was also immensely busy, in part as the feted father of the soon-to-be-enthroned XVIIth Karmapa and in part because of his own preparations for the journey, which essentially involved arranging things at home to be looked after in the family's absence. Members of their immediate community vied for the honour of caring for the family's livestock and Karma Döndrub diplomatically divided the responsibilities so as not to offend anybody. Overnight, his family's status had changed profoundly: they had become the closest thing to nobility that the community knew.

At Karlek Monastery, Apo Gaga's family gathered with an official party that had travelled west from Tsurphu. Also assembled to honour the boy were monks and lay people from the nearby Karma Gön Monastery, which had itself been founded by the very first Karmapa. It was 8 June 1992. The *tulku* was given a cleansing ritual and dressed in new robes. From this moment, the boy would be tended exclusively by monks.

Offerings from the Tsurphu lamas were showered on the *tulku*, and each item was rich in symbolism. His parents, extended family, Lama Amdo Palden and the Karlek monks were also the recipients of precious gifts from the west. All who had played a role in the boy's early years were remembered, their contribution gratefully recognised.

The local community offered its best horses for the first leg of the journey, for the single day that the party would need to travel by horseback. The gaiety and beauty of the grand parade of travellers distracted Apo Gaga's sisters from their sadness.

Loga and Karma Döndrub nodded to each other in silent pride as they caught glimpses of their young son, up near the head of the line of horses. When the three brothers – Yeshe Rabsel, Apo Gaga and Tsewang Rigdzin – managed to ride together, Loga swallowed the sob that was rising in her throat. With the knowledge she never again would be responsible for her son's intimate needs came the sensation that part of her had been permanently disabled. She could not help but worry for her middle son's future, despite the extraordinary honour that had transformed his life. Tibet was a different country to that which it had been when she was a young girl. All the high lamas had been forced to flee to India and, despite the recent softening, Loga fretted over her son's future.

As for the boy himself, his spirits had never been higher. He had the look of someone travelling home after a long journey. Thirty-three years had passed since the XVIth Karmapa had left Tsurphu and Tibet in early 1959. By that time, news of the destruction of monasteries further east had reached Lhasa and its surrounds. The PLA, in its efforts to smash Tibet's alleged feudalism, were particularly harsh on the monks and high lamas. Remaining in Tibet any longer would have left the Karmapa in grave danger of imprisonment, torture and even death. Not long after the Karmapa's departure, the Dalai Lama would also flee his home.

Leaving the nomads' high country meant leaving the horses behind and transferring into a convoy of four-wheel-drive vehicles. Loga noticed that her middle son, her *tulku*, seemed reluctant to dismount from his horse into the waiting arms of a monk. How long would it be, she wondered, before he rode on horseback again beneath the wide bright skies of Kham?

The next six days of the journey blurred into a series of breaks in elaborate, decorative Tibetan picnic tents. Fine food was being so lavished upon them all that the younger children, including Apo Gaga, seemed to no longer have any appetite. Loga worried about the waste of it all.

The one constant on those days of driving westwards was the Tibetans lining the road. Everywhere, fine Tibetan clothing had been reclaimed from storage and was now being worn in defiance of the days of the Cultural Revolution when such pride in tradition was forbidden. The locals proudly wore their traditional garb with a sense of joy. Here and there, a Mao hat or jacket blended seamlessly with the sheepskin and woven Tibetan fabric. The smell of the journey became a mixture of the distasteful odour of petrol fumes, and the familiar heady aroma of burning juniper. In her mind's eye, Loga imagined an unbroken chain of *khatags* marking their journey all the way from Lhatok to Tsurphu, such was the abundance of the white silk blessing scarves along their path.

On the day before the convoy's arrival at Tsurphu, an official welcome party led by Tsurphu's abbot, Drupön Dechen Rinpoche, greeted the *tulku* below a sacred mountain. The Karmapa's *dharma* throne had been positioned inside a ceremonial tent, and the boy was invited to sit on it for the first time.

Loga had become accustomed to seeing her fit, agile son carried almost everywhere. Admittedly, his new, ornate robes proved cumbersome for him but it was curious to see a young boy lifted from a jeep and carried to a tent as if he were an invalid. Apo Gaga, for his part, seemed to take this sort of attention in his stride. Indeed, he seemed to enjoy the contact with the monks and would often mischievously pat their heads as though they were the small children and he the wise father. Now the *tulku* was lifted from his jeep and carried past the row of monks and gathered lay people, all holding their white *khatags*. Loga noticed that her son had assumed a particularly serious demeanour and she found herself holding her breath in anticipation of something momentous. The monk placed the boy at the tent's opening and helped him arrange his robes. Apo Gaga hesitated for a moment before stepping inside, as if awaiting some unseen sign. When the boy eventually stepped across the threshold, a great triple thunderclap tore through the brooding silence below the dark clouds. Loga felt goosebumps rise on her skin and watched those around her involuntarily raise their hands to their foreheads in a gesture of prayer. Some of the older Tibetans spontaneously threw themselves down on the grass and began prostrating. The triple thunderclap symbolises one thing to Tibetans: fame.[25]

The following morning, Loga stole a little time with her son before the daunting events of the day ahead, the day he would arrive at Tsurphu. Apo Gaga, Loga noted, seemed preoccupied. For the first time, he seemed anxious about what lay before him.

'Are you worried that something will go wrong?' she asked her son.

'No, no.' He shook his head dismissively. 'It's the monastery. I can already see the broken buildings . . .'

As the convoy entered the Tölung Valley, which heralded the end of its journey, the picturesque scene ahead of them almost made Loga forget her son's reference to the damage that had been wrought in Tibet, and specifically at Tsurphu, between the country's occupation in 1950 and the end of the Cultural Revolution in 1976. In 1966, the PLA forced local Tibetans to demolish their beloved monastery. Soldiers had gone on to use Tsurphu's most precious statue for target practice before having it dynamited. Re-building did not start until 1982.

A river meandered through the dazzling yellow of fields in bloom, and the air was thick with juniper smoke. Tibetans lined the road in awed welcome. After a stop at Nenang Monastery, the party continued on its way and Loga could see her own tension mirrored on her husband's face beside her. Although her son was in a vehicle ahead of them, she was certain she could sense his anticipation. *Khatags* were now being flung at the jeep in which her son rode and the chanting of '*Karmapa khyenno*' – 'Karmapa think of me!' – filled the air. For the first time, Loga's son was openly being called Karmapa. For the first time, the people were making their own demands of him.

Horsemen rode out from Tsurphu Monastery wearing fine gold robes and carrying what looked like rifles. For a moment,

Loga wondered whether her son's life was now in danger but she chased this notion from her head. No, whatever the men were carrying was purely ornamental and rather than making her son a target, being the Karmapa would render him untouchable.

The horsemen were followed by gold-clad monks bearing incense and banners. Others formed an orchestra and yet others, wearing the masks of figures from myths and religious stories, danced and spun before them.

The *tulku*'s convoy now drew to a complete halt and the boy, in his gold brocade, was deposited atop a beautiful white stallion. On Apo Gaga's head was a hard riding hat covered in more gold brocade; an ornate umbrella, carried by a monk, hovered above him constantly. The image of Loga's son in all his finery was so at odds with that of him enjoying his favourite childhood pastime – riding his pet goat – yet it suited him just as well.

The details of the extraordinary gathering now started to blur for Loga; she had never seen so much pageantry. What's more, arriving at the Karmapa's monastery made Loga's permanent separation from Apo Gaga tangible. Her son was carried inside the temple, where he would receive many hundreds of devotees and bless each one of them. Outside, in the monastery's forecourt, a Tibetan opera was in full swing. Loga felt her eyes grow wider and wider in amazement until shutting them was the only way she could steady herself. When she glimpsed her son, sitting on the high throne in the temple, she saw clearly that, to him, this great whirl of colour and activity was perfectly normal. As for Loga, she joined her husband in gazing longingly at the mountains behind the monastery.

TIBET: LHASA UNDER OCCUPATION

The first PLA troops, numbering several thousand, marched into Lhasa towards the end of 1951. Their arrival marked the true beginning of Chinese communist occupation. The army and the party cadres were charged with transforming Tibet into a social-

ist society.[26] From the outset, the arrival of the Chinese troops –
despite their exemplary behaviour in accordance with PLA rules
– placed grave pressure on the environment; there was simply
not enough fuel for their cooking needs and soon an acute shortage of food developed. This initial environmental strain would
go on to multiply exponentially over the decades, as China
transformed herself from occupier to colonist.

As the Chinese started demanding food and lodging by right,
and no longer saw fit to pay for these essentials, the Tibetans'
anger became tangible. They started to clap and spit at the
Chinese soldiers (a traditional attempt to drive out evil), children threw rocks and stones, and monks wound the loose ends
of their robes into bunches that were used to whip away any
Chinese soldiers who approached them. As early as 1952, dissatisfaction at the Chinese presence in Lhasa was voiced through
a popular resistance movement and posters declaring the
Chinese enemies of the faith. The Chinese cadres, who genuinely
believed their various undertakings to bring reform to Tibet
were necessary and should therefore be welcomed by the
Tibetans, were alarmed at the anti-Chinese sentiment. Already
the first Tibetan revolutionary group was forming and some
Tibetans started openly demanding the withdrawal of Chinese
soldiers and cadres, or at the very least the limiting of their
numbers. Another concern of the people related to the Dalai
Lama; ordinary Tibetans felt it was imperative that he retain his
traditional power and status. Clearly, the Chinese government
were interested in him only as a compliant puppet, not as a true
leader. Monks and religious institutions must also be protected.

The Tibetans' flight into exile had already commenced,
although it was not described as such at the time. When Tibet's
two acting prime ministers, who had gained tremendous popular
support for their ongoing struggle for their people, were forced
to resign as a direct result of Chinese pressure, many Tibetan
aristocrats travelled to India under the pretext of going on a
pilgrimage. There they joined the other wealthy Tibetans who
had taken up residence in Kalimpong – the first Indian city
beyond the Sikkimese border – for the interim. Members of the

Dalai Lama's family had also left Tibet to attend school in India and this development was of particular concern to the Chinese. Their departure made it clear to any interested foreign parties that, despite Chinese officials' best efforts, they could not convince the Dalai Lama's own family that communism was a boon to Tibet.

The Dalai Lama's eldest brother, Thubten Norbu (who had become Takster Rinpoche), fled his own monastery – Kumbum in Amdo – where he was being held by the Chinese. They had been attempting to indoctrinate him into communism and wished for him to then go to Lhasa and convince his brother, the Dalai Lama, to accept Chinese rule. If Thubten Norbu would not agree to undertake this mission, the Chinese promised to kill him. After fully explaining to his brother what was going on in eastern Tibet, Thubten Norbu escaped to India.

Already the secular communist government sought to promote a religious leader to further its own ends. The communists went on to demand the Dalai Lama and the *Kashag* recognise the Panchen Lama, a high-profile lama in the Dalai Lama's Gelug school, fully. Indeed, the Chinese sought to elevate the Panchen Lama to a status akin to that of the Dalai Lama. So important was the Panchen Lama to the communists that one of the clauses of the 17-Point Agreement concerned his status. Traditionally, the Panchen Lama occupied himself with religious affairs, leaving all secular matters to the Dalai Lama. The IXth Panchen Lama, however, became active beyond religion and ultimately fled his monastery, Tashilhunpo (situated at Shigatse, to Lhasa's west), back in 1923 when a conflict arose between it and the Tibetan government. When he died in 1937, the Nationalist Chinese had seized the opportunity to gain influence in Tibet by giving their support to a child named as the Panchen Lama's tenth incarnation. The boy had been enthroned at a monastery in Amdo by the time the communists came to power, but the Tibetan government still refused to recognise him. The young Panchen Lama reportedly sent telegrams to Chairman Mao, conveying good wishes and support 'on behalf of all the people in Tibet'.

Finally, in April 1952, the fourteen-year-old Panchen Lama arrived in Lhasa, escorted by more than 1000 Chinese troops. Tibetans were somewhat divided, some referring to him as 'the Chinese Lama' while others – notably those from Shigatse – were pleased that the Chinese were endowing him with what they saw as his true and rightful status. After much negotiation between Lhasa and Tashilhunpo, the Panchen Lama returned to Shigatse where he was formally re-enthroned.

30 September 2003
Lineage: the sixth Karmapa
The boy lama: one for Tibet,
one for the free world
Tibet: living under communism

30 SEPTEMBER 2003

Half an hour east of Dharamsala is the Norbulingka Institute, dedicated to the preservation of Tibetan culture in both its literary and artistic forms. Like Chonor House up at McLeod Ganj, the place feels utterly at odds with the dust and poverty of rural India. Named after the Dalai Lama's summer palace, the institute is, quite simply, a refuge. The Norbulingka's gardens are beautifully laid out and I follow stone paths through the trees, parting veils of flowers before me. Everywhere is the sound of running water and birdsong and I feel far from the tourist thrum of McLeod Ganj.

I am going to stay in the Norbulingka Institute's guesthouse for a few days, as the centre is within easy reach of the Karmapa's 'temporary' residence at Gyuto Tantric University. In my simple room, the fan hums overhead, barely stirring the dank smell of the monsoon that finished some weeks ago. Here in the Himalayan foothills, everything feels musty, instead of marigolds, I smell damp. From my room, I look through a vine-covered fence into a field where two buffalos graze, resplendent in their great bestial blackness.

It is no idle claim to say that the Norbulingka Institute strives to preserve Tibetan culture. Here, new arrivals from Tibet are taught the ancient art of *thangka* painting, taught to sew clothing in Tibetan styles, and learn to fashion and paint traditional Tibetan furniture. As I wander around the institute's grounds, the whirr of sewing machines draws me to a doorway. Inside, a group of women work with myriad pieces of coloured silk, creating magnificent appliqué wall hangings depicting Tibetan pastoral scenes. One of these – an image of yaks in a green meadow below snow-capped peaks – I will carry home with me. It will nurture my family's dreams of a land we have not yet seen.

Lama Phuntsok, the Karmapa's private secretary, is coming to meet me. His apparent reluctance to make a fixed appointment sees me tormented by pangs of anxiety. I sit in the guesthouse's communal lounge room, trying to focus on Robert

Thurman's most recent book on Buddhism, *Inner Revolution*; if nothing else, there is time to think.

I wait for two hours, reading in fits and starts, before abandoning my book and deciding to walk along the shady paths outside. On tenterhooks, I somehow feel that everything hinges on this meeting with the secretary. If I am honest with myself, I admit that I am not even confident of meeting the Karmapa. Over the past few months of planning and correspondence, although I've had nothing but encouraging feedback about my project from exile government employees and the Karmapa's private secretary, I have been able to get no clear sense of what access to the great lama, if any, I'll be granted.

When I return to the guesthouse, the flash of maroon robes in the foyer announces that Lama Phuntsok himself is real, rather than some ever-polite persona created by the Karmapa's administration to placate people like me. He stands, waiting for me, grinning easily. He appears younger than I had anticipated – a slim, fit-looking man with spiky black hair, greying at the temples, sporting a thinnish moustache and a narrow, vertical goatee. I try to make my smile big enough to erase the doubt from my face. We shake hands warmly but I cannot be sure of whether my expression is successfully hiding my anxiety. I offer him tea, which he declines, and invite him to come and sit with me in the lounge room. For all the world, he gives the air of someone just passing who thought they'd drop in, not of a cleric coming to meet some unknown writer who has taken it upon herself to undertake a book on his master. (Later, when I glimpse him in documentary footage at the XVIth Karmapa's side, I realise that his youthful appearance was just that, appearance.)

We make polite conversation and I learn that Lama Phuntsok is widely travelled and has spent time in the US and Europe, as well as in India and Nepal. Indeed, for some time he was based at one of the Karma Kagyu's two principal Western monasteries, at Woodstock in upstate New York.

After seemingly endless small talk, Lama Phuntsok ventures, 'So you would like to write a book on the Karmapa?'

'Yes', I tell him uneasily. 'That's my plan. That is what I intend.'

Quickly I proceed with my spiel, telling him I wish to write about a contemporary Tibetan in a way that will illuminate, for Western readers, the lives of modern Tibetans, both inside Tibet and in exile. I make this sound eminently achievable, perhaps to give myself courage more than anything else.

Lama Phuntsok seems rather pleased by what I've told him and I offer him a letter from my publisher, hoping that what is clearly set out as a done deal won't offend him. With very little fuss, after all that we are making an appointment for me to meet the Karmapa the next day.

In the early evening, I climb to the roof of the Norbulingka Institute's temple. To the west is Dharamsala and to the east, Gyuto Tantric University. The university cum monastery is a Gelug institution – that is, it belongs to the Dalai Lama's Gelug school, not the Karmapa's Karma Kagyu school – but this is where the Karmapa has been housed since shortly after his arrival in India. He has not yet been granted permission by the Indian government to travel to his own monastery, at Rumtek in Sikkim. I look east, trying to imagine my meeting with His Holiness, the XVIIth Karmapa, scheduled for eleven o'clock tomorrow morning. A headline in London's *Daily Telegraph* proclaimed him a '900-year-old teenager'.[27] Is it possible that the Karmapa is standing on the roof of Gyuto's very own temple, looking west and thinking of the very same meeting?

I am joined at my eyrie by a large, plump-faced, smiling Tibetan monk. In broken English he tells me he's from Kham, and I learn that he's a geshe (doctor of philosophy) and a teacher. We share a fond appreciation of the mountains rising behind the temple to the north. He points towards Dharamsala, telling me that he can clearly see the Dalai Lama's residence. Try as I may, I cannot discern it from its surroundings.

I am drawn to Geshe's great warm, toothy smile. I find myself smiling at him so he'll smile back; he needs no prompting.

LINEAGE: THE SIXTH KARMAPA

The VIth Karmapa, Thongwa Dönden (1416–1453), was born in eastern Tibet, not far from where the XVIIth Karmapa would be born around 550 years later. It is reported that straight after his birth he sat up and laughed, and that when his umbilical cord was cut 'celestial fragrance permeated the countryside'.[28] When only four months old, he grew excited at encountering one of the students of the previous Karmapa. The student inquired after the child's name and the infant replied that he was the Karmapa. When the boy was taken to Karma Gön Monastery and shown pictures of the previous Karmapas, he announced 'That is me!' and claimed that the Vajra crown was his, too. Apparently, nomads saw flowers rain from the sky for three days before Thongwa Dönden was finally proclaimed the Karmapa.

The VIth Karmapa is said to have cured epidemics by conferring blessings and ended a drought by playing with water. Ordained at nine, he spent his life composing prayers, founding and restoring monasteries, having sacred books printed and spreading the *dharma*.

THE BOY LAMA:
ONE FOR OCCUPIED TIBET,
ONE FOR THE FREE WORLD

Stories of heroes, and of prospective heroes, are never quite as simple as their champions would like them to be. The tale of the young XVIIth Karmapa, as it happens, was already tainted by controversy before he was enthroned. The stories told by the different parties, it seems, are as polemic as the two very different histories of Tibet that are promoted by the Chinese and the Tibetans.

The XVIth Karmapa died in a Chicago hospital in November 1981; he had been in the US teaching. After his death, the responsibility of managing his affairs and continuing his work until the day that his XVIIth incarnation should attain his majority, fell upon the shoulders of the Tsurphu *labrang* (Tsurphu administration). The *labrang*, made up of the Karmapa's General Secretary and close disciples, serves the Karmapa over the generations in his different incarnations. For the first time in the 800-odd years of the Karmapa's existence, however, the Tsurphu *labrang* would be forced to operate during this sensitive period between Karmapas outside Tibet, from the Karmapa's seat in exile at Rumtek Monastery in Sikkim. The XVIth Karmapa was the first Karmapa to die while he and the *labrang* were in exile. Rumtek monastery was established as the Karmapa's seat after the XVIth Karmapa fled Tsurphu, and Tibet, in 1959.

Individuals also have a role in this process, as the responsibility of passing on the spiritual lineage from one incarnation to the next usually falls to one key disciple or root guru. Not only does the Karmapa's prediction letter often get handed to this key disciple, but the sacred teachings do as well, and it falls to this disciple to transmit the teachings to the Karmapa. In this way the lineage has continued.

Over the centuries, different emanations of great Kagyu lamas had been entrusted with this key role of root guru. Prior to the end of the eighteenth century, the incarnations of Shamar Rinpoche and Gyalstab Rinpoche had featured in the process. Over the last 200 years, the Tai Situ and Jamgon Kongtrul emanations have been honoured with the role. While the holder of the prediction letter, or Last Testament, plays a significant part in finding the Karmapa's incarnation, the Karmapa – because of the details given in his letter – is nonetheless said to 'self recognise'.

After the XVIth Karmapa's cremation, his General Secretary requested that the Karmapa's four 'heart sons' – Tai Situ Rinpoche, Shamar Rinpoche, Jamgon Kongtrul Rinpoche and Gyalstab Rinpoche – form a council of regents to take joint responsibility for the spiritual affairs of the Karma Kagyu lineage. They were referred to as the four seat-holders and were charged with the responsibility of locating the Karmapa's prediction letter and bringing forth his next incarnation. Each one was to act as sole regent for a period of three years on a rotating basis. The Tsurphu *labrang* would support each regent in his endeavours during his period of office. In December 1982, thirteen months after the death of the XVIth Karmapa, his General Secretary of some thirty-four years died unexpectedly. A new General Secretary, Topga Yulgal, was appointed during the term of the first regent, Shamar Rinpoche.

In the past, Karmapas have handed their prediction letters to a trusted lama with instructions about when exactly the letter should be opened and read. When the XVIth Karmapa died, however, none of those close to him were aware of the existence of such a letter. As the years passed, and no letter was unearthed, the prediction of the Vth Karmapa must have weighed heavily upon the regents. Deshin Shekpa had warned that troubles for the lineage might arise 'after the XVIth in the rosary of Karmapa [and] before the XVIIth'. As the years passed, the Karmapa's devotees – estimated to number a million within Tibet and a couple of hundred thousand in the West – became more and more vocal in their demands that the XVIIth Karmapa be recognised. During the decade after the XVIth Karmapa's death, different regents called meetings to make announcements, and rumour and speculation were rife, yet all to no material end. A number of children across the Himalayan region were put forward by various people as the Karmapa, one of whom was a Bhutanese prince.

During the period, it was not uncommon for a lama to announce that such and such a woman was carrying the incarnation of the XVIth Karmapa, only to result in the woman giving birth to a girl child. One self-proclaimed Karmapa discounted the fact that he had been born before the XVIth Karmapa's death as mere detail, insisting that he had inhabited a body without a soul before the Karmapa's soul eventually came to him.

The Karma Kagyu lamas seemed divided about where the reincarnation, once found, should live. Some insisted that it would be impossible for the XVIIth Karmapa to live within

Tibet, even should he choose to be reborn there. Should the child be born in Tibet, therefore, he must be smuggled to India and the safety of Rumtek before any official recognition could take place. Others were already carefully doing the groundwork that would result in the XVIIth Karmapa being accepted by the Chinese authorities.

Some seven years after the Karmapa's death, Tai Situ Rinpoche recalled that his master had given him a sealed protection amulet back in December 1980, telling him, 'This is your protection amulet. In the future, it will confer great benefit.' Although protection amulets typically do not contain objects that require scrutiny, Tai Situ Rinpoche ultimately decided to open the precious gift. It contained the prediction letter for the rebirth of the XVIth Karmapa. It would, however, be years, not months, before Tai Situ presented the letter to the other regents.

The four seat-holders of the Karmapa met at Rumtek on 19 March 1992 to review the letter. At the first official discussion of the letter, none of the four regents was reported as having any doubt about its authenticity. From it, they determined that the XVIth Karmapa had been reborn in the Lhatok region of Kham in eastern Tibet ('*lha*' meaning divine, and '*thog*' meaning thunder) in a community bearing the sign of the cow. The year of birth, according to the Tibetan calendar, coincided with that of the one used for the earth – the Wood Ox – and was therefore 1985.

They wasted no time in planning to send a search party. As it happened, Jamgon Kongtrul Rinpoche had already arranged to be in Tibet in June so it was agreed that he should represent them in leading the search. What's more, as the grandson of Ngabo Ngawang Jigme, he might be able to arrange the cooperation of both Chinese and Tibetan officials.

Jamgon Kongtrul Rinpoche had been sent a new car – a BMW, no less – by his brother in the US and wished to commence his auspicious journey in this powerful yet somewhat unlikely vehicle. On the way to the airport, Jamgon's driver lost control of the car. Three of those riding in it were killed, including Jamgon Kongtrul Rinpoche. It was 26 April.

Speculation continues to this day about whether the accident was orchestrated to prevent him from undertaking the crucial journey on which he was about to embark. The two regents who were at Rumtek at the time, Tai Situ Rinpoche and Gyalstab Rinpoche, decided that the search should not be delayed and appointed Akong Rinpoche and Sherab Tarchin as their representatives.

Akong Rinpoche, who was one of the two co-founders of Samye Ling, the Tibetan monastery in Scotland, had particularly close ties with the XVIth Karmapa and was attending his funeral rites at Rumtek. The fact that he had travelled to Tibet a number of times in recent years doing charitable work made him an ideal member of the search party. Sherab Tarchin was treasurer of Gyalstab Rinpoche's organisation.

Prior to the pair's departure, the details of the prediction letter were dispatched to the abbot of Tsurphu Monastery. By this time, it had become clear to Tai Situ Rinpoche and Gyalstab Rinpoche that Shamar Rinpoche's cooperation in the matter of searching for the boy described in the letter would not be forthcoming.

All was not well among the regents. Shamar Rinpoche had refused to stand down at the end of his agreed term as sole regent because the three other regents had accused him of trying to transfer the Karmapa's land into his own name. While the allegations were never proven in court, they were to have serious ramifications. The rotating regent-ship dissolved, and with the support of the *labrang*'s General Secretary (Shamav's cousin), Shamar Rinpoche himself became sole regent.

The advance search party from Tsurphu Monastery arrived at Loga and Karma Döndrub's home on 21 May 1992. The two regents' representatives, Akong Rinpoche and Sherab Tarchin, subsequently verified the boy's identity upon meeting him. From Delhi, Tai Situ Rinpoche and Gyalstab Rinpoche confirmed that their master's reincarnation had been found via an intermediary in Lhasa. Armed with this auspicious news, they headed north to Dharamsala to inform the Dalai Lama and to seek his confirmation of the boy's recognition. The Dalai Lama was, in fact, in Brazil at the time of their arrival, but, through his office, they conveyed to him the salient points. The Tibetan leader, after some consideration, issued an informal confirmation of the reincarnation.

On 12 June, Tai Situ Rinpoche and Gyalstab Rinpoche arrived at Rumtek to announce that not only was the XVIIth Karmapa's reincarnation being installed at Tsurphu Monastery, but that the Dalai Lama had given the boy his approval. Shamar Rinpoche arrived soon after, apparently to dispute these claims. Accompanied by soldiers from the Indian Army, Shamar Rinpoche reportedly made his way through the monastery's courtyard and into the shrine room, clearly angry. Members of the public, particularly the gathered Sikkimese, protested at the army's arrival at the monastery. With the assistance of the Sikkimese police, who were stationed outside the monastery, the soldiers were persuaded to leave. The involvement of the Indian Army came about, allegedly, because it had been suggested to the Indian government that the Chinese were manipulating the entire dispute as they were intent on gaining power first at Rumtek and then across Sikkim.

Subsequently, and after meetings on 29 June with Tai Situ Rinpoche, Shamar Rinpoche and Gyaltsab Rinpoche, the Dalai Lama went on to issue a document known as the *Buktham Rinpoche*. It was his official confirmation of the recognition of Apo Gaga as the reincarnation of the XVIth Karmapa. It was dated 30 June 1992.

> The boy born to Karma Döndrub and Loga in the Wood-Ox Year (of the Tibetan calendar) identifies with the prediction letter (left by the late Karmapa) and is hereby recognized as the reincarnation of the XVIth Karmapa. With prayers for his well-being and for the success of his activities.
>
> The Dalai Lama, as translated by Kalon Tashi Wangdi.

The Dalai Lama had already told Tai Situ Rinpoche that he himself had had a special dream regarding the Karmapa's rebirth. In it, he had found himself in a beautiful green valley replete with lovely streams. It was cradled by low mountains and apparently, upon waking from this dream, the Tibetan leader felt intense happiness. 'Some source told me that this is the place where Karmapa is born,' the Dalai Lama subsequently told film-maker Clemens Kuby, and the source to which he refers is clearly other-worldly. The description he gave of the scene seemed to correspond with the details of Apo Gaga's birthplace.[29]

Those supporting Shamar Rinpoche insist that his is the opinion that matters in the Karmapa's recognition because he, they claim, is the highest ranking of the Karma Kagyu lamas after the Karmapa. Historically, his incarnation once was. However, the Shamar incarnation has spent its fair share of time beneath a dark cloud. In 1793, the Xth Shamar Rinpoche (1742–1792) was deported from Tibet for anti-government activities and the Shamar incarnation was officially banned. His monastery was subsequently confiscated. No Shamar appeared in the Kagyu lineage tree after the Xth, but it is rumoured that he reincarnated in secret for the next 200 years. The current Shamar was only recognised by the XIVth Dalai Lama, informally after China's invasion of Tibet and formally once the Tibetan leader had gone into exile, and at the express wishes of the XVIth Karmapa. Tibetan religion and culture were, at the time, under threat.

It is alleged by Shamar Rinpoche's followers that the power play over which of the four 'heart sons' would emerge as the key disciple began as early as at the XVIth Karmapa's cremation ceremony. One story has it that a mysterious charred ball flew from an opening in the Karmapa's funeral pyre and landed in Tai Situ Rinpoche's right hand. The other story purports that the ball simply rolled to the north of the pyre, in the direction of Tibet, and that Tai Situ Rinpoche was not even present at the time. Apparently he later took the object, which was now speculatively being referred to as the Karmapa's heart, to his own rooms. The two versions of this story illustrate the public moment of divide. To some, it suggests that Tai Situ Rinpoche was clearly the chosen disciple, and, to others, that he simply wished to fashion events to make things appear in this way.

One camp has it that Tai Situ Rinpoche's relationship with the XVIth Karmapa had irrevocably broken down. Yet it was he, not Shamar Rinpoche, who was with the Karmapa at the moment of his death and clearly intimacy existed in their relationship at the time. It is widely believed that great Buddhist masters choose their moment of death and it seems unlikely that mere coincidence saw Tai Situ Rinpoche at his master's bed at that propitious moment.

Shamar Rinpoche's camp insists that the moment Shamar laid eyes on the prediction letter that Tai Situ Rinpoche produced for the recognition of the young Apo Gaga, he pronounced it a forgery. Whether Shamar voiced his doubts at that meeting or not, things assumed a momentum of their own when one of the four regents flashed the envelope containing the letter as they emerged from their meeting at Rumtek on 19 March 2002. Devotees had gathered from far and wide once it was known that the four regents were meeting at the monastery.

Jamgon Kongtrul Rinpoche was said to be the peacemaker between the two factions but what followed, as we already know, was his sudden and tragic death.[30] While Shamar Rinpoche was trying to have forensic tests done on a copy of the prediction letter, the search was already in full swing.

Apparently it was on 11 June that Shamar Rinpoche issued his first public statement doubting the veracity of the letter; by this time, Apo Gaga's life had already irrevocably changed. (Later, Shamar Rinpoche would hint that he was on the trail of another candidate; a senior, trusted confidant of the previous Karmapa had approached him to say that he was in possession of the Karmapa's instructions, but that the time was not yet ripe to make them public.)

Despite his doubts, on 17 June Shamar Rinpoche signed a statement saying that he no longer had any concerns over the prediction letter's authenticity. On the same date, he attended a meeting with the Chief Minister of Sikkim, along with other important Kagyu lamas, and stated that they had resolved their differences over the recognition of the XVIIth Karmapa and had unanimously agreed upon the boy named by the Dalai Lama. In a letter to the Tibetan leader, dated 29 June, Shamar Rinpoche once again accepted the recognition of Apo Gaga.

Here it is worth remembering that a power struggle between the different schools of Tibetan Buddhism has simmered away beneath the surface for centuries. At different times in Tibetan history, one or the other of the schools has been the most dominant. The Dalai Lama's Gelug school has held the most prominent position in Tibetan society since the seventeenth century. At that time, the Mongol Army, under Gushri Khan, attacked Tibet and, with it, the Xth Karmapa's camp. The Xth Karmapa, Chöying Dorje, fled Tibet and, ultimately, the Vth Dalai Lama assumed temporal power in 1642. While the current Dalai Lama has called for the end to rivalry between the different schools of Buddhism, for some the power struggle is still very much alive. When the Dalai Lama endorsed the recognition of Apo Gaga as the XVIIth Karmapa, some Tibetans accused him of interference.

Shamar Rinpoche's supporters contend that back on 29 June Shamar Rinpoche first presented the Dalai Lama with details about this other possible candidate but, nonetheless, the Dalai Lama's official confirmation of Apo Gaga's recognition was issued the following day.

The General Secretary, Topga Yulgyal, who was appointed by Shamar Rinpoche, was subsequently forced to resign for 'indiscipline' as a result of a resolution of the Kagyu International General Assembly. The Deputy General Secretary, Tenzin Namgyal, was then elevated to the role of General Secretary. The meeting, which was held at Rumtek's Dharma Chakra Centre between 30 November and 3 December 1992, was attended by more than ninety-five per cent of the lamas and followers of the Karma Kagyu school. Shamar Rinpoche did not attend. Despite figures from that meeting suggesting the opposite, Shamar Rinpoche's Western supporters continue to argue that the vast majority of Karma Kagyu Buddhists support Thaye Dorje as the XVIIth Karmapa.

A second 'incident' took place at Rumtek Monastery in August 1993 and would go on to become significant in terms of legal proceedings that ensued. On the second of the month, Tai Situ Rinpoche and Gyalstab Rinpoche arrived at the monastery to conduct ceremonies for the *Yarney*, the rainy season retreat. Upon arrival, they found that the doors of the Shrine hall were locked and so they sent out messages to find one of the Assistant Shrine Masters who held the key. A monk official was located but he refused to open the doors, apparently upon orders from Shamar Rinpoche. Local worshippers were arriving and became distressed that the two lamas were being barred from the hall. Tensions rose as more monks supporting Shamar arrived and the police were called in. The local constabulary eventually persuaded the Assistant Shrine Master to hand over the key and the doors were opened. The keys were subsequently given to Tai Situ and Gyalstab Rinpoche who placed them in the hand of a different official.

Notably, Shamar Rinpoche went on to claim that on that date, 2 August 1993, the Karmapa Charitable Trust and its trustees had been 'dispossessed' of the Karmapa's properties by the government of Sikkim and Gyalstab Rinpoche. Although Tai Situ Rinpoche was one of the trustees at the time, he did not join the suit – Shamar, the trust itself and two other trustees comprised the plaintiffs – that has attempted to prove this dispossession illegal.

The Karmapa Charitable Trust had been established back in 1961, two years after the XVIth Karmapa's flight from Tibet. The founders comprised twelve residents of Sikkim, as well as the Karmapa – both as an individual and as the head of the Tsurphu *labrang*. The Karmapa acted as sole trustee. It was established 'for the benefit of the followers of the Karmapa and the Karmapa himself'[31] and the money conveyed to the trust at its instigation totalled a little more than 250,000 rupees. On the death of the XVIth Karmapa, the trust was to be administered by a group of trustees until such time that the XVIIth Karmapa reached twenty-one years of age.

The assertion that the trustees were 'dispossessed' of the

Karmapa's properties on 2 August 1993 indicated that at least some trustees believed the trust had inherited or controlled the XVIth Karmapa's entire estate.

Despite statements he had issued to the contrary, Shamar Rinpoche clearly continued to disbelieve that the boy who had been enthroned the XVIIth Karmapa was genuine. Indeed, in January 1994, his own candidate, whom he had smuggled out of Tibet, reached Delhi and was subsequently enthroned at the Karmapa International Institute (Delhi) on 17 March 1994. On three different occasions, over the ensuing years, Shamar Rinpoche petitioned the Dalai Lama to recognise his candidate, Thaye Dorje. Despite the Dalai Lama's requests for proof to confirm Thaye Dorje's recognition, Shamar managed to produce nothing conclusive, at least in the eyes of the Dalai Lama. Certainly, there is no other prediction letter.

On the third occasion that Shamar petitioned the Dalai Lama, and after the commencement of legal action decreeing over the Karmapa's estate in Sikkim, he put a most curious request to the Tibetan leader. Shamar Rinpoche proposed a compromise solution that would entail the Dalai Lama decreeing Ogyen Trinley Dorje the Karmapa for the Tibetans in occupied Tibet, and his own candidate, Thaye Dorje, the Karmapa for the free world. One can only assume that the Karmapa 'for the free world', under this scheme, would become a very wealthy man.

TIBET: LIVING UNDER COMMUNISM

Once the Chinese had solved the issue of shortages by arranging the import of food and goods from India, public anger towards them was tempered. Under the Chinese administration, printing plants were established and a Tibetan newspaper was published every ten days. For the first time, Tibetans could read of international news in their own language. Some wealthy Tibetans even began to send their children to school in China.

Road building had been progressing at a great rate – initially Tibetans were well paid for their labour – and by the end of 1954 the Qinghai-Tibet Highway had been completed. It was now possible to drive from Lhasa to Beijing, more than 3000 kilometres away, in twenty days. These roads, however, were not merely a means for transportation. Not only did building roads provide the Chinese with the opportunity to organise political study for the Tibetans while they worked in road gangs, but the roads themselves helped shore up the PRC's control over Tibet.

From the Chinese perspective, the spread of communist ideals was progressing satisfactorily within Tibet. China's control over the Tibetans seemed tighter by the day. More significantly, things were progressing well for them internationally. In 1954, China had signed a trade agreement with India, part of which outlined 'Five Principles of Co-existence', otherwise known as the *Panch Sheela*. While ostensibly addressing the issue of trade, the agreement implied India's acceptance of Chinese sovereignty over Tibet.[32] Thus Tibet's southern neighbour, with whom she shared the origins of Buddhism, became the first member of the international community to trade away Tibet's independence. She would not be the last. One writer, in his book about the Tibetan diaspora, suggested that the agreement was testament to the Indian prime minister's admiration for the communists' anti-colonial stance.[33] In four years' time, Achary Kripalani, the leader of an Indian socialist movement, described the agreement as 'born in sin to put the seal of our approval on the destruction of an ancient nation'.[34]

In 1954, a Tibetan delegation that included the Dalai Lama, Panchen Lama and the XVIth Karmapa, attended the National People's Congress in Beijing. The Dalai Lama hoped his presence there would help Tibet maintain its autonomy, but ultimately the Chinese gained more from his presence than the Tibetans. The Chinese used the Dalai Lama's attendance and the semblance of his participation (all talks were conducted in Chinese, which he had not mastered) as international propaganda and apparent proof that the Tibetans accepted Chinese rule.

During the Dalai Lama's visit to Beijing, in March 1955 the

Preparatory Committee for the eventual establishment of the Autonomous Region of Tibet (PCART) was formed and comprised representation by three groups, one headed by the Dalai Lama and another by the Panchen Lama. Once PCART was functioning, the implementation of communist reforms in Tibet, previously carried out by the Chinese military, would be handled by the new body. On the one hand, the establishment of PCART gave the semblance of more Tibetan participation in decision-making but, on the other, it was specifically engineered to speed up the integration of Tibet into the so-called motherland.

The Dalai Lama's status and power had already been significantly eroded, despite clause 4 in the 17-Point Agreement that vowed to maintain his position. PCART had given power not only to the Panchen Lama, but also to a group called the Chamdo Liberation Committee, which was comprised of both Tibetans and members of the PLA's invading force. The Chinese also fostered involvement in politics by different groups, including leaders from other Buddhist schools. This change marked the first time those from other schools had been involved in Tibetan politics since Gelug rule had been established in the seventeenth century under the Vth Dalai Lama. Although the *Kashag* was permitted to exist, its power had been eroded even more severely than the Dalai Lama's.

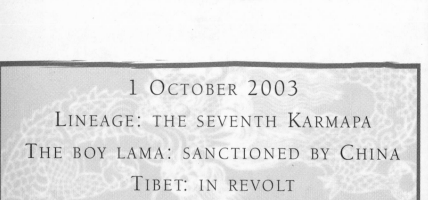

1 OCTOBER 2003
LINEAGE: THE SEVENTH KARMAPA
THE BOY LAMA: SANCTIONED BY CHINA
TIBET: IN REVOLT

1 OCTOBER 2003

This is the day I meet His Holiness the XVIIth Karmapa. Somewhat inauspiciously, it happens to be Chinese National Day.

My meditative ritual during these days at Norbulingka will have some formality. This morning, as I will do every morning, I walk to the temple and linger to watch the Tibetans in their prayers before the great golden Buddha. I move on and climb the stairs to the temple's roof. As I had hoped, the air is clear and for the first time I can see many, many kilometres to the south. Instead of the cultivated plains and clusters of houses that I'd expected, there are forested hills rolling away before me. As isolated as this part of India is, the Tibetans are, I think, fortunate to have landed here. Life further south, in semi-tropical southern India where the largest Tibetan settlements are located, is a far cry from what it was in the so-called land of snows.

Here at the Norbulingka Institute, as at Chonor House, the walls are decorated with Tibetan birds and animals, some mythical, most real. In the café, bird murals surround me and I feel that I'm dining in a snow-dusted aviary. Bird book in hand, I struggle to identify them: the Tibetan partridge, the Himalayan woodpecker, the brown hawk owl, the black-necked crane . . . Above me, appliquéd onto white cloth, are cloud motifs in red, blue and green. In the room in which I sleep, tigers and rabbits dance below the ceiling.

As with so many things I cherish about Tibet, a number of these animals and birds are now extinct, or threatened within Tibet today. Chinese soldiers and settlers hunted the once-protected wildlife, killing exponentially more than Tibetan hunters ever had, and deforestation on a massive scale saw many other animals perish. During the Cultural Revolution, Mao ordered that Tibetans should kill a quota of birds and insects each day, as these creatures were deemed detrimental to the economy because they fed on crops.

Mao's attitude towards religion and culture was no less brutal.

Given the limitations of my traveller's wardrobe, I choose a long skirt and simple T-shirt – complete with scarf at my throat for modesty's sake – in which to meet the Karmapa. Westerners, I gather, often struggle to know how to dress appropriately for audiences with Tibetan lamas. My favourite story about dressing for the lamas concerns a Californian woman. To her audience with the Dalai Lama, she is reported to have worn a pair of fairy wings.

I take a taxi east from the Norbulingka to Gyuto and we turn into a simple, unmarked lane. There are no signs, no indicators that this is the home of a great *tulku*, let alone of the only incarnate lama endorsed by both the Dalai Lama and the Chinese government.

Gyuto Tantric University is an austere place, lifeless and dull when compared to the verdant Norbulingka Institute. The temple complex itself, rising before the mountains, is handsome enough but the place lacks the energy of the living. On either side of the courtyard in front of the temple is newly built accommodation for monks. I hear that 400 of them will one day be housed here. For the moment, the rooms are empty and I stand alone in the monastery's courtyard which is the size of a football pitch. I feel the eyes of an Indian security guard upon me from way up on one of the temple's terraces. Eventually a Tibetan woman comes by – she's been shopping for food – and asks if I'm here for the audience. She does not like me standing out there alone and ushers me inside with her, urging me to sit in an ante room around one side of the temple.

This entrance hall resembles an airport waiting room, without the bustle. Three uniformed female police sit, bored, at a table. Three more lay security personnel, Indian men, sit at a table opposite, appearing to be equally bored. I'm offered a plastic chair that is placed at the women's table and I, for some time, endeavour unsuccessfully to make eye contact with each of them. One is knitting, one is fiddling with the curly cord from a telephone that never rings and the third is reading a newspaper in a lacklustre manner.

I ask them whether they're here every single day; yes, yes,

they tell me. It must be very boring, I venture. Yes, yes it is, and they are immediately animated by the topic of exactly how boring it is for them. They are three beauties, each one of them slim with lustrous black hair, worn in plaits. The youngest of them has a red marking in the parting of her hair and a rather fine nose stud.

'Maybe you'd like to see my photos,' I offer, and produce my first Mother's Day card with its selection of family photos. There's a family portrait – Isla in the backpack I am wearing and Paul, my husband, stands holding our German shepherd, Lola, in his arms; it was taken after Paul and Lola won the local dog-and-master swimming race. Another is of Isla lying on her dog, apparently asleep. There's an image of her in my arms with the sun shining in such a way that her hair – indeed, her whole demeanour – appears golden.

One by one, the female guards are drawn in, the first to succumb is the softest of the three, apparently the youngest. She confides that she too has a baby, aged only six months, who's being cared for by his grandmother. The woman is clearly undone by the golden image of Isla and sighs in a fit of longing for her own son.

Soon, a man and his young son arrive. They are clearly known to the guards, who ask how the boy is today. I estimate him to be five or six years old. When he starts to hunch forward, reaching towards his toes and moaning, I ask his father whether he's okay. Yes, yes, the man tells me, his son is just excited. The three of us are ushered into a smaller waiting room to sit on soiled white sofas.

I inquire whether the man is Tibetan. No, Chinese, he tells me, then quickly explains that he was raised in the West and now lives in Singapore.

'He does not speak,' the man blurts out in anguish, and for a moment I think he's telling me of an audience he's had with the Karmapa. 'He's been diagnosed with autism.'

I gather that the man does not, or cannot, accept his son's diagnosis and he goes on to tell me that he's brought the boy to the Karmapa for blessings. They've seen him before. I feel a pang of sadness for the pair, although at the moment the boy seems quite content. Once again, I bring out my family snaps and the child is quickly enchanted by the images of my lovely dog.

The boy's father gives me a history of the treatments they've tried. It is a pitiful tale and I can sense how much hope he places in the Karmapa.

When I tell him I'm writing a book on the Karmapa and ask if I could make contact with him in a few months' time about their meeting and its repercussions, the man's demeanour changes completely. This, he tells me, is a very private matter. Yes, of course, I nod, smile, do not point out that he already poured out the entire story without any prompting from me.

Lama Phuntsok strides into the room, clearly expecting only one visitor for his master. He questions the man about his arrangements and it seems that another of the Karmapa's retinue told him to bring his son today. Clearly, Lama Phuntsok cannot turn away the man and his son.

The Indian security personnel arrive and the child starts wailing. We are already twenty minutes late for our hour's audience. The man fusses over his and his son's possessions, taking an inordinately long time to gather up their gear before leaving the room. I am ever conscious of the clock ticking.

We are led along a maze of corridors and through a drab kitchen, in which everything looks and smells of dull green vegetable matter (on the way back, I realise that this is the kitchen in which the Karmapa's own meals are prepared and am struck by the indignity of these arrangements). We climb flight after flight of stairs before I am seated on a veranda outside the audience room. The boy and his father are ushered inside but not before more fussing with their bags, all the while the child wailing, louder and louder. The guards try to silence the boy and I cannot help but wonder whether the Karmapa is the type to be disturbed by the sound of raw distress. The moment the two disappear behind the Tibetan curtain hanging in the doorway, the boy falls silent. I wait and wait, and realise that the distraction caused by the pair has made my own anxiety dissipate.

The Tibetan security guard standing outside the Karmapa's

rooms tells me that the father and son should be visiting Sakya Trinzin, the head of the Sakya school, in Rajpur rather than the Karmapa and I am distracted by the notion that important religious leaders might specialise in different miracles. Finally the boy and his father emerge, the elder wearing a *khatag* and both wearing cute little red ties around their necks that remind me of something from a boy scout's uniform. In haste, I try to examine the boy's features for any sign of change.

I bumble into the Karmapa's audience room, awkward with the great silk expanse of my specially chosen *khatag*. After dismissing a number of ordinary-looking *khatags* in shops in McLeod Ganj, I settled on a white silk scarf that looks positively voluminous, purchased in the temple at the Norbulingka Institute. My notebook and pens are tucked under my arm because I have not been permitted to bring my bag with me. Lama Phuntsok has advised me that if I carry no electrical equipment into my audience with the Karmapa – neither tape recorder nor camera – I do not have to apply to local police for permission to interview him. As I am in India on a tourist visa, I decide that this arrangement will be satisfactory for the moment, despite the chore of note-taking.

The XVIIth Karmapa is tall (six foot, or so I'm told) and lean and his face has the clean, clear lines and planes of a fine sculpture. His dark eyes are utterly arresting and I keep my own fixed on them as I fumble through the scarf-offering routine in which I attempt to unfurl my carefully folded *khatag* so the Karmapa can place it around my neck. He takes the scarf from me before I have a chance to drop it on the floor and places it around my neck with a grace that I envy. Tibetans traditionally offer the white scarf, itself seen as a symbol of truth, to high lamas and officials on special occasions. I sink to the floor to perch on my bare feet before him.

The Karmapa's light brown skin is smooth and glowing; he radiates well-being and strength. He is every bit as handsome as he appears in photographs and as ageless as he looks in the old video footage of him that I've watched. I doubt that he has ever shaved his face. There is a warmth emanating from this young/old *bodhisattva* that I had not anticipated. We study each other with some curiosity, exchanging shy smiles. I am profoundly surprised to feel that I'm in the presence of someone familiar to me.

I cannot help but noticing that this young man – who is eighteen in Western years but nineteen in Tibetan – is beautiful. He has a strong jaw and broad forehead and the arm that escapes from his robes is lightly muscled. His fingers are long and finely shaped. Later, while studying his photos with a friend in Sydney, we pronounce him the Keanu Reeves of Tibetan Buddhism.

Although I try to ignore everyone but the Karmapa and Lama Phuntsok who is to translate for us, I'm aware that there are at least four others in the room as well. There is one of the policewomen, a man who I guess is from the Indian Intelligence Bureau, a second Indian woman in plain clothes and the Tibetan security guard. There may be another of the Karmapa's aides hovering there behind me, but it does not matter; I find it hard to shift my attention from the *tulku* sitting before me, so drawn am I to him.

Lama Phuntsok and I are sitting on the floor. It feels as though we're sitting at the Karmapa's feet but, in reality, a low table separates us from him. The Karmapa's audience room is a simple, light space with minimal decoration. At most, there might be a pair of *thangkas* on the wall behind the Karmapa but otherwise the room is empty and bright. A pair of doors to his right opens onto a terrace that overlooks the monastery's forecourt. I am surprised to note that the Karmapa is sitting on a moulded, clear Perspex sofa with a cushion on it. Tibetans are known for their finely carved, ornate furniture and I am a little bothered by the absence of it here.

I do not explain myself to the Karmapa, as I believe that Lama Phuntsok has already done so, but begin by offering him one of my family photos, wanting to put myself in a context that is not just professional. I imagine that this testimony to my healthy family, complete with dog, shows the young man before me so much. I tell myself, and hope to convey to him, that I have not come to him to ask something for myself.

With notebook propped on my knees, we speak of the Karmapa's early years, back when he was the small boy fondly dubbed Apo Gaga by one of his sisters.

The young Karmapa is at pains to stress the beautiful simplicity of his family's nomadic life, so very far from cities and the distraction of modern, material concerns. His parents raised him as a strict Buddhist, he informs me, and as a child this meant being mindful of the worth of all beings. It meant never hurting even the smallest of insects. The family's religious practice, the Karmapa adds simply, was his primary childhood influence.

As a young child, the Karmapa helped look after the small kids and lambs among his parents' livestock. There was nothing like a pet dog, he tells me, no doubt thinking of my own family dog from the photo I had showed him. The family would have owned as many as eighty or ninety sheep, goats and yaks. Although we're talking numbers at my urging, the Karmapa returns again to the subject of material simplicity. From that simple life he learned that the fewer your belongings, the less you suffer. I wonder whether I'm imagining the wistful longing in his voice.

I tell him that I've heard that the Chinese authorities within Tibet are once again trying to impose regulations on Tibetan nomads that will radically change their lifestyle, as they did during the Cultural Revolution. Were such restrictions already apparent when the Karmapa was a boy?

From the side of the room we are interrupted by the vigorous throat-clearing of one of the plain-clothes Indians. I guess this is to remind the Karmapa that he may not criticise China while he's on Indian soil.

The Karmapa insists that as a child he was unaware of such restrictions. Childhood, for him, was clearly a simple, golden time.

I ask whether the young Karmapa's attachment to Karlek Monastery, at the tender age of three or four, had been, in part, his own choice. Was it he who had instigated it? This is, of course, a leading question. I am inviting this serious young man to seduce me with stories that prove his status as the true reincarnation of the XVIth Karmapa. It is difficult to forget that there is another young man – one with very powerful supporters – who also claims to be the XVIIth Karmapa.

Instead, he tells me that a three-year-old has no free will in such matters, and I am left feeling a little silly. Later, I will become preoccupied with the notion of free will in a life like that of the Karmapa.

He goes on to remind me that his parents had promised their not-yet-conceived son to Amdo Palden.

The man I take for an Intelligence Bureau agent walks forward, tapping his watch, telling me that my time is up. We will not be permitted to go even a minute over time, despite the fact that the Karmapa's first private audience of the day – with the boy and his father – didn't start until twenty minutes after it was scheduled to. I feel stricken; we have covered so little territory.

I take my leave of the Karmapa and turn to walk from the room. After two steps, I turn to bow to him, suddenly mindful that this great lama might be offended by the sight of my back. The Karmapa is smiling at me and maintains eye contact as I make my clumsy backwards retreat.

Outside on the terrace beyond the audience room, the Indian security man asks again and again whether I'm a 'Buddha student'. I reply in the affirmative, by no means a lie, but I know he doesn't believe me. At this stage I have not yet decided whether the Indian security presence is for the Karmapa's protection or is there to silence him.

Back in the room of soiled white sofas, I wish the father and son well, commenting that the boy seemed at ease in the Karmapa's presence. The father is distant from me now, no doubt worrying about what he's already told me that he might not care to see in print.

A Western Buddhist nun has arrived who seems to be just passing the time of day there in the room. When she sees my notebook, she immediately wants to know whether I'm a journalist. I tell her no, I'm not. Her accent declares her American.

The man and his son leave and the nun draws me towards

her. She wants to know how the Karmapa seemed to me and confides to me that she's heard his cook has gone to work at the Tibetan Children's Village (founded more than forty years ago by the Dalai Lama's elder sister, the Tibetan Children's Village offers home and education to Tibetan children).

Worried about his diet, the nun has baked the Karmapa some wholemeal bread. She produces a squashed lump from her maroon shoulder bag and I'm touched to see the little note attached to it. The nun wastes no time in declaring the Karmapa's situation – here at a monastery that's not his own, under virtual house arrest – a disgrace. She's delighted when I agree with her. She tells me that she's undergone some sort of court case here in India for agitating on the Karmapa's behalf and that she subsequently had to leave the country so things could cool down. I feel myself inching away from her on the shabby sofa, lest the Indian intelligence man come back to question me and find the two of us shoulder to shoulder.

Had I come to the Karmapa for his blessing, she wants to know. No, I tell her, I just came to speak to him about his life, mainly about his childhood.

'You spoke to him about his life?' The nun is in raptures and I imagine she would have been less surprised had I told her the Karmapa and I had engaged in astral travel together. Everyone, she explains, comes to him to speak about their own lives, to ask him to solve their own problems. She quizzes me again about my discussion with the Karmapa and seems inordinately pleased by the thought of the conversation we had.

As I leave, the nun beseeches me to tell the world about the Karmapa's situation. Yes, I tell her, I will certainly do that. (A few weeks after my return to Australia, I receive a postcard from McLeod Ganj featuring the image of the Karmapa. I read it on the pavement outside my house as Isla searches the letterbox for snails. The card says 'thank you for giving this young monk your interest in his life, his pet goat and the years before he became a political captive' and for a moment I am transported back to the light-filled audience room atop Gyuto Tantric University. The Karmapa has sent me a postcard! I read on in some confusion and then realise the card is from the American nun, who calls herself 'rinpoche' and clearly wants me to join her in some sort of political action on the Karmapa's behalf.)

I share a taxi back to Norbulingka with two of the Karmapa's attendants who look for all the world like teenagers out to have some fun away from their home and duties. They are probably the same age as their master.

The institute's tranquil gardens are abuzz with life – human life as well as the characteristic insect and bird life. White four-wheel-drive vehicles in the driveway emblazoned with 'BBC Himalaya' announce there has been a new arrival in my absence, the words 'with Michael Palin' appearing in smaller lettering. The café terrace is all hard British accents and people in ripped jeans standing around looking bored, unimpressed by the slow service and limited vegetarian menu. I sidle over to one of the Brits to ask whether Michael Palin is actually there, and stop myself just in time. The dishevelled man before me is the best-selling author himself.

Within the café is a group of French tourists – our paths already crossed up at McLeod Ganj – and the room is full of the nasal twang of their Provençal French. Their Tibetan guide comes to sit with me for a while to make concerned inquiries about the progress of my book. The young man clearly thinks the subject of the Karmapa too sensitive to be written about by someone like me. He's concerned I might offend the Indian government and seems to think that the fact that the Karmapa is largely confined to a few rooms on top of Gyuto, unable to go to his monastery in Sikkim or leave the country, is perfectly acceptable.

What is freedom, anyway? The Dalai Lama, he tells me, has no freedom. While I'm not in a position to disagree, this comment plays on my mind for weeks afterwards. The young man does, however, share my view that the Indians' treatment of the Karmapa is heavily influenced by the Indian government's fears of angering the Chinese. In addition to the fact that the Indians suspected the Karmapa of being a Chinese spy when he arrived in their country, they may feel that if they send him to

Sikkim, in India's northeast, it will be akin to giving the Chinese an invitation to invade the Indian state (Sikkim had been an independent kingdom up until 1975).

We speak again of freedom and I suggest that the Karmapa may have been able to do more for the Tibetans when he was in Tibet. I also suggest that the Karmapa should be given permission to travel in the West, to see his Western followers. I venture that in the West the Karmapa might finally experience some real freedom.

The Tibetan is scornful of this notion. India, he informs me, is the most democratic country in the world. As proof of this, he tells me that while the Dalai Lama lives there in exile as a religious leader, he is officially barred from engaging in political activity in India; we both know that the Dalai Lama is as religious as he is political. The Tibetans' leader, although he now calls himself merely a simple monk (and is known internationally as the Tibetans' spiritual, not temporal, leader) never stops working for the Tibetans both within Tibet and in exile.

LINEAGE:
THE SEVENTH KARMAPA

Chödrak Gyatso (1454–1505), the VIIth Karmapa, was born in northern Tibet beneath a sky filled with coloured lights. He said *'Ama-la'* – 'mother' – at birth and auspicious symbols were found on his body such as *dharma* wheels on the soles of his feet. When he was only seven days old, he began to speak. As a very small infant, he announced, 'There is nothing in the world but emptiness.' He was recognised as the Karmapa at only nine months of age by an antecedent of Gyalstab Rinpoche.

With Gyalstab Rinpoche, the young Karmapa travelled the countryside in a group that must have had the feeling of a travelling monastery. The Karmapa and his monks moved from place to place with their tents, including a particularly fine shrine tent with a golden roof that was decorated with precious relics. As a very young boy, the VIIth Karmapa brokered peace between the warring Nagas and Bhutanese and was an advocate for the freeing of hostages and political prisoners. A dedicated vegetarian, Chödrak Gyatso preached that animals' lives must be saved wherever possible.

Like the Karmapas who preceded him, Chödrak Gyatso was a great scholar. He was also the author of a number of seminal Buddhist texts and he established monastic universities. He was active within the various communities surrounding him and inspired people to recite *'Om mani padme hung'* repeatedly for their own and others' benefit.

THE BOY LAMA:
SANCTIONED BY CHINA

As she had anticipated, Loga now saw her son less and less over the course of the summer, in the lead-up to his enthronement. His days were so crowded with meetings, with audiences, that there was no time for him to behave as a son any more. Yes, Loga and Karma Döndrub still had a role to play in their son's life but it was largely ornamental.

When the government officials came to meet their son, Loga and her husband were present, witnesses to the awkward way in which these representatives of a secular government negotiated their meeting with the young *tulku*. While the officials made the customary offering of *khatags*, this, it seemed, was the extent of their reverence. They expected the boy to sit at the same level as they did and to shake their hands, as they would with anyone they considered their equal. The *tulku*, instead of displaying affront, took to the business of handshaking with good grace and gusto. Although the Chinese may have wished it to appear that they played a decisive role in the XVIIth Karmapa's recognition, their real function was to sanction his appointment.

The young Karmapa was provided personal attendants to

meet his every possible need. Suddenly he commanded a chamberlain, a butler, an appointment secretary and a correspondence secretary. At each of his general audiences, he was watched over by his own personal guard. When the boy went walking, beyond the monastery and up into the mountains, a whole procession of attendants accompanied him, including one monk who would almost constantly hold the boy's arm lest the precious child should slip from the path and injure himself.

His mother, despite her son's host of carers, worried for him most in the middle of the night. She would wake when all was still and quiet, aware only of what she perceived as unnatural silence. Within the room her family shared, she heard only the breathing of her husband, two sons and youngest daughter. She missed the sound of each of her other children in their sleep as they lay under sheep skins in the family's tent. She missed the sound of the movements of their livestock, of the creatures snorting and snuffling in the night. She could barely imagine her son, should he wake in the night in his silent room atop the monastery that he shared with only one attendant. It was summer now, but when the winter came how would he ever be warm enough without the bodies of his siblings pressed up against him in the night?

When Tai Situ Rinpoche and Gyalstab Rinpoche arrived from India in July; the circle was joined. Now they, these incarnate lamas who had been with the boy when he was a man in his previous lifetime, were his true family once more. It was they who would guide and teach him, and they who would be afforded the time to sit with him and play. Their presence in the young Karmapa's life, particularly that of Situ Rinpoche, was as essential to his development as a religious leader as his mother's milk was to his development as an infant.

Once the Karmapa's root gurus had arrived, two monumental events took place, events beyond which there was no turning back. The sacred hair-cutting ceremony symbolised the first crucial step on the path to the boy's full ordination. The ceremony took place in what many Tibetans would argue was the most holy place in Tibet: in the Jokhang Temple in Lhasa before the statue of Jowo Rinpoche. This is the statue of Shakyamuni Buddha (the buddha who was born as Prince Siddhartha) which King Songsten Gampo's Nepalese wife brought from Nepal in the seventh century. Of all the other Karmapas, the only other who shared the honour of having his hair ritually cut at the Jokhang was the XIIIth. Normally only the Dalai Lama's and Panchen Lama's hair-cutting ceremonies were held at this most sacred of sites. The choice of venue was to enforce the status the Chinese authorities wanted the Karmapa to hold, that of the pre-eminent religious figure in the land. The political manoeuvring went both ways, though; in full view of the gathered Chinese officials – representatives of Tibet's occupying forces – the Karmapa was presented with a *khatag* that was a special gift from the exile leader, the Dalai Lama, who had also given his endorsement of the boy's recognition. These were extraordinary times.

The second of the ceremonies, which was as large as the first was intimate, was that of the enthronement, held on 27 September 1992 to coincide with the eighth new moon. This was the final process in the young boy's recognition as Karmapa and was attended by more than 20,000 people. The shrine room at Tsurphu, festooned with brightly coloured fabrics and samples of the offerings devotees would be making to the Karmapa that day, was divided in a somewhat unusual manner. On the left-hand side sat the religious hierarchy, and on the right-hand side sat representatives of the government that had once ordered the destruction of Tibet's monasteries.

A representative of the central government's Religious Affairs Bureau put into words what had, until this moment in Tibet's history, seemed impossible. The XVIIth Karmapa's reincarnation was officially approved by the communist government, making him the first high incarnation to be so anointed. This involvement represented both the government's need for a malleable young Tibetan it might groom for its own ends, and its desire to be seen to allow Tibetans freedom to practise their religion.

99

TIBET: IN REVOLT

It was in the frontier region of eastern Tibet that rebellion first took hold in early 1956. Land reform was to be introduced in Kham and Amdo before it was attempted further west in the central region of U-Tsang. It involved land and livestock being taken from the monasteries, aristocrats and other landowners, and managed by the so-called peasants and officials. The Chinese were surprised to encounter resistance among the villagers who, for the most part, could see no reasons for such changes.

Fighting broke out and in February 1956 thousands of villagers sought shelter in Changtreng Sampheling Monastery. The Chinese laid siege to the monastery and eventually an aeroplane was called in to drop bombs. The *Khampas*, Tibetans from Kham who became known as notorious resistance fighters surrendered and hundreds of Tibetans – monks and laymen – were killed. The story of the monastery's destruction spread throughout eastern Tibet and soon the Chinese had laid siege to a second monastery at Lithang, once again sending in bombs to end the impasse.

Gradually, horror stories from Kham and Amdo trickled west. The Chinese were using sophisticated artillery against rebels, monks and ordinary villagers alike. There was wholesale destruction and monk and lay leaders were being imprisoned, tortured and killed. Buddha had been declared a reactionary. In one of the Dalai Lama's meetings with Chairman Mao, during the spring of 1955, the great helmsman told the Tibetan leader that religion was poison. He went on to explain how it reduced the population because monks and nuns bore no children, and how it failed to contribute to material progress.[35] Gradually, policies were introduced to severely restrict religious practice, while monks and nuns were harassed and publicly humiliated.

Those *Khampa* resistance fighters who had not surrendered fled into central Tibet where initially their stories were seen as both incredible and unwelcome. Resources were already strained in Lhasa, forcing some *Khampas* to seek refuge in India, taking news of the revolt in eastern Tibet with them.

It is ironic that Tibetan resistance to Chinese rule in the fifties was directly related to the people's commitment to the Dalai Lama, given that he and his office represented the cornerstones of the 'feudal' world the Chinese believed the Tibetan people would be so grateful to break with. The Chinese greatly underestimated the Tibetans' devotion to their temporal and spiritual leader, and continue to do so. The Tibetans' belief in his wisdom and goodness remains one of the fundamental tenets of what it is to be Tibetan. What's more, most Tibetans regarded the taxes they paid to the monasteries and aristocratic landowners as a somewhat onerous fact of life rather than as the equivalent of servitude, which is how the Chinese portrayed the workers' relationships with their landlords. Despite Chinese officials' endeavours to completely undermine the power of the Dalai Lama and the Tibetan aristocrats, behind the scenes the Chinese courted them and sought their assistance.

One group of Tibetans posted notices demanding the Chinese leave Tibet and campaigned for Tibet to maintain its army and currency. It also assisted refugees from the east and the Lhasa poor, who had been so adversely impacted by price rises caused by the influx of Chinese. Far from receiving support from the *Kashag*, the rebellious group received criticism. The *Kashag* insisted that politics should remain its responsibility alone, in accordance with Tibetan tradition.

In November 1956, the Dalai Lama, the XVIth Karmapa and members of the *Kashag* left Lhasa for Sikkim at the invitation of both the Sikkimese crown prince and the Indian government. They had been invited to attend the 2500th anniversary of the Buddha's birth. The Panchen Lama had also received an invitation from the Indian government to attend the celebrations but he and his entourage were not given the head-of-state reception accorded to the Dalai Lama. A visit to India by the Chinese premier, Zhou Enlai, was carefully scheduled to coincide with the Dalai Lama's trip. Zhou, who was known as a talented diplomat, was to be on hand to counter any bad public relations the Dalai Lama might cause for China.

It was common knowledge among Tibetan officials that the

Dalai Lama was considering remaining in India, which made every step of the visit politically charged. Prime Minister Nehru informed the Dalai Lama through an intermediary that he should return to Tibet as he was the only one who could unite his people. Nehru went on to tell the Dalai Lama in person that India could be of no assistance to the Tibetans and that they should work with the 17-Point Agreement. However, he did promise to speak to the visiting Chinese premier about conditions in Tibet.

Should the Dalai Lama have remained in India, it would have put enormous strain on the Sino-Indian relationship, which was already under pressure because of the development of Chinese ties with Nepal. While Nehru's advice might seem both unhelpful and uninformed in a contemporary context, Tsering Shakya in his book *Dragon in the Land of Snows* reminds us that Nehru, of all people, knew what it was to fight for a country's independence. Not only had he fought the British for India's independence, but he had been imprisoned for his efforts.

The Dalai Lama's brothers, Gyalo Dhundup and Thubten Norbu, were keen for him to remain in India and Thubten Norbu had been conferring with America's Central Intelligence Agency regarding covert US action in Tibet. Zhou Enlai himself demanded a meeting with the Dalai Lama in which he insisted that the Tibetan leader not visit exile Tibetans in Kalimpong (which was now something of an outpost for Tibetan revolutionaries). The Tibetan leader took the opportunity to complain to the Chinese premier about the increasingly difficult conditions in Tibet, as did each Tibetan with whom Zhou Enlai came into contact. Apparently the premier listened with concern to the complaints, arguing that they could be best addressed upon the Tibetans' return home.

Revolt in Tibet had by now spread to Lhasa from the east, and Chinese authorities clearly feared a major uprising. A couple of months later in January 1957, Zhou Enlai met the Dalai Lama a second time in Delhi, carrying a message from Chairman Mao. Communist reforms in central Tibet, such as redistribution of land, could be delayed for five years, or even longer if necessary. However, should there be an uprising in Tibet, the PLA would quash it categorically. Given India's lack of support to the Tibetans and the uncertain nature of the United States' potential assistance, the Dalai Lama decided that he could be of more assistance to his people from within Tibet than from India or any other place of exile. Once again, he would endeavour to work with the Chinese.

2 OCTOBER 2003

LINEAGE: THE EIGHTH KARMAPA

THE BOY LAMA: CHINA'S PAWN?

TIBET: FLIGHT OF THE DALAI LAMA

2 OCTOBER 2003

Although I've heard so many similar stories, tales of Tibetans' faith and devotion still have the power to move me profoundly. One of the staff at the guesthouse tells me his own story and only because I ask. Tenzin is in his mid-twenties but looks younger, as though he may have only just started shaving. A single man from Amdo, Tenzin tells me he was neither a freedom fighter nor a monk. Indeed, when he was growing up he had so little knowledge of politics that he didn't realise that Lhasa, to the west, was also occupied by the Chinese.

When Tenzin finished school, he made a simple yet fundamental decision. He would leave Tibet and walk over the Himalayas to India so he could see the Dalai Lama. He knew the journey was very risky but had already decided that if he died en route – whether it be in the mountains or at the hands of a Chinese border patrol – he would quite simply offer his life to the Dalai Lama. Tenzin is no zealot; he's not crazy and he's not exceptional. He's just an ordinary Tibetan who in 1998 decided that seeing the Dalai Lama once was more important than his own safety, indeed, than his own life. Nearly fifty years after China's occupation there are still those who, like Tenzin, have not heard a word of what the Chinese have tried to tell them about their leader. In the face of this sort of faith, I marvel that the communists ever believed they would 'reform' the Tibetans.

Although today I will visit another high Kagyu cleric, Tai Situ Rinpoche, Lama Phuntsok has told me that I have been granted a second private audience with the Karmapa tomorrow. With no idea of whether I will get to meet the Karmapa twice or twelve times, I have to take each day as it comes, gathering information on him and his life wherever I can find it. I feel like a bowerbird, swooping earthwards mid-flight for shiny treasures.

I leave the grounds of the Norbulingka Institute with Arun, who has become my driver. Really I've become his tourist and I am quite certain that I would be unable to leave the premises and approach any of the other waiting drivers in their white taxi vans without causing a major uproar. I have been claimed.

We are driving east, our destination Sherab Ling Monastery, which was founded and is still presided over by Tai Situ Rinpoche, the Karmapa's guru and root teacher. Not only was he the one to whom the previous Karmapa handed his letter of recognition, giving details of his rebirth, but Tai Situ Rinpoche bears a particular responsibility for the transmission of the teachings of the lineage. In interviewing him, I hope to get not only a sense of the Karmapa as a young student, but also an understanding of the politics that keep him at Gyuto. Little do I realise, at this point in my journey, the extent to which the Indian government has politically silenced Tai Situ Rinpoche.

Tai Situ Rinpoche's status as root guru to the XVIIth Karmapa was foreseen in centuries past by Chogyur Lingpa, a famous Tibetan *tertön* (a psychic or seer who reveals previously hidden teachings) who was born in 1829. When Chogyur Lingpa visited Karma Gön Monastery in Kham, he had a vision of Guru Rinpoche surrounded by the twenty-one manifestations of the Karmapa, fourteen of whom had already taken birth. He recounted the vision in some detail to the monastery's abbot, who instructed artists to bring it to life in a mural. Of the section of his vision pertaining to the XVIIth Karmapa, Chogyur Lingpa said, 'Nearby, at the foot of a lush tree on a rock mountain, [is] the seventeenth incarnation with Khentin Tai Situpa [Tai Situ Rinpoche]. This image symbolises that through the unity of their minds, the tree of the Buddha's doctrine will flourish, laden with the ripe fruit which is the essence of the teachings of the lineage of Gampopa.'[36] I've little doubt that this bond between the Karmapa and Tai Situ Rinpoche, as forecast nearly two centuries ago, gave the disputed letter of recognition all the more weight in the Karma Kagyu community.

I will subsequently learn that Shamar Rinpoche challenges the application of this prediction to the situation of the current Karmapa. This prediction, he asserts, should apply to the relationship between the previous XVIth Karmapa and Tai Situ Rinpoche. As another child, Shomar alleges, had been recognised as the XVIth and died, the Karmapa we know as the XVIth should really have been the XVIIth.[37]

The Norbulingka Institute has become my haven and it's a shock to be at large in India again. Arun drives with a foot ever on the accelerator and a hand on the horn; the brake is rarely used. His reaction to an obstacle on the road ahead is not to slow down but to hit the horn and speed up. Once I relax my white-knuckle grip on the handle above my head, I actually begin to enjoy myself.

In my quiet neighbourhood in Sydney, I am constantly surprised at how few people one sees on the streets; I can go for a week without even glimpsing one of my immediate neighbours. Here in India, it seems most of life is carried out beyond the four walls of the home, or certainly this is the case for those with less. Alongside the road, men sit and talk, the elderly tend their grandchildren and women work either in the fields or over some food preparation. Today is a public holiday – Mahatma Gandhi's birthday – so there is a sense of occasion added to the everyday feeling of people being out and about. Many people are sporting their finery: women wear gold-flecked saris, dazzling nose jewellery, their teeth flashing a brilliant white when they smile; men wear trousers with perfect creases ironed into them and crisp, clean shirts; children's clothes are notably clean and occasionally I spy a young girl done up kewpie-doll-style, all pastel flounces and tulle. I gape in wonder each time I see a family of four on the one moped and this is no uncommon sight. For a while, we drive behind a couple on a moped – the woman holding a sleeping child whose head lolls back unsupported, bouncing alarmingly as the bike flies up out of potholes. Eventually, the woman pulls the child in towards her breast and I feel my own chest relax. I am certain the child is the same age as Isla.

We pass the leafy, green fields of the Zen Tea Plantation, bustling market squares, Hindu temples and army barracks. We cross rivers and streams, their banks festooned with clothes drying in the sun. Arun greets the cows, goats, donkeys, bicycles, buses and other cars with which he shares the road in an egalitarian fashion, playing his horn for all of them. We drive east, through Palampur and beyond, all the while the outline of the

Himalayas rising and falling to the north. We are moving into less populous country; Delhi is far, far behind me.

After ninety minutes of driving, we begin to see the first signs announcing Sherab Ling and start the climb up into the pine forests. A couple of cars heading in the opposite direction are crammed with young monks in their yellow sleeveless shirts. I am heartened by the rapid succession of smiling young faces.

We are now driving neck and neck with another taxi and I see a white arm clutching the ceiling grip. I guess that this is someone else who has come to have an audience with Tai Situ Rinpoche. High lamas are clearly everybody's property.

Sherab Ling is both a great building and a concrete bunker, with the monk's accommodation rising starkly around an empty courtyard. The fourth side of the square comprises the monastery's temple and Tai Situ Rinpoche's reception rooms.

Tai Situ Rinpoche's other visitor is a Western Buddhist nun; she is pale and her skin looks papery dry. The nun is pleased that I've been told to come and see Rinpoche today because, she says, at least this signifies that something is happening. And something certainly is happening. The waiting room into which we are ushered is already crowded with monks who sit on the seats that line the room's walls. They are all clutching their *khatags* and envelopes that must, I guess, contain money. We could be in a doctor's waiting room in the West, with each of us seeking an answer to our own special question, along with some spiritual healing. I remain conscious of the clock ticking, see my interview with Tai Situ Rinpoche dissolve into nothing. As we wait, lay Tibetans start to arrive as well.

Lama Tenam comes to greet me. He bears a striking resemblance to actor Bob Hoskins. For three years, since the Karmapa's arrival in India, Lama Tenam had worked as the Karmapa's private secretary and translator. He wastes no time in giving me the ground rules for my interview with Tai Situ.

'No political questions,' he warns me.

'So,' I venture, 'may I ask him his thoughts on the security surrounding the Karmapa?'

Lama Tenam replies that I may not. No. I remember that Tai

Situ Rinpoche himself was barred from India for a four-year period between 1994 and 1998. The Indian government, under the Foreigner's Act, has absolute discretion over the comings and goings of non-citizens and, as such, was never obliged to give a reason for this barring. The Indian media reported that charges had been brought against Tai Situ Rinpoche (by Shri Narayan Singh) for sedition but were subsequently dropped.

Monks come and go. Tibetan pilgrims come and go. An elderly Tibetan with a hand-held prayer wheel, his hair carefully braided into about a dozen plaits, his white shirt freshly ironed, comes and goes. The Western nun, who tells me she's a Dane living at Samye Ling, a Tibetan monastery in Scotland, has her own audience and leaves, and still the Tibetans come, still the monks come. An Indian family arrives, each one of its members wearing a red bindi on their forehead, and is admitted to Tai Situ Rinpoche's inner sanctum – parents, children, aunts, grandchildren – and still I wait. All the while, I strive to engage Lama Tenam in discussion about the Karmapa. While he is polite and friendly, he clearly sees it as his master's role to answer my questions, and proves both charming and evasive.

My stomach growls and Arun, the driver, arrives to check on me. 'No worries, no worries,' he tells me breezily when I confess that I still haven't had my interview. I don't feel quite so casual myself as I start to contemplate the drive back to the Norbulingka Institute on those winding, pot-holed roads in the dark.

I am to be given the prized audience – the last interview so we have plenty of time! – but eventually Lama Tenam, perhaps tired of my ceaseless chatter and grumbling stomach, ushers me into Rinpoche's room even though there are still more monks waiting to be admitted.

Tai Situ Rinpoche, seated on his low throne, appears a small man but has a big warm smile that puts me immediately at ease. Self-consciously I present my *khatag*, my money offering, the letter from my publisher and my business card. He's perfectly happy, he tells me, to have my small black tape recorder under his nose.

During our interview, Tai Situ Rinpoche speaks with palpable emotion about meeting the XVIIth Karmapa for the first time, describing it as 'the best moment in my life'. I have already become accustomed to placing such questions in their context; were I to ask, for instance, when Tai Situ first met the Karmapa, he would ask me to which incarnation of the Karmapa I was referring.

Rinpoche repeats that the intensity of joy he felt on meeting the Karmapa is indescribable and something never to be repeated in this lifetime. He is clearly trying to invite me to understand this, so I stop to think before pushing on. Effortlessly, I imagine myself meeting my beloved father again, albeit in a different incarnation, and I get it. My eyes fill with tears, as do Rinpoche's.

We talk about his relationship with the XVIth Karmapa, whom Tai Situ first met when he was only a year and a half old. He confesses that he doesn't remember this meeting but explains that when he was five or six he had to flee his monastery in eastern Tibet because of the Chinese invasion, and took refuge with the Karmapa at Tsurphu. Less than a month after his arrival at Tsurphu, the Karmapa and his own entourage, including Tai Situ Rinpoche, were forced to flee to Bhutan. It was 1959. 'We escaped,' says Rinpoche simply. And it's no exaggeration to call this migration an escape, as the Chinese, both at the time of occupation and during the Cultural Revolution, sacked the monasteries, razing many of them to the ground. Monks, along with nuns, those deemed Tibetan aristocrats, and landowners suffered the most cruelly under the Chinese.

The Karmapa and his *labrang* travelled to Sikkim, as did Tai Situ Rinpoche. We talk of the early years in Sikkim when the XVIth Karmapa was building Rumtek Monastery, near Gangtok, and establishing the exile seat of the Karma Kagyu there. Not only had Sikkim been deemed an ideal place for its position, immediately across the Tibetan border, but its royal family had close personal connections with Tibet and Tibetan Buddhism.

'In those days, there were no roads there so you had to go on horseback for four or five hours to get to Rumtek from Gangtok. I visited many, many times as a little boy of seven or eight and I was there until I was twenty-two.' Tai Situ Rinpoche tells me that by the time he was twelve, however, the Karmapa had already completed the transmission of teachings to him.

He explains that his role was to continue with the work of his previous incarnation and, under this guise, he came to the region in which he now resides to found his own monastery, Sherab Ling. When he arrived there was nothing – no people, no roads, no electricity, no shelter. Although the monastery is now complete, Tai Situ Rinpoche tells me that there are still so many things he wishes to do. Back in the days of the XVIth Karmapa, despite the fact that Tai Situ was at Sherab Ling and the Karmapa at Rumtek, at opposite ends of the Himalayas, the two saw each other frequently.

While Tai Situ Rinpoche made three visits to Tsurphu Monastery after the XVIIth Karmapa had been recognised, in order to transmit the teachings to the Karmapa, the Chinese eventually refused him permission to visit again. Tai Situ tells me sadly that he does not know the reason for this change of heart on the part of the Chinese. Then he stresses that he does not wish to dwell on these negative aspects.

Am I a cricket fan, Tai Situ wants to know. I reply in the negative. As I'm Australian, I have been asked this question repeatedly since I arrived in India. Actually, I tell Rinpoche, my only sport – and it's barely such – is yoga. We chuckle for a moment over this meeting of East and West.

Rinpoche goes on to explain that he sees his role in his relationship with the Karmapa as that of the cricket bat. I am left to assume that in this analogy the Karmapa is the wicket. Tai Situ Rinpoche tells me it is his duty – indeed, his honour – to deflect the ball again and again. In this way, he explains, he is of service to the Karmapa. I ponder this comment, delivered in the context of the Chinese authorities denying him permission to visit, because this is as political as we'll get.

Tai Situ Rinpoche talks with some distress of his first meeting with the XVIIth Karmapa after he had arrived in India.

'As soon as I got the message, I took off.' He hadn't seen his student in nearly seven years. 'He seemed so weather-affected: his eyes were red, his skin was so dark. It was wonderful to see him and wonderful to see him safe, but at the same time it was sad . . . I knew how he had looked in his past life and then to see him after the journey . . . It took about a week for him to get here and he'd lost so many kilos.'

'What does the Karmapa need now in order to reach his full potential?' I ask, hoping that this will prompt Tai Situ to speak to me about the conditions under which the Karmapa is forced to live at Gyuto.

'Everything that happens around him is his activity; around him is the smell of rose, the colour of rose, the petal of rose. Everything is part of the rose.' Rinpoche does not even stop to think, just insists that the young Karmapa is already fully realised. 'Whatever is going on around him is his activity. You are writing a book, some people are writing newspaper articles, other people are asking him questions about their lives, their philosophies . . . All of these are his activities . . . Even when he is sleeping, someone is talking about him, someone is writing about him. All of these are his Buddha activities or this is how I see it.'

I understand Tai Situ Rinpoche to be speaking about the Karmapa's manifestations, suggesting that all these things going on around him are happening because the Karmapa has willed them to. The 'Buddha activities' to which Rinpoche refers are what we Westerners might call special powers. I listen to all of this, nodding as though it makes perfect sense. I smile politely at the thought that my book is something I've undertaken because I've been called to it. Then, slowly, the smile slips from my face and my jaw drops.

(Later, when I recount this conversation to my friends at home, almost without exception, they share my moment of eerie realisation. One of them, however, a lawyer, is wholly dismissive of the notion that I was 'called' to write my book. This notion, she insists, is utterly self-serving. For my part, depending on how the writing is going, I myself will alternate between awe and dismissiveness.)

'I really wish you could read Tibetan because his writings are unbelievable,' Tai Situ Rinpoche continues, and I drag myself back to the moment and try to concentrate.

I venture back to the delicate area of politics, asking about the rift in the Karma Kagyu school over the recognition of Ogyen Trinley Dorje as the XVIIth Karmapa and referring to the issue of the other candidate and his supporters.

The so-called 'Lama Wars' was never confined to public mud-slinging. In 1993, it went legal when a pair said to be Shamar's followers, Dugo Bhutia and Karma Gompu, filed a writ in the Gangtok High Court challenging the recognition of Ogyen Trinley Dorje by the Dalai Lama and others. The writ was dismissed in August 1994. The next suit came in 1996 and this time was against the state of Sikkim, challenging its recognition of the XVIIth Karmapa. It was withdrawn within a month.

Tai Situ Rinpoche asserts that he doesn't understand the purpose of the other group or the reason for all the false things they're claiming. 'Everybody knows the sun is over there,' he tells me, gesturing in a westward direction towards Gyuto Tantric University. He explains that the dispute is all part of Buddha activity but says he doesn't understand why some people need to learn in that way. 'I have lots of friends who do bungy jumping,' he says, making a joke of one of the most serious brawls in the history of Tibetan Buddhism. 'They really want to do it, but I don't have to do it myself . . . I'm not against bungy jumping but I will not do it. It's like that . . . they are creating some things which are absolutely unnecessary.'

I cannot help but wonder whether Tai Situ Rinpoche is making a sly reference to the controversial Dane, Ole Nydahl, one of Ogyen Trinley Dorje's rival's key supporters. Nydahl has founded Buddhist centres across the world and is, notably, a keen parachutist. He likes to advocate jumping to his *dharma* students as a Buddhist exercise. He himself, with more than eighty jumps to his name, attempted to parachute in lotus position. The result was a major lesson for him in pain and suffering, resulting in many broken bones.

When I tell Tai Situ Rinpoche that he's answered all my questions and that the interview is over, he looks delighted and promptly turns off my tape recorder.

'So how are you doing here in India?' he asks me in a tone of voice that suggests we can get down to a real conversation now.

We swap reflections on India and on Australia, a country he once visited. I produce my family snaps. Tai Situ Rinpoche is captivated by my dog, the lovely Lola. Is she a German shepherd, he wants to know and I tell him yes. He has four, he tells me, although one of them has gone wild. We smile at each other and nod a lot, agreeing that they are beautiful dogs. I show him a second photo, the one of Isla lying on top of her dog. This produces a response of even greater delight and Tai Situ gestures to Lama Tenam who is hovering in the corner.

When I finally emerge into the waiting room that is still abuzz with devotees, I feel that this man, who is called upon by so many for such different things, has genuine concern for my well-being and for the success of my book. After all the waiting and uncertainty about what exactly was being offered me, I suddenly feel myself gliding in just that way the *Sunday Times* journalist did after he interviewed the Dalai Lama. Without even noticing that it had happened, I feel that I've been blessed.

Down in the courtyard, where young monks are now noisily gathered, a lay Tibetan is being trailed by one of Tai Situ Rinpoche's German shepherds who bears a striking resemblance to my Lola. My photos come out again and the young monks – some of them not yet ten – are thrilled to see this other shepherd who looks so much like their own. They keep tossing the biscuits to the dog and placing the photo of Lola beneath her nose. 'Dolma, meet Lola in Australia.' (Four months later, the monks from this monastery will be honoured in Hollywood. Their CD, *Sacred Tibetan Chant*, will be awarded a Grammy in the best traditional world-music category. I can easily imagine their simple delight and the way they will have tossed even more biscuits to Dolma, their canine mascot.)

Arun and I drive away, once again passing a site of extraordinary devotion. On one side of the road is an ornate wall and a massive *stupa*, at the foot of which some young monks and the old Tibetan with the plaits and prayer wheel are worshipping. On the other side of the road, the forest's pine trees are laced with string upon string of prayer flags in varying states of decay. I mentally dub the spot 'the avenue of airborne prayers'. Further along the road, our approach scatters a group of young monks out promenading with their saffron-yellow umbrellas raised above their heads. I am filled with an inexplicable sense of joy as we drive west, the Himalayas turning purple in the dusk.

LINEAGE: THE EIGHTH KARMAPA

The VIIIth Karmapa, Mikyö Dorje (1507–1554), was visited by the IIIrd Tai Situ Rinpoche when he was only nine days old. The Rinpoche found that the circumstances of Mikyö Dorje's family home and his parents' names closely matched the details in the prediction letter written by the VIIth Karmapa. Tai Situ Rinpoche gave the parents particular instructions to follow and, upon doing so, the baby said, '*Emaho*! Do not doubt me, I am Karmapa!'

When Mikyö Dorje was five, another boy was put forward as the Karmapa. The VIIth Karmapa's regent was sent from Tsurphu to eastern Tibet to meet the two boys and investigate. On seeing Mikyö Dorje, the regent began to spontaneously prostrate before him. Tests were devised for the two boys, nonetheless. Not only did Mikyö Dorje pass them, but he clearly proclaimed once again that he was the Karmapa. He was enthroned the following year.

The VIIIth Karmapa was a talented artist whose religious paintings had a profound influence on such art throughout Tibet. It is reported that he once carved a marble image of himself and asked it whether it was a good likeness. The statue replied 'Yes, of course!' and the Karmapa then went on to leave the impression of his fingers in a lump of leftover stone. Mikyö Dorje travelled constantly with the large monastic community that come to be known as The Great Camp of the Karmapa. He spread the *dharma* and blessed thousands of people during the course of his travels in the region.

THE BOY LAMA: CHINA'S PAWN?

A Tibet Information Network report claimed that Tibetans suspected the Chinese of attempting to manipulate the Karmapa for their own purposes and, in particular, to undermine widespread support for the Dalai Lama. During two tours of China, the Karmapa had been introduced to a number of leaders and officials.

In reaction to the Karmapa's 1994 tour, protests allegedly took place at Tsurphu Monastery. Posters appeared that denounced the Chinese government for not permitting the Karmapa to visit India. Six monks were subsequently detained.[38]

The Karmapa, according to a Beijing journal, said he had 'received an education in patriotism' and would, at Jiang Zemin's behest, 'work hard for the unification [sic] of the motherland and national unity'. Li Ruihuan, Chairman of the Chinese People's Political Consultative Conference, was already claiming that the Karmapa would significantly impact the development and stability of Tibet.[39]

Just as the Chinese authorities in Tibet had hoped to wield ultimate control over the Xth Panchen Lama (the Chinese have appointed their own candidate, Gyaltsen Norbu, his successor), they similarly had extremely high hopes for the young Ogyen Trinley Dorje. They had, perhaps, by the 1990s, understood Tibetans well enough to know that their religion and religious figures would remain an abiding force in their lives, regardless of communist propaganda denouncing Buddhism. We also know that Chinese communist leaders have long believed that once the XIVth Dalai Lama dies, international concern for the plight of the Tibetans will die with him. Perhaps in the leadership's mind, the missing link was a Tibetan religious figure who would, in the Dalai Lama's absence, unite Tibetans both within Tibet and in exile.

What the Chinese leadership had under-estimated, however, was the strength of character of one exceedingly bright young *tulku*.

To some Tibetans in exile, and it is difficult to be certain whether or not these are confined to the supporters of Shamar Rinpoche, permitting the incarnation of the XVIth Karmapa to be installed with Chinese approval at Tsurphu Monastery in Tibet represented only one thing: collusion with the occupying forces. To many others, it represented an attempt to work in a positive manner with the Chinese government within the frame-work of occupation. To present-day Tibet-watchers, it might seem like a precursor to the Dalai Lama's 'middle way' approach, in which he seeks genuine autonomy for his people within the framework of the People's Republic of China. In 1988, in what has become known as the Strasbourg Proposal, the Dalai Lama relinquished his claim for independence and instead called for genuine autonomy for his people.

What is without doubt is that the Chinese leadership had extremely high hopes for the young Karmapa. Not only did they bestow on him all manner of privilege, but they ensured that he was guarded with the sort of zeal one might reserve for a sophisticated secret weapon. Prior to the young Karmapa's arrival at Tsurphu, an agreement had been made between senior Tibetan clerics (including Tai Situ Rinpoche) and the Chinese leaders that stated that while the Karmapa would live in Tibet he would be permitted to travel to Rumtek Monastery in Sikkim and have good access to his teachers in India. Like so many deals struck between the Tibetans and Chinese authorities over the last half-century, this one was never honoured. Not only was the young Karmapa denied permission to travel to India, but ultimately his teachers were no longer permitted entry to Tibet.

Professor A. F. Thurman (a.k.a. Robert Thurman, father of movie star Uma), well known as a close friend of the Dalai Lama's, spoke of his meeting with the young Karmapa, aged only nine, in an interview with *The New York Times*. He remembers him as 'very sweet', but also recalls that Chinese security guards prevented him from talking to the Karmapa. 'We had a very cordial and jolly lunch with his father,' Thurman said, referring to Karma Döndrub. 'His father, a hardy nomad, was wearing a big Dalai Lama button, and was going on and on about how he wanted to go to India.'[40]

The fact that the young Karmapa's father was permitted to wear a Dalai Lama badge is telling. It suggests that back in 1993–34 the 'thaw' in Tibet, as instigated by Hu Yaobang (Communist Party general secretary from 1980 to 1987), was still discernible, at least around Tsurphu Monastery and perhaps throughout central Tibet. The thaw dates back to the early eighties, post-Cultural Revolution. The Third Work Forum on Tibet, held in Beijing in 1994, put an end to it and, in 1996, displaying pictures of the Dalai Lama in public was banned.

At the time of the Karmapa's escape, an American journalist commented on how the Tibetans believed the Chinese were attempting to co-opt Tibetan Buddhism's leadership.[41] He went on to cite the case of the XIth Panchen Lama.

As it happens, with the case of the XIth Panchen Lama the Chinese may have found their compliant pawn, although at this stage it remains to be seen. Gyaltsen Norbu, though, is unlikely to unite Tibetans within Tibet, let alone elsewhere. Tibetans, quite simply, do not see him as genuine. When the Dalai Lama announced the identity of the Xth Panchen Lama's reincarnation in 1995, the Chinese authorities reacted in fury, claiming that it was their role to make such a recognition and not the Dalai Lama's. So as not to be seen to follow the Dalai Lama's lead, and in order to re-establish their authority, the Chinese leaders 'disappeared' the Dalai Lama's chosen Panchen Lama, Gedhun Choekyi Nyima, and installed their own candidate. Gyaltsen Norbu's parents were paid-up party members. Almost a decade later, Gedhun Choekyi Nyima and his family's whereabouts remain unknown.

It is reported that the XVIIth Karmapa repeatedly refused to issue any public statement endorsing Gyaltsen Norbu as the XIth Panchen Lama. The Tibetans themselves had made their own decision about the two boys. When the Karmapa was taken to Tashilhunpo to meet China's Panchen Lama for the first time, the crowd bowed to the Karmapa and ignored the young Panchen. Not even six months before he eventually left Tibet, Ogyen Trinley Dorje himself showed reluctance to prostrate before China's Panchen Lama. As if he had not already jeopardised enough his relative freedom within Tibet, the young Karmapa would not bow to pressure to denounce the Dalai Lama.

One Western journalist, Isabel Hilton for *The New York Times*, wrote that when party representatives asked the Karmapa to read a speech they'd written for him in 1998, he hesitated. 'Do you wish me to say that I am giving this speech on your behalf?' the Karmapa reportedly asked the officials. No, the representative explained, the speech was to read as though it was in the Karmapa's own words. 'In that case,' the Karmapa asserted, 'I have no need of this text.' No speech was delivered.[42]

It is difficult to know what to make of reports of a failed assassination attempt on the young Karmapa's life in mid-1998. On the day in question, the young Karmapa was out at a picnic with his monks, about two kilometres from the main monastery buildings. It started to rain but the Karmapa had refused to return to the monastery immediately because he sensed that there was some danger. Indeed, while he was out, two Chinese men were discovered hiding beneath blankets in the Tsurphu library, adjoining the Karmapa's room. It is alleged that they were armed with knives and explosives. Although the pair was detained, the report alleged that the detention period was minimal. They had, they said, been paid to kill the Karmapa by an unnamed Lhasa person and would have received an additional fee had they been successful. Tibet Information Network reported that despite the seriousness with which the Karmapa's monks viewed the event, the local authorities discouraged further investigation and would not increase security at the monastery. Had the Karmapa already become too unmalleable?

TIBET: FLIGHT OF THE DALAI LAMA

When he returned from India to Tibet in early March 1957, the Dalai Lama was welcomed by thousands of his people. Hundreds of refugees from Kham were camped around Lhasa and the Tibetan leader was greeted by new stories of the destruction of monasteries. The communists' decision to delay reforms in Tibet related not only to their perception that the environment there was not yet ripe – in that the Tibetans were not yet ready – but also to China's failing economy. Tibetan leaders, including the Karmapa, were asked to try and quell the revolt in Kham, but they had only limited success. Despite the fact that reforms were to be delayed in Kham and Amdo, as well as in U-Tsang, the Chinese could never win back the trust of the Tibetans who had witnessed the destruction of their monasteries. Revolt continued to spread.

Notably, the Dalai Lama and the *Kashag* never openly encouraged the *Khampa* resistance, knowing that the Tibetan government could not offer material support. In early 1958, a pan-*Khampa* resistance movement calling itself *Gushi Gandruk* or 'Four Rivers, Six Ranges' – the ancient name for Kham that united all its ethnic groups – was born. The group, reportedly numbering more than 15,000, gathered at a town outside Lhasa. Not only were arms in exceedingly short supply, but the *Khampas* did not have the support of Tibetans from central Tibet. The *Kashag* itself was placed under extreme pressure by the Chinese to expel the *Khampas* or risk wide-scale bloodshed.

In December 1957, five *Khampas* who had been covertly trained by the CIA in guerilla warfare were parachuted into central and eastern Tibet. The two who were dropped into central Tibet were under orders to make direct contact with the Dalai Lama and seek his approval for CIA involvement. The official who was their contact with the Dalai Lama refused to make the introduction, out of fear for his own safety. The Dalai Lama was never informed of the guerillas' arrival and the Americans went on to direct their attention towards forging links with the *Khampas* alone.

By the beginning of 1959, anti-Chinese sentiment had taken hold among all sections of the Tibetan community and revolt had spread throughout Tibet. Celebrations surrounding *Losar* (Tibetan New Year) and the associated *Mönlam* (Great Prayer Festival), were likely to be particularly significant as the Dalai Lama was to take his final monastic examinations at that time. As *Mönlam* had been a time of conflict and Tibetan nationalism since the Chinese invaded, officials were concerned that there would be trouble again this year and the Chinese officials in Lhasa made preparations to defend themselves. Among the Tibetans, there was intense worry for the Dalai Lama's safety and a suspicion that the Chinese might attempt to remove him from Lhasa.

When Tibetan officials heard that the Dalai Lama was to attend a dance performance at the PLA headquarters on the following day, 10 March, some were convinced that he was walking into a trap. Whether a trap had been laid for their leader remains unclear, but some sources suggest that the Dalai Lama himself had innocently arranged the event by expressing polite interest in seeing the dance group. The rumour spread that the Dalai Lama was to be abducted by the Chinese. Despite the fact that the Chinese were openly issuing invitations to Tibetan officials, the Chinese suggestion that the Dalai Lama should attend the performance without his bodyguards only confirmed the Tibetans' suspicions.[43]

The Chinese claimed that the mayor of Lhasa was warning citizens that the Dalai Lama was planning to visit PLA head-quarters and that 'the Hans' (the Chinese) intended to kidnap him and take him by plane to Beijing. By mid-morning on 10 March, thousands of Tibetans had gathered outside the Norbulingka to protect their leader and prevent him from walking into danger. They vented their rage on two Tibetan officials who were regarded as arch collaborators, one of whom was killed. The Tibetans clearly felt that the *Kashag* and Tibetan aristocrats had let them down badly and betrayed both the Dalai Lama and Buddhism. A member of the *Kashag* attempted to disperse the crowd to no avail, while over at PLA headquarters the dance performance went ahead as planned, attended by most of the Tibetan hierarchy (whom the Chinese later accused of instigating the revolt), including the Dalai Lama's family, but without the Dalai Lama.

The Dalai Lama wrote in his earlier memoir *My Land, My People* that he felt he was standing between two active volcanoes, engaged in correspondence with the Chinese leadership from behind the high walls of the Norbulingka. Through his letters, he told the Chinese that he did not endorse the demonstrations outside the Norbulingka's walls and that his advice to officials about breaking up the group had not been taken. Later, he explained that he took this tone only to gain time, but it resulted in convincing the Chinese that the Dalai Lama was being held by force. The crowd, instead of dispersing, only grew. Tibetan officials were divided between those who supported the revolt and those who did not. Those in favour of the revolt had gathered below the Potala Palace in the days proceeding 10 March. Ultimately, the crowd renounced the 17-Point Agreement, claiming it had already been broken because the status of the Dalai Lama had not been maintained.

Members of the *Kashag* saw no alternative but to remove the Dalai Lama from Lhasa for his own safety and made plans for his escape, along with that of his two tutors, his family and the *Kashag* itself. By 17 March, the Chinese had started shelling parts of Lhasa and two shells landed near the Norbulingka. The state oracle had also declared that it was no longer safe to remain in the palace. That evening, dressed as a soldier, the Dalai Lama crossed the Kyichu River and left Lhasa.

Later, the Chinese would accuse the CIA and the Tibetan exiles in Kalimpong of instigating the revolt and the Dalai Lama's escape, but there is no evidence to suggest that this was the case. After three days of revolt in Lhasa, the *Kashag* authorised the limited release of arms from government arsenals to the people, but it wasn't until 20 March that the PLA was ordered to retake the city. Two days of intense fighting ensued and the Tibetans, who were ignorant of the Dalai Lama's fate and feared he had been captured, started to surrender, often using white prayer scarves tied to sticks to do so. According to the Chinese,

4000 people were arrested. According to the Dalai Lama, there was no accurate record of those killed at the time of what became known as the Lhasa Uprising. A PLA document subsequently captured by Tibetans estimated that between March 1959 and September 1960 there had been 87,000 deaths as a result of military action.[44]

On 23 March, the Chinese flag was hoisted over the Potala Palace (the 1000-chambered winter palace of the Dalai Lamas) for the first time. Fifty-odd years later, the Chinese propaganda would proclaim to the world that they were 'restoring' the UNESCO-listed Potala Palace. Should the Dalai Lama ever return to Tibet, however, he would not be permitted to reside there. As the palace, according to communist China, was now a world heritage site, it belonged to the people.[45]

Although the Dalai Lama and his group had initially hoped that they could set up a new government elsewhere in Tibet, it quickly became clear to them that, despite promises of help from the CIA, this was far too dangerous an undertaking. The Chinese premier had already announced that the rebellion had effectively 'torn up' the 17-Point Agreement and he went on to promote the Panchen Lama into the Dalai Lama's role of Chairman of PCART, although the Panchen Lama's status in this role was only 'acting'. On 30 March 1959, the Dalai Lama crossed the border of India into exile. He has not returned to his country since.

I cannot shake a poignant image of hide coracles (traditional Tibetan boats) crossing the Kyichu River behind the summer palace by night. It is no coincidence that the boats, in my mind's eye, appear as vulnerable as the Dalai Lama and the Tibetan exile community during their years of exile.

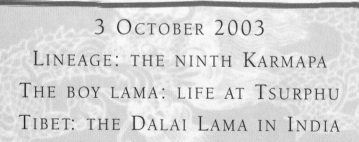

3 OCTOBER 2003
LINEAGE: THE NINTH KARMAPA
THE BOY LAMA: LIFE AT TSURPHU
TIBET: THE DALAI LAMA IN INDIA

3 October 2003

My simple room at the Norbulingka Institute has become a place for writing, yoga, sleep and contemplation. From the desk, pulled up against the windows, I gaze out through a veil of leaves and red flowers that look like miniature hibiscus. This verdant tangle between me and the neighbouring field is always alive with birds and insects; there are myna birds, green-flecked birds that look like finches, and enormous bees. From this vantagepoint, I think of the concrete walls of Gyuto Tantric University at which the Karmapa must gaze.

I leave for my second audience with the Karmapa with little time to spare. This time I walk boldly through the monastery's central courtyard, the yellow three-storey monks' accommodation silent on either side of me. Today, I feel not so much watched as part of a still life. The guards recognise me immediately, give me friendly smiles and ask what news I have of my daughter. I tell them proudly that her father baked her a banana cake. I don't tell them that she's lost her favourite furry pink jumper and that she cries when she's left at her day-care centre.

As I arrived, I had noticed another woman entering the courtyard and checking her watch and, once again, feel possessive of my short time with the Karmapa. It turns out this second visitor is well known to the security people, although she asks, rather crudely I think, for 'the sister'. Her English is heavily accented by Chinese and I gather that 'the sister' is the Karmapa's sister. This glamorous Chinese woman has been staying at the Norbulingka Institute too, and although I glimpsed her there only once, I had been told that a close friend of the Karmapa's sister was in residence.

When 'the sister' arrives, I see that she and the Chinese woman are not close friends at all. They are awkward and constrained with each other; two more different individuals would be difficult to find. Ngodup Palzom is petite, shy and wholly unembellished in her maroon nun's robes and a deep red fleecy top. At her feet is a salt-and-pepper-coloured pooch, possibly a Lhasa apso. Ngodup Palzom's hair is cut short and her body language suggests that she's very unsure of herself. I take an immediate liking to her. The Chinese woman, by contrast, is tall and immaculately dressed. She wears gold drop earrings, hair down to her waist and a heavy gold watch. From her bag, she produces a tiny mobile phone and electronic organiser. She gestures towards the gold ring on Ngodup Palzom's finger, telling the nun that the finger on which she's placed the ring is where other women wear their wedding rings. The Tibetan woman laughs in nervous embarrassment and changes the ring to another finger. It is clear that it is a gift from the Chinese woman.

I strike up conversation about the dog with Ngodup Palzom. She tells me that the dog follows her everywhere, even sleeps with her. The Chinese woman feigns disinterest, but I'm sure she's paying close attention to our conversation. I show Ngodup Palzom a photo of Lola. The Chinese woman asks where I come from and when I tell her Australia she says, 'Me too!' She pronounces the word Chatswood – the name of a suburb in northern Sydney – with such a dodgy accent that I doubt that she's ever been there. She subsequently tells me that she spends most of her time in Hong Kong. I try not to study the two women too closely but I am fascinated. I, the novelist, am convinced that the Hong Kong Chinese is a spy.

My one-hour audience with the Karmapa that was supposed to start at eleven o'clock is getting shorter and shorter and I sit fuming in the room of the grubby white sofas. At a quarter past eleven, I rise and go to ask the guards the reason for the delay. With no explanation as to why, I am told that the Karmapa's daily audience has been reduced from one hour to half an hour. I leave the women to their awkward silences when a monk I have not seen before comes to summon me.

Eventually, I ascend to the Karmapa's domain. At least I don't have to vie for his time with an anxious child and his stricken father. Today I have been permitted to take my bag into his room with me, which makes the whole ceremony of *khatag*-offering less troublesome.

The Karmapa seems pleased to see me, and today I offer him a card with some money and a little koala badge. I also give him one of my favourite Free Tibet T-shirts but I immediately feel foolish; the 900-year-old looks at the thing as though it is profane. I had read that in Ogyen Trinley Dorje's spare time he listens to rap music and plays Nintendo; such a modern lama would, surely, wear a T-shirt upon occasion. Evidently not. Nonetheless, I try to explain that the T-shirt is actually quite humorous. It depicts three monks meditating. Two are on the ground, weighed down by balls and chains labelled China, while the third has ascended above them, the chain attaching him to his own lead ball broken. The slogan reads only 'Free Tibet'. Later, Lama Phuntsok assures me that had the T-shirt's sleeves been maroon or gold, one of the monks might have felt inclined to wear the thing.

The Karmapa strikes me as an intensely physical person. He sits on his incongruous Perspex throne, leaning forward towards me, and clenches and unclenches one of his hands, letting it lift and fall onto his leg. This one action, repeated constantly, suggests to me a far greater physical repression. The young man almost crackles with pent-up energy. Were he an animal, it would be a sleek, powerful lion, rippling with strength and yet measured in his every movement. When I mention the Karmapa's physicality to one of his close advisers, the man tells me that this is nothing; when the boy arrived from Tibet, his physical frustration was much more apparent.

I do not wish to question the Karmapa about the controversy surrounding his recognition nor about the other candidates for the title of the XVIIth Karmapa. While I know a reasonable amount about the challenger, Thaye Dorje, I am happy to remain largely ignorant of any others. I do, however, wish to give him every opportunity to speak about recollections from his previous incarnation and his powers.

At the time that the search party was looking for the XVIIth Karmapa the seven-year-old Apo Gaga insisted his family move to their summer pasture and had already packed his few belongings onto his pet goat's back in preparation. Did this mean, I ask him bluntly, that he knew that the party was coming for him, and he also knew then that he was Karmapa?

No, he tells me, that's not what these actions meant. From time to time he did this: placed his few belongings on the goat's back – that's all.

I try to learn whether the Karmapa immediately knew members of the search party from his previous life. No, he tells me, although there were some in the party who had been acquainted with the XVIth Karmapa.

We talk of his journey from Kham to Tsurphu Monastery, west of Lhasa. Karmapa tells me that he remembers feelings of excitement on that journey and also when he arrived at the monastery. He was certain that he'd have a wonderful time at Tsurphu but the reality of the situation was not so. It is as though Tsurphu itself was somehow not what he remembered it to be, although these are not the words the young Tibetan used. (Tsurphu was being rebuilt when the Karmapa arrived and when the young boy first came to the monastery, the main temple was the only part of the complex whose rebuilding had been completed. Under the newly enthroned Karmapa, this work continued.)

Of the enthronement, the Karmapa remembers mostly a blur of people and noise. I, after watching video footage of the event a number of times, recall more or less the same thing.

I am both intrigued and frustrated that in my discussions with the Karmapa there's not a sound bite to be had. Admittedly, we converse through a translator, but the Karmapa is determinedly giving me nothing sensational, nothing contentious. I provide him every opportunity to tell me stories that will 'prove' that he is indeed the reincarnation of the XVIth Karmapa but he does not take the bait. He doesn't even nibble. He is resolutely his own man, dignified, deep thinking and sincere. While on the one hand this makes him a little impenetrable, I like him for it very much.

I am very conscious of the extent to which the Karmapa's story may be used to push forward different issues. Indeed, I myself wish to use his story to illustrate the plight of contemporary Tibetans. I had heard that the Karmapa had refused to bow to the Chinese-appointed Panchen Lama and ask him about his meetings with the boy. He was certainly present at Gyaltsen Norbu's enthronement but does not comment on whether he was supportive of him or not. He tells me that, at the time, he had already heard the rumours that the boy was simply a 'Chinese plant', so these impressions clouded the Karmapa's mind when he met him. He insists that he was under no pressure by the Chinese to formally approve this young Panchen Lama and was fully aware, from Chinese radio and the Voice of America, that Gedhun Choekyi Nyima (the boy recognised as the Panchen Lama by the Dalai Lama) had disappeared.

When I ask, the Karmapa tells me he cannot identify the exact moment that he decided to leave Tibet. He made his final decision some time in 1999, he recalls, and this was when his plans were crystallised.

Did he believe that he would survive the hazardous journey and make it to India, I ask. The Karmapa tells me no, he didn't believe this and comments that it would be difficult for anybody to be certain of such a thing. He never felt one hundred per cent convinced, but around the time he was planning his trip he had a dream in which His Holiness the Dalai Lama appeared. This, he said, helped him believe that he would arrive safely.

Although the Dalai Lama and the Karmapa head two different Tibetan Buddhist schools, the Dalai Lama is unequivocally the Karmapa's leader just as he is for every Tibetan. Has the Karmapa ever dreamed of returning to Tibet with the Dalai Lama, I wish to know, wondering whether he has already prophesised what would be the Tibetan event of the century.

'No,' Karmapa tells me, 'I haven't had this dream but it is most certainly my aspiration to return to Tibet with the Dalai Lama, as it is for most Tibetans.'

My final question of the day for the Karmapa is about whether he would like to visit Australia.

'Yes,' he tells me with certainty, 'I would. Many, many things must fall into place beforehand, however.'

Indeed they must, I think as I leave him there in his handful of rooms atop Gyuto Tantric University. I have heard that the Karmapa must seek permission to simply visit the monastery's main temple, which is right there beneath his own quarters. While he is outright barred from entering Sikkim, I am told that the only place he may go, without seeking police approval first, is the Dalai Lama's compound.

As I drive with Arun towards the Norbulingka Institute, I realise that I did not doubt a single word the young Karmapa spoke to me. Something about him, his demeanour, niggled at me. As I recall driving from Gyuto two days earlier with a pair of laughing monks, I suddenly put my finger on it. The Karmapa might wear a mantle of fierce intelligence, but it fails to conceal a profound sadness.

Later, I tell my friends that I had my own personal question for the Karmapa that I never asked. This question for the Karmapa only came to me for the first time when I was in his presence. Western devotees ask their Buddhist teachers all manner of life questions, not simply confining their talks with these men to the topic of religion. Seemingly from the air in the Karmapa's presence came the sudden urge to ask him whether Paul and I should have a second child, but at both audiences our time together had been filled with the young man's own life. My friends and I agree, laughingly, that I, in my non-asking, answered my own question. What's more, I would hate to be given advice that I might not follow.

Some weeks later, in Sydney, I meet a Western Buddhist nun who tells me that one of her students recently returned from India, having had a very intense guru–student relationship with the Karmapa. The nun tells me that the Australian woman constantly sought the Karmapa's advice but never took it. When she finally decided to leave India and went to see him one last time, he apparently warned her that she would suffer for not having taken the advice that she herself sought. I query the nun – surely he didn't mean it literally – and the nun insists that he did. She goes on to tell me that the Australian woman has been very sick ever since her return home. When I hear this story, I gulp with relief at what might have befallen me had I sought the Karmapa's advice and not heeded it.

Some of his monks have described the Karmapa's gaze as

wrathful and, while I never experienced such a look from him, I find his personal power almost palpable. The joy that emanates from the Dalai Lama, however, is noticeably absent in the Karmapa. In the presence of his guards and attendants, I felt quite stifled; one can only imagine how this young man must feel himself.

While my two audiences with the Karmapa have been rich and intense, I am frustrated that each day there are hours and hours during which I sit in my room at the Norbulingka Institute, having already conducted all the other formal interviews I had planned for the trip. While I could sit there another week and see the Karmapa a couple more times, I feel a powerful pull to travel to Sikkim in the east. I decide that I must be able to picture the Karmapa at the monastery that was, apparently, his ultimate destination when he left Tibet.

Lineage: the ninth Karmapa

The IXth Karmapa, Wangchuk Dorje (1555–1603), was born in eastern Tibet at a place in close accordance with the details of his predecessor's prediction letter. Near his family's house, an image of the *bodhisattva* Chenrezig had miraculously appeared on a rock. Shortly after his birth, he is said to have announced 'I am the Karmapa!' and arranged himself into a seated, cross-legged position in which he remained for three days. He was soon reciting the Sanskrit alphabet and within eighteen days was walking.

News of the extraordinary child spread to Karma Gön Monastery, from where Tai Situ Rinpoche sent a party to investigate. The *rinpoche* ultimately recognised the boy as the Karmapa and, notably, the political authorities in central Tibet also endorsed the boy. The secular powers were all too aware of the Karmapa's importance as a willing or unwilling leader. Wangchuk Dorje was enthroned when he was six and Shamar Rinpoche conveyed to him the essential teachings. Much of his study took place while travelling with his monks in The Great Camp of the Karmapa.

Wangchuk Dorje was known both as a political mediator and a committed restorer of monasteries. He identified many young reincarnations of senior Kagyu lamas, teaching and caring for them devotedly. His travels as Karmapa took him to Bhutan and Mongolia. He was invited to China and Sikkim but was unable to make the visit to either place. Nonetheless, he had three monasteries built in Sikkim that he consecrated from Tibet. One of these was Rumtek which, when rebuilt, would become the seat of the exiled XVIth Karmapa. The XVIIth Karmapa, on leaving Tibet, expected that he would reside there himself.

THE BOY LAMA: LIFE AT TSURPHU

Not long after their son's enthronement, Loga and Karma Döndrub, along with their other two sons and their daughter Mönlam, left Tsurphu to return to Kham. It was time to go home to their other daughters and to their livestock. Their middle son, after all, was being looked after by his monk attendants as if he were more precious than life itself.

One day Loga and Karma Döndrub would take a house in Lhasa so they could be near their son for extended periods, but for the time being they needed their old life. The young Karmapa had quickly become accustomed to commanding those around him and he showed every sign of coping extremely well without his parents and siblings. The Karmapa's parting from his younger brother, Tsewang, was particularly tender. The youngest of Loga's children would himself go on to be recognised as an important *tulku*. Loga and Karma Döndrub would not be left without a son; instead of taking his vows as a monk, Yeshe Rabsel would marry and have children of his own.

The young Karmapa's studies began in earnest and his days were carefully divided between lessons, rituals and audiences. In his studies, he showed the aptitude of a great intellectual and the restlessness of a seven-year-old boy. During the breaks that were an integral part of his schedule, he would rush outside to play on the flat roof beyond his quarters. The young monks who assisted the Karmapa in play were as delighted by the plastic, mechanical toys as he was himself.

At other times, the young Karmapa, would sit in his room and dream. From these dreams – which some might call visions, and others, prophecies – sprang the recognition of other important Kagyu reincarnations.

When a high Kagyu reincarnation dies, the administration of that lama's monastery contacts the Karmapa, requesting that he identify the new incarnation. Standard procedure is for three requests to be made before the Karmapa replies that the time is right to recognise the rebirth. Then, in writing, he gives the circumstances of the *tulku*'s rebirth.

Jamgon Kongtrol Rinpoche was one of the XVIth Karmapa's four regents, and was entrusted with administering the Karmapa's affairs between the time of his death and the moment that the Karmapa's next incarnation gained his majority. Jamgon Kongtrol, however, never saw the happy day of his master's seventeenth enthronement because he was killed in the car crash when he set out to lead the search party that was heading for Bagor, in the Lhatok region of Kham.

The Karmapa had already responded three times in the negative to the requests that he recognise Jamgon Kongtrul Rinpoche's reincarnation. It was not yet time. Mid-1995, however, his response differed. Next year, he promised, there would be news.

In May 1996, two representatives of Jamgon Kongtrul Rinpoche's administration travelled to Tsurphu to meet with the eleven-year-old Karmapa. On the day of the meeting, a massive *thangka* was being unfurled on a hillside opposite the monastery. Story has it that the moment the young Karmapa handed a letter describing details of the rebirth to Jamgon Kongtrul's representatives, a thunderclap resounded in the sky. It was followed by a sun shower, or what the Tibetans call the 'rain of flowers'.[46]

The Karmapa had written:

> From here, in the direction to the south, the place is a
> distance of seven days on a good steed. A son was born
> in the Year of the Pig to a father whose name includes
> *ga* or *ma* and to a mother whose name includes *tha* or
> *kha*. There are eight in their family. As for the place:
> in front of a great black mountain, its view partially
> obscured by the mountains to its right and left.
> Between, a mighty river rushes forth. The house is two
> storeys and well built; its door faces east. This vision of
> his birthplace has appeared to me. As for the *pujas* to be
> performed, if one hundred thousand *tsok*-offering *pujas*
> of the Protector and as many *pujas*[47] of Gyalwa Gyamtso
> as possible are done, his activity as the glorious protec-
> tor of beings and the doctrine will be ensured.
>
> I therefore grant this letter describing the signs of
> Jamgon Rinpoche.
>
> Karmapa Ogyen Trinley Dorje
> 11 April 1996[48]

Jamgon Kongtrul's monks went on to seek further clarification
from the young Karmapa, who sketched for them in his exercise book an idyllic scene; there were mountains, a rainbow
overhead and the family's home. He drew a detailed layout of
the house and the surrounding buildings, telling the monks
that the building was two storeys high and its door faced east.
The mountain, he claimed, was the one there in front of
Tsurphu and the house in question was to the mountain's
south. After further questioning, the young Karmapa produced
the name of an area to the south of Lhasa, and other names of
the bordering regions. The Karmapa also revealed that it was
towards the end of the Year of the Pig that the incarnation had
been born.

Apparently, the Karmapa had been having regular visions of
the mountain in question, the one that lay before Tsurphu. In the

visions, rainbows appeared over the mountain, and within them the luminous image of Jamgon Kongtrul Rinpoche.

Eventually, and after searching for some time, the party found a young woman who seemed to know the child for whom they were looking. As the monks approached the house to which she was leading them, a woman emerged with a baby strapped to her back; he was dressed in the maroon and gold of Tibetan monks. The names of the parents began with two of the letters the young Karmapa had identified. According to one of the searchers, the baby kept looking at him and smiling in a particular way. He was quite unafraid. The mountain, and the details of the young *tulku*'s home, were just as the Karmapa had described them.

Upon the search party's return to Tsurphu with photographs for the Karmapa, the young Karmapa turned to a house he'd built from Lego. He wanted to know whether the *tulku*'s house looked anything like the one he had built. The members of the search party were not at all surprised by the strong resemblance between the house of Lego and the real one.[49]

The young Jamgon Kongtrul Rinpoche was undisputedly an exceptional child, as was the young Karmapa himself. As a toddler, Jamgon Kongtrul stoically, even beatifically, endured hours of ritual and ceremony, first at his enthronement at his predecessor's monastery in Nepal and then again and again as part of daily life. I would hazard to say that most children of this age – he was not yet two when he was enthroned – can barely sit still for the duration of their meal, let alone tolerate hours of wearing ornate robes and being gaped at by myriad strangers.

The Karmapa, while still only a boy himself, would go on to recognise other *tulkus* in a similar fashion. Each of the boys would prove to be exceptional babies who had already developed extremely quickly. Rapid physical maturation is one of the traits of a high *tulku*.

TIBET: THE DALAI LAMA IN INDIA

The attitude of Indian Prime Minister Nehru to the plight of the Dalai Lama and his people back in 1959 seems to be echoed by Indian policy towards the Karmapa today. Nehru explained that the government of India's policy towards Tibet was informed by three conflicting influences: '(1) the preservation of the security and integrity of India; (2) our desire to maintain friendly relations with China; and (3) our deep sympathy for the people of Tibet.'[50] Despite professing deep sympathy, Nehru was accused within his own parliament of selling Tibet to the Chinese.

Initially, Nehru hoped giving asylum to the Dalai Lama would not be seen as in any way supporting Tibet politically. The PRC had recently given refuge to a Nepalese communist and Mao had dismissed this act as nothing more than adhering to international protocol. Nehru clearly intended that China should regard India's handling of the Dalai Lama in the same light, as a solely humanitarian gesture. He was also said to have referred to the 'tremendous bond' between India and Tibet that had grown over centuries of spiritual and cultural exchange.[51]

When the Dalai Lama issued his first statement from exile mid-April, worded in the third person, the Chinese alleged that it was not written in the Dalai Lama's style and implied that it had been drafted by Indian officials. One historian mooted the theory that Nehru himself had written it.[52] When the Dalai Lama issued his second statement, this time in the first person and stressing the authenticity of the previous one, China's criticism of India became even more strident. India stood accused of 'expansionism' and was officially condemned for interfering in the internal affairs of China.

Nehru sought to keep the media away from the Dalai Lama, claiming to be concerned that the journalists were merely after sensation. More likely he was in damage-control mode, determined to protect India's fragile relationship with China. The Dalai Lama's story was, of course, serious political news and his people were relying on him to inform the world of their plight. This situation prompted the international press to suggest that the Indians were holding the Dalai Lama prisoner. While the Indians maintained that they were protecting the Dalai Lama from the media, their tight hold over him was perhaps not quite so well intentioned. Under the circumstances, the Dalai Lama was in no position to make comments that might be construed as anti-Chinese propaganda.[53]

In the short term, the recently arrived Tibetan refugees were confined to Mussoorie in the Indian state of Uttarakhand in the Himalayan foothills, where they were unable to contact foreign governments. They had intended, on arrival in India, to declare a government-in-exile and appeal to the United Nations. However, when Nehru and the Dalai Lama met on 24 April, the prime minister told His Holiness that the Indian government would never recognise such an exile government. By this time, the XVIth Karmapa and Sakya Trinzin had fled Tibet as well.

4 OCTOBER 2003

LINEAGE: THE TENTH KARMAPA

THE BOY LAMA: FLIGHT

TIBET: UN INACTION

4 October 2003

Today is my last day at the Norbulingka Institute. I will attend one of the Karmapa's public audiences at Gyuto, later in the day, but when I wake before six I am buzzing with excitement and a sense of my own well-being. I would not have thought that India could do this for me – but then, why not?

At the monastery, dozens of mainly Western devotees and tourists mill around and I am immediately sensitive to the jockeying for position that's going on. I presume that those at the front of the queue to enter the Shrine hall will be those who sit closest to the Karmapa. The public audiences are held on a regular basis, twice a week on Saturdays and Sundays. Up until recently, the public audience or teachings were also held on weekdays.

Around the side of the main building, in the grubby reception rooms, the same bored Indian security personnel greet me like a friend. I find it intriguing that they are less suspicious of me now that I've been to see the Karmapa already; their suspicion is not aroused by my returns.

I hang back, so the more zealous devotees can move into the Shrine hall before me. I am very conscious that I've been privileged to see the Karmapa privately – if that's how you could describe our meetings – and try not to feel smug about this. Everyone is patted down and I cannot help but feel, as I've done before, that these searches are conducted in a haphazard, inefficient manner, as if simply for show. It's as though the most important thing is that the Indians are seen to be protecting the Karmapa, rather than truly protecting him.

Within the temple, we all sit in rows on the floor, latecomers crowding in closely, impinging on others' personal space. It's not that the Shrine hall is full – there's plenty of space towards the back of the room – but clearly the idea is to be as close to the *bodhisattva* as possible. Later, friends of mine who sit right at the front of the room report that the small salt-and-pepper-coloured dog, the one I met the day before trailing the Karmapa's sister, is running in and out of the room, sharing the eager anticipation of the devotees and heralding his master's arrival.

It is hardly surprising that the majority of those at the Karmapa's audience are Western women; he is, after all, the Keanu Reeves of Tibetan Buddhism. I am somehow heartened to see that there are plenty of Tibetan women present as well. I would be disconcerted if this was all a spectacle for the tourists. While the Western women range between their early twenties and late fifties, the Tibetans are spread across a much broader spectrum. In front of me is an ancient grandmother, her waist-length plaits steely grey, coloured string woven into them. A few rows before me is a young Tibetan mother with a tiny baby, closely swaddled in the heat of early autumn.

When the Karmapa finally strides towards his throne on the stage before us, the elderly Tibetan woman in front of me performs full prostrations with all the vigour and ease of the young Western devotees. The prostrations remind me of a speeded-up version of a yoga practice called salute to the sun; the hands move up to the forehead in prayer before being swept down the body and onto the floor in front, followed by the knees and then the whole body until the figure is, indeed, prostrate on the floor.

There is a moment of hushed anticipation as the Karmapa fixes a small microphone to his robes before he starts to chant. His deep resonant voice fills the Shrine hall and I find it surprisingly transfixing. I realise that during my audiences with him I've been so focused on my questions and his answers relayed to me through a translator that I haven't managed to actually hear his voice. The chanting continues for only a matter of minutes but it seems to stretch on and on and on, somehow an end in itself. When it does cease, abruptly, I wonder whether it's my imagination or whether there's a palpable sense of loss in the room.

The Karmapa's attendants, including Lama Phuntsok, now form a line to their master's right. Those sitting at the front of the room begin to stand, *khatags* and envelopes in their hands, to process before the Karmapa; they know the drill, they've done this before. First, one monk takes the *khatag* from the devotee, unfurls it, then places it over the devotee's outstretched hands.

He or she then shuffles forward to the next monk standing closer to the Karmapa, who takes the *khatag* from the devotee's hands and places it around his or her neck. Some devotees have an envelope with a money gift for the Karmapa and they hand this to him directly. All is closely monitored for irregularity or potential threat. All who file past the Karmapa receive a silky red blessing cord, tied with a single knot, from his own hands. He and I make eye contact well before I reach his feet and, once again, I experience a surge of joy at the smile this otherwise serious young man offers me. Unintentionally, unwittingly, I have transformed from interviewer to devotee.

As I shuffle towards the back of the temple, I notice the young Tibetan mother and her baby once again. I had meant to watch them as they filed past the Karmapa, eager to see what sort of special blessing he would bestow on the youngest of his devotees. As it happened, I was too engrossed in the moment, and in my own connection with the man, to follow the course of others.

Although I do not stay to witness it, I am painfully conscious that Gyuto will be dead again, once the throngs leave for the day. Later, in Dharamsala, I find a photo of the Karmapa on one of the high terraces above the temple. He stands alone, beside an unfurled flag – his own – and waves. The image in itself is poignant, but even more so when a friend tells me that the Karmapa stands up there up on the terrace, waving, after each of these public audiences.

I am told that the Karmapa's entourage at Gyuto numbers about forty. At Rumtek, in Sikkim, his community would number up to 600. One is a thriving monastic community that's the repository for the Karmapa's prized possessions like the replica of the Vajra crown; the other is a concrete shell, awaiting the Gyuto monks.

Back at the Norbulingka Institute, I hastily gather my belongings, settle my account and wait, once again, for Lama Phuntsok. This time he will come to me with the Karmapa's sister Ngodup Palzom. He arranged this meeting for me at my request, after Tai Situ Rinpoche suggested that she was the best person with whom to discuss the Karmapa's childhood.

When they arrive, Ngodup Palzom is every bit as timid as she appeared at Gyuto the day before and Lama Phuntsok works hard, cracking jokes and trying to relax her. He seems to be having the opposite effect.

'The sister', as well as having a fine gold ring from her Chinese/Hong Kong/Australian 'friend', has a smart little red mobile phone like Lama Phuntsok. Although the image of a Tibetan monk or nun with a nifty little mobile phone did not fit into the set of preconceptions with which I travelled to India, I am now quite fond of it. While we make small talk in the lounge room, waiting for our tea, Ngodup Palzom receives a pair of virtually incomprehensible text messages in English from someone she hardly knows. The messages are meant to be jokes and one, I note, is flirtatious. She looks utterly bewildered as I try to explain their meaning to her. She is a babe in the woods.

Rather than asking Ngodup Palzom to spell her name for me, I ask her to write it. I quickly realise that this must seem like a daunting test to her as she struggles to form each character. When she has finally written the words for me, she seems pleased to have achieved such a thing in front of a strange Western woman. She baulks, however, when I ask whether I might tape our conversation. I end up with my notebook on my knee, once again.

Ngodup Palzom tells me she is eight years older than the Karmapa. As the first boy after so many sisters, Apo Gaga was all the more deeply cherished and received no lack of attention from them.

'He was so gentle and caring,' Ngodup Palzom tells me of her brother, 'that we loved him all the more. When he was very young, he showed great compassion towards all sentient beings. He would take care of the very smallest creatures. Nomads have to kill their own livestock in order to eat. On those occasions, my family had to make sure that our brother was far away.'

I can see, on Ngodup Palzom's round face, the depth of her feelings for her brother. While he felt pain for all those sentient beings, she felt pain for him.

When she was only five or six years old, Ngodup Palzom

became a nun at Karma Gön Monastery, which was a two-hour ride from where the family lived. Ngodup's father, Karma Döndrub, decided that she should become a nun and she was the first child in the family to take vows. She did not stay at the monastery, though, as only monks are resident there. One of Ngodup's sisters, Kalzang Paldzom, also became a nun. The Karmapa's brother, now known as Tsewang Rigzdin Rinpoche, is still in Tibet at Karma Gön Monastery. He is sixteen years old. The abbot, however, fled Tibet and, only in his early twenties, resides at the nearby Tashi Jhong Monastery.

I comment that it seems that an inordinate number of the family's children took up a religious life.

'Tibetans try to minimise the mundane in life,' Ngodup Palzom announces, then tries to explain when she sees my look of confusion. 'Instead they try to devote as much energy as possible to going to heaven.'

I, too, would like to minimise the mundane in life, I am thinking, but see the logic in the familial distribution of duties. There are some who work at the physical chores, and others who work at the spiritual ones.

Life after Apo Gaga's recognition was not so radically different for Ngodup Palzom's family. They continued to live as they had before, but would also travel to Tsurphu to visit their boy, the Karmapa.

Ngodup herself seems to me, in some way, to have taken part of the weight of her brother's responsibility onto her own shoulders. I can see that she is the one from her own family who bears a strong duty of care towards him. Over a period of seven years, Ngodup travelled back and forth between Tsurphu Monastery and Lhasa, where her family had taken a house. She tells me that during those days her responsibility was to look after the house, but I sense that her unspoken duty was to look after her brother, also.

I ask Ngodup Palzom whether her brother has changed over the years since he was enthroned, knowing that the answer has to be yes.

'My brother underwent many teachings and has given so

many teachings and audiences himself,' she tells me. 'Each time I visited him I saw that he had made progress. He has to take care of so many people, so many sentient beings. He can no longer choose how he spends his time.'

Ngodup tells me that before her brother was recognised as the Karmapa they could spend as much time together as they wished. Now she has to respect him and his duties. When they're together these days, their most pleasurable time is spent talking about their parents and their old home, along with the sharing of thoughts and ideas.

I ask Ngodup what she wishes for her brother and her answer is very simple.

'I would like him to be able to learn more, and to have more time for spiritual development.'

Of course Ngodup Palzom is a nun herself but, nonetheless, I remain impressed by the place Buddhism holds in her life. I am reminded that even for the Tibetans who do not call themselves religious, Buddhism provides an essential life philosophy.

Ngodup left Tibet and travelled to Nepal in November 1999. Her aim, she explains, was to travel on from there to India, to see the Dalai Lama. Unbeknown to her, her brother was making plans for a similar journey, although his was not sanctioned by the state as hers had been. She recalls that she arrived in Dharamsala on 3 or 4 January. Her brother arrived there on the fifth. I choose not to question her about what she knew and did not know of her brother's plans; the story she tells to anyone who asks is that she had no prior knowledge of his escape.

'It was *karma*,' Ngodup Palzom tells me quietly, when I comment on the coincidence of her and her brother arriving in Dharamsala within days of each other. '*Karma*.'

What does Ngodup Palzom wish for herself, I want to know. Does she wish to undertake formal studies as a nun, for instance? No, she tells me, she just wants to stay with her brother.

I try to explain, through Lama Phuntsok, the nature of the book I hope to write. It seems important to convey to the young woman that I will not pretend to know her brother intimately, but seek, in telling his story, to tell a broader story about Tibet.

Perhaps I expect scepticism from this young woman, who has seen me only twice, but that's not what I get. What I get is heartfelt gratitude that quickly feels like a burden. We both so want me to be up to the task I have set myself.

What would she like from Australia, I wish to know. An intermediate English textbook, Ngodup tells me – such a modest request that I'm very happy to meet. Later, when I send the book to Gyuto Tantric University, I imagine her and her brother poring over it together and being reminded, once again, of how far they are from the rest of the world. Some months later, I learn that the book never reached them. I cannot help but wonder whether the Intelligence Bureau would prefer that their charge not gain proficiency in English.

This afternoon I am to bid farewell to Lama Phuntsok, also. He has been my fixer and adviser in India and I feel a debt of gratitude to him. When I explain that I'm leaving for Dharamsala that afternoon and then travelling on to Sikkim, I can see from the expression on his face that he's amazed that I will be there in Dharamsala then and gone again so quickly.

'You should return and spend a month,' he tells me. How I wish I could and how these words will ring in my ears over the following weeks and months.

Later, I meet two friends in a Dharamsala bar. One is Sophie, with whom I travelled from Delhi, and the other is another publishing friend who, after many years at the top of her field, chose to move to India and manage the construction of Tenzin Palmo's nunnery. Tenzin Palmo, from London's East End, became a Buddhist nun and published an immensely successful book, *Cave in the Snow*. My friend Monica worked on its Australian launch. I cannot help but feel bemused that we three ex-publishing women have left quite regular jobs and ended up here, flirting with Tibetan Buddhism in our own different ways.

Over weak Indian beer and the now unfamiliar cacophony of bar-room voices, I speak of my reaction to the Karmapa and his gentle sister. I tell them that I am surprised and a little overwhelmed by how protective I feel towards the pair.

I realise that, should the most intriguing story concerning

their lives fall in my lap tomorrow, I would not share a word of it unless I was sure that it could not harm them.

LINEAGE: THE TENTH KARMAPA

Chöying Dorje (1604–1674), the Xth Karmapa, is rumoured to have taken seven steps towards the north, south, east and west at birth. Enthroned at the age of eight, Chöying Dorje was already an accomplished debater of philosophy, and an artist and poet. He was graced with one of the typical Karmapa traits of foresight.

While studying at Tsurphu Monastery, the King of Tsang, in central Tibet, became the Karmapa's patron. The king's son became embroiled in a dispute with two of the large Gelug monasteries near Lhasa, and the Gelugs called upon the assistance of the Mongol chiefs, seeking to suppress the other schools of Tibetan Buddhism. In anticipation of having to flee central Tibet, the Karmapa gave away many of his possessions and his money to the poor, and appointed a regent. When Gushri Khan's Mongol armies attacked the Karmapa's own camp, Chöying Dorje remained fearless and appeared alternately to the soldiers in his own form and in the forms of an eagle and a deer. Ultimately, he fled, leaving his followers – or so it is said – with an image of him flying through space holding the hand of his chief attendant.

Chöying Dorje fled to Bhutan, where he lived in the wilderness for some three years. He subsequently travelled on to northern Yunnan, near Kham's border with southwest China, where the inhabitants welcomed him warmly. The local king developed a plan to drive the Mongols from Tibet and establish the Karmapa as head of state. The Karmapa, however, dissuaded him, arguing that waging war was against the Buddha's teaching. Chöying Dorje lived in Yunnan for thirty years, but often travelled into Tibet disguised as a beggar to find the Kagyu lineage incarnations who had been born there.

Chöying Dorje was finally able to return to Tibet as the Karmapa because the political climate had changed considerably. The Vth Dalai Lama had become both the spiritual and temporal leader, as would each of his subsequent reincarnations right up until that of the present, the XIVth Dalai Lama, Tenzin Gyatso. The Karmapa bestowed teachings on the Dalai Lama, who subsequently proclaimed that Tsurphu Monastery should be protected from political disturbance.

THE BOY LAMA: FLIGHT

On December 28, 1999, under the cover of a dark night, my senior attendant and I escaped from my monastery in Tibet and fled to India to seek refuge. The decision to leave my homeland, monastery, monks, parents, family and the Tibetan people was entirely my own: no one told me to go and no one asked me to come.

His Holiness the XVIIth Gyalwa Karmapa Ogyen Trinley Dorje,
27 April 2001 (press statement)

The young Karmapa, his monks and his teachers had by now made so many requests to the Chinese-controlled government for permission to travel that they must surely have lost hope that a state-sanctioned visit to India would ever occur. Two hundred Tibetan monasteries had put their names to a petition to the Chinese government, requesting that the Karmapa be permitted access to his teachers. All to no avail.

As we now know, the fourteen-year-old would leave behind his mother, Loga, and his father, Karma Döndrub, who proudly wore a Dalai Lama badge and dreamed of one day travelling to India and meeting the Tibetan leader himself. The boy would also leave behind two brothers and five sisters, not to mention the dozens of devoted monks who had become family to him during the seven years he resided at Tsurphu Monastery.

The Karmapa knew enough about how things worked within Tibet to understand that his departure would make the lives of his immediate family and entourage extremely difficult. There would be no reunions with them in India in a few months' time. This was a momentous decision for anyone to make, let alone a fourteen-year-old boy.

The plan for his escape was the product of detailed research on the part of those who would travel with their master, and of deep contemplation on the part of the Karmapa himself. The escape party would number six in total; in addition to the Karmapa, the two key players were also high lamas – Lama Tsutrim and Nenang Lama. Tsimpön Drubgnak, the Karmapa's long-term, older attendant, would also make the journey. The men were chosen for their unique skills, as well as for their long-term allegiance either to the Karmapa or to Tsurphu Monastery. At the last minute, two drivers would be invited to participate in the great escape: Tsewang Tashi, the only layman among them, although formerly a monk from Nenang Monastery; and Dargye. If there was hesitation on the part of any of them, it was, apparently, only because of concerns for their master's safety.

On 27 December 1999, the Karmapa announced to his monk and lay fraternity at Tsurphu that he was entering a strict, twenty-one-day retreat. This was the trigger that moved the escape plan into its final phase. The four-wheel-drive vehicle that would transport the party was brought to the monastery and those who would be travelling with the Karmapa started to spin the tales that would give their absence, at least initially, a legitimate appearance.

At Tsurphu, Lama Nyima, the Karmapa's tutor who normally stayed in his master's quarters by night and served him by day, would remain to make the various devotional noises that would normally be associated with the Karmapa's retreat. Lama Nyima knew that he was putting his life at risk, but if his master reached freedom then this would be an acceptable price to pay. The cook, Thubten, would come and go, bringing his master's meals and taking the empty bowls away afterwards, and all would appear perfectly regular. Lama Tsultrim and the driver Dargye had already received permission to travel away from the monastery in the vehicle they'd been preparing for the last few days.

The journey itself would take at least seven days. While it was likely that they would be driving off-road over difficult terrain, they knew also that they would have to walk. The departure time was confirmed in code over the telephone. The party had decided upon ten-thirty pm, when the monks who were guarding the monastery that night would be absorbed in some particularly gripping television viewing. What's more, those on the security shift – some of whom were known to be Chinese sympathisers – would be unlikely to venture outside in the biting cold of that winter's night.

In his own room, the Karmapa was making his final preparations to leave all he knew and loved. He had written a letter of explanation, stating that he was leaving so he could receive the *dharma* from his teachers, as he had requested many times. In it, he also promised that he would be returning to Tibet and asserted that he was not turning against the country, or the Chinese. Alongside his own letter, which would be widely misquoted by the Chinese, he left a letter from the Dalai Lama in which the Tibetan leader had specifically asked the young Karmapa to 'serve the teachings in Tibet'. In the tradition of so many other great lamas who had fled Tibet before him, the Karmapa changed into lay clothing for his escape journey, wearing a scarf, hat and glasses to make his disguise all the more convincing.

The Karmapa, along with his tutor and his attendant, quietly left his room and home of seven years, descended a flight of steps and climbed out through a window onto the roof of one of the monastery's shrines. Below, Lama Tsultrim was waiting and one of the drivers stood quietly nearby. Suddenly, a security guard appeared and the Karmapa was halted in his tracks. After some brief discussion, the guard moved on and away.

In a matter of moments, the young Karmapa had dropped from the roof and onto the ground near the car. His older attendant was helped down behind him. This was the point of no return; the young Karmapa must not be seen in the monastery's grounds wearing lay clothes.

Lama Nyima returned to the Karmapa's rooms to receive the phone call from Nenang Lama who was awaiting the Karmapa down the valley.

'What is the situation?' Nenang Lama asked him.

'The scripture has been sent,' replied Lama Nyima. 'Please take good care of the scripture.'

These words confirmed that the Karmapa was, indeed, on his way.

The group left without further delay by a side road. At the end of the Tölung Valley, Nenang Lama and the second driver joined the party with a load of provisions.

The six men drove westward through the cold night, none of them able to sleep. Pre-dawn and Shigatse's streets were deserted; the travellers were able to buy petrol for the main tank and for the reserve tanks on the roof, as well. Instead of heading south, direct to Nepal and freedom, they continued westwards.

Careful research undertaken during the previous months had borne fruit. The lamas had identified a road leading to an unguarded border crossing that was unlikely to be buried in snow at the time. It was towards this that they were driving. Through their research, they had already identified the danger spots and had a good idea of the routines of the guards at any checkpoints they might encounter.

This journey represented a far cry from the Karmapa's other trip west in 1992 when he was a young *tulku* being taken to Tsurphu for his enthronement. It was, however, every bit as significant.

Ahead of the party lay the mighty Brahmaputra River, which traverses southern Tibet. Although the river was frozen at this time of year, crossing it was still hazardous. The Karmapa's next great obstacle was an army camp at Dranggo, close to the Nepalese border. The group halted before reaching the camp, to wait until the early hours of the morning before passing anywhere near the sleeping soldiers. The young

Karmapa kept reassuring his anxious companions, telling them not to be afraid.

Eventually, when the last light at the camp had been dimmed, the party moved forwards, the lights on their vehicle also extinguished. Suddenly, a light appeared from nowhere ahead of them and four of the party, including the Karmapa, leapt from the vehicle into the darkness. They would climb the nearby mountain and hope to intercept the road to meet up with their vehicle on the other side of the camp. The other two would continue in the car.

The night was pitch black and the Karmapa and his companions had to scramble up the steep slope, clinging to shrubs and shredding their hands in the process. All the while, those on foot feared for those in the vehicle.

The driver illuminated the vehicle's headlights and the two drove on, unchallenged. Beyond the camp and near the mountain pass, the pair stopped to wait for the other four, once again extinguishing their lights. Minutes stretched to hours and the pair set out on foot themselves to try to find the Karmapa and his companions. Eventually, the moon appeared in the sky, casting its gentle light on the mountain. Finally, the Karmapa glimpsed the vehicle's silhouette in the distance. Once reunited, the travellers sped away; to be anywhere near the army base at dawn would have spelled disaster.

Ahead of them lay a fork in the road: in one direction was Mount Kailash and in the other, the Nepalese territory of Mustang. Only 200 metres beyond the fork in the road, in the direction of Kailash, lay a second army base. Using the last of the darkness for cover, the group continued towards Mustang. The bitter cold of the night had, once again, brought them safety; the soldiers, who would normally have been guarding the road were sheltering inside.

The only clue that the XVIIth Karmapa had passed from occupied China into freedom was the presence of a humble stone beside the road. On one side was painted the word China and on the other, Nepal. The Karmapa was leaving behind his people, the Tibetans, just as his predecessor had done in 1959.

Ogyen Trinley Dorje had been far and away the highest-ranking incarnate lama (who had his people's devotion) remaining in Tibet.

Crossing into Nepal did not ensure safety. Ordinary groups of Tibetans were often returned to Chinese territory by Nepalese border guards and this, after all, was no ordinary group. It is possible that the travellers believed they'd encounter less trouble in Mustang than in Nepal proper. The kingdom is predominantly ethnic Tibetan and not only was the current king married to a Tibetan noblewoman but he was outspoken in his support of the Dalai Lama. One journalist claimed that it was the king himself who granted the young Karmapa safe passage.[54]

The Mustang terrain over which the group had to travel was wild and arid. At one point, the vehicle in which the group was travelling became hopelessly bogged. The Tibetans had to continue on foot until they reached a village in which one of Nenang Lama's relatives lived. It was early morning on 30 December and the travellers were given a hastily gathered assortment of horses that they were to leave at Lo Monthang, Mustang's capital.

The vision that is Lo Monthang must have appeared otherworldly to the weary Tibetans. A fortified city at 3770 metres above sea level, its red battlements are in stark contrast to the rugged mountains surrounding it. Here, in a kingdom as isolated as Tibet had once been, the Karmapa and his men were well fed. The family with which the group sheltered questioned the Tibetans about their identity and purpose. All the while, the young Karmapa masqueraded as a simple monk and devoted attendant to Nenang Lama, keeping his head down.

When locals arrived to speak to Nenang Lama, they were full of queries about Tsurphu and the young Karmapa. They were, they insisted, keen to meet him one day and hoped the lama could arrange things for them. Story has it that Nenang Lama assured Mustangis that they would indeed meet the Karmapa. And, without knowing it, they had.

From Lo Monthang, the party continued on fresh horses towards Jomson in Nepal, where there was a small airport. The route was perilously steep and at times the travellers led their horses rather than trust their lives to the animals' four legs. Rather than risk their luck flying out of Jomson and on through the busy Nepalese resort town of Pokhara, the group decided to trek further, over treacherous alpine paths, to Manang. There, the danger of being apprehended by the authorities was deemed smaller and the Tibetans would raise little curiosity. At this point, the party finally split up, the two drivers and their guide from Lo Monthang striking off together. Eventually, Tsewang Tashi and Dargye would be reunited with their master in India.

The Karmapa, along with Lama Tsultrim, Nenang Lama and Drubngak, continued his trek through the night. In another world, millions of Westerners greeted the new millennium with fireworks and champagne. So much for the free world: in Mustang, the Karmapa and his companions walked and rode in turn, right through the first day of the New Year and on into the night, crossing mountain passes of more than 5000 feet. Although Mustang had once sheltered Tibet's resistance army, the Nepalese government, who controlled it, was extremely sensitive to the will of the communist Chinese who occupied the territory to the kingdom's north.

In addition to the extremely arduous terrain, the young Karmapa was suffering from some sickness and one of his companions was plagued by a stomach disorder. Altitude sickness can kill, and quickly, so one can only imagine the anxiety that travelled with the party of exhausted Tibetans. Fit, well-equipped Western trekkers would normally make acclimatisation stops when trekking in this region but these were a luxury the Tibetans clearly felt they could ill afford.

After crossing the highest of the passes – Thorongla at 5416 metres – the monks faced the knee-shattering descent on foot. Below a deserted helipad lay a trekker's lodge where the travellers found warm food, comfortable beds and telephones. After arranging a helicopter for the next day, they made a call to Tsurphu, hoping to reach Lama Nyima to check on his safety and on whether the escape remained a secret. The confusion they encountered at the other end of the line told them that the Karmapa's departure had been well and truly discovered.

When the helicopter eventually arrived the following day, it was much smaller than the one they expected and could take only three of them at a time, and did so in two trips. The helicopter ultimately took the Karmapa much further than had originally been planned, all the way to Nagarkot, beyond Kathmandu.

The next phase of their journey had already been planned. From Nepal, Nenang Lama had made telephone contact with Tai Situ Rinpoche's attendant, Lama Tenam, via the latter's mobile phone. Taxis took the group, overnight, from Nepal to India and a bribe saw them pass uneventfully through the Indian border town of Rauxal. Tibetans, who are classified as Chinese citizens, are not permitted to exit Tibet without special papers, which the group did not possess. At Gorakhpur, they boarded a train for Lucknow.

From Lucknow, the travellers hired two cars to drive them through the night to Delhi. Despite the party's exhaustion, it was deemed prudent to race through India to the Dalai Lama's protection. Only then could the fourteen-year-old, who meant so much to the Chinese, possibly relax.

In Delhi, the Tibetans changed cars again and, on 4 January, the Karmapa and his companions drove north through the region's notoriously thick fog. Beyond Chandigarh, one might imagine that despite the omnipresent fog the travellers had started to experience the contentment of a journey approaching its end. This feeling of well-being, however, would have been all too short; on this leg of the journey, the car in which the Karmapa was travelling drove off the road and into a tree.

Miraculously, nobody was hurt, but further delays ensued until another vehicle could be rented for the party.

When the Karmapa finally arrived at McLeod Ganj pre-dawn on 5 January, he was a mere shadow of the man who had left Tsurphu Monastery a week earlier. Still dressed in the lay clothes in which he had travelled, the Karmapa was thin and tired, his hands were badly lacerated and his cheeks chafed by the cold wind. As was his way, the Karmapa reassured all those who felt distress and concern for him.

For the final phase of his long journey, the Karmapa dressed in monk's robes that had been provided for him. Ogyen Trinley Dorje and his companions were driven the short distance along the steep, narrow McLeod Ganj roads and up the sweeping driveway to a closely guarded compound through the iron gates. When the Dalai Lama and the young man finally met, the two great incarnate lamas touched foreheads. That moment, on a cold January morning, marked the beginning of a powerful and sustaining personal relationship. It represented the meeting of old and new Tibet.

TIBET: UN INACTION

Once again, in April 1959, there was talk of presenting Tibet's case at the UN and this time it was the Australian Minister for External Affairs[55] who made the suggestion while visiting South Korea. Britain, repeating herself, advised against taking Tibet's case to the General Assembly for a range of reasons: she and others had already recognised Chinese suzerainty over Tibet; there was a chance that the PRC might be invited to join the UN in order to properly discuss the matter; Britain might herself be censured for her own behaviour in certain states under her dominion; and finally, no UN censure would prompt the Chinese to withdraw from Tibet. In the meantime, the UN was being widely criticised in the international press for its failure to act on Tibet.

Within India, Nehru was under siege. The Chinese regarded India's granting of asylum to the Dalai Lama as a breach of the *Panch Sheela* agreement and the Indian people themselves, not to mention the opposition parties, were also highly critical of Nehru's stance on Tibet. Nehru would not permit the Tibetan exiles to contact other foreign governments directly, so opposition politicians started to undertake this task themselves.

In July 1959, the International Commission of Jurists (ICJ), led by one of India's most prominent lawyers, issued a preliminary report stating that 'on the part of the Chinese, there has been an attempt to destroy the national, ethnical, racial and religious group of Tibetans by killing members of the group and causing serious bodily harm to members of the group . . . these acts constitute the crime of genocide under the Genocide Convention of the United Nations of 1948'. The ICJ further found that Tibet was an independent country and wrote, 'From the present report there emerges also, it is submitted, a prima facie case of the worst type of imperialism and colonialism, coming precisely from the very people who claim to fight against it.'[56]

In *Freedom in Exile*, the Dalai Lama wrote that even he only fully understood the magnitude of the bloodshed in Tibet when he read the ICJ report. It starkly documented his people's crucifixion, vivisection, disembowelling and dismemberment at the hands of the PLA. Those who shouted 'Long live the Dalai Lama' on their way to execution, had their tongues ripped out.[57]

Eventually, the Indian government permitted the Dalai Lama to hold a press conference nearly three months after he had arrived in India. The Tibetan leader claimed that no matter where he was with the *Kashag*, Tibetans recognised them as the true government of Tibet. At that press conference, the Dalai Lama finally repudiated the 17-Point Agreement, claiming that it had already been violated by the Chinese.

At the end of September, Malaya and Ireland wrote jointly to the UN Secretary-General, requesting that 'The Question of Tibet' appear on the agenda for the forthcoming fourteenth session. Both countries wrote of the violation of human rights in Tibet, avoiding the controversial political issue of China's occupation. Despite the Soviet Union's strident opposition and technical objections from other nations, the issue of human rights violation in Tibet was finally tabled and a resolution proposed. After debate in which opposition to the resolution fell into two camps, those aligned with the communists and those Western nations who were afraid of a precedent being set that would adversely affect their own territories, a resolution received a two-thirds majority and was approved. One of its two points demanded 'respect for the fundamental human rights of the

Tibetan people and for their distinctive cultural and religious life'. The Indian delegation did not vote on the grounds that its own stance would influence that of the other nations.

While it is unlikely that anyone, even the Tibetans, believed the resolution would soften China's stance toward Tibet, it was a significant public-relations victory for the Tibetans. Indeed, Nehru's prediction that public censure of the Chinese might have an adverse result within Tibet may have been accurate. A subsequent letter from the US Secretary of State to the Dalai Lama, supporting the principle of self-determination for Tibet, also served to aggravate the Cold War, yet gave no tangible assistance to the Tibetans.

A second resolution was passed on Tibet at the UN in 1961, this one having been proposed by Thailand and Malaya. Despite its call for self-determination for the Tibetans and its expression of hope that member states would 'make all possible efforts as appropriate towards achieving the purpose of the present resolution', this second resolution had no more impact than the previous.

5 OCTOBER 2003

LINEAGE: THE ELEVENTH KARMAPA

THE BOY LAMA: EYES OF THE WORLD

TIBET: SMASHING THE THREE EVILS

OF THE PAST

5 OCTOBER 2003

I am woken before six by the chanting, rising in waves from the *Tsuglagkang* (the Dalai Lama's temple) which is just below the terraced gardens of Chonor House. The chanting is mingled with other devotional music that sounds almost carnivalesque.

Unable to lie in bed a moment longer, I go to the terrace to look down at the temple and listen. I sit for a few minutes but am drawn inexorably to the temple itself.

The temple's grounds are humming with Tibetans in their morning prayer. Unlike the Catholic churches of my childhood, this is a vital scene and Tibetan lay people and monks alike chant; read from long, flat prayer books; prostrate; whirl their prayer wheels; drink tea and eat Tibetan bread. I sit among them for a while without feeling self-conscious, and my eyes keep filling with tears. The word 'exile' is ringing in my ears. Elderly women in *chubas* prostrate with the grace of young dancers, their lined faces easily breaking into intense, creased-eyed smiles.

I move from the temple to the courtyard that lies before the entrance to the Dalai Lama's compound and, from the activity within the steel gates, I can tell that he's about to go somewhere. Cars are being prepared, a Tibetan official arrives with a large suitcase, and a magnificent German shepherd prances back and forth in anticipation of action. I cannot deny that I long for a glimpse of the Tibetan leader in his exile home.

From the temple, comes the sound of horns and cymbals and from further up the hill in McLeod Ganj the sound of earth-moving equipment – woefully inadequate as it is – that's attempting to shore up the village from the ravages of the monsoon and over-development. Hotels of five or six storeys cling to the steep slopes and between them are pot-holed, unpaved roads.

Tibetans are gathering at the foot of the drive leading from the Dalai Lama's residence. Some hold *khatags*, some prayer wheels, and an ancient Buddhist monk holds a brazier of burning juniper. Other Tibetans pull green switches from the nearby diadora trees. All watch the driveway expectantly, as I do myself. I have a breakfast date with my friends for which I am already late but I cannot drag myself from this roadside vigil. More elderly Tibetans wander down the hill from the temple to join the guard of honour.

Stray dogs are repeatedly chased from the road and there's a good deal of pretend stone-throwing, hissing and angry gesturing towards them. I find the dance of the dogs, who run back onto the road at each opportunity like wilful children, quite amusing but it's clear the Tibetans don't share my amusement. I, a Westerner familiar with the Dalai Lama's laughter and jokes during his public appearances, cannot imagine for a moment that he would be bothered by the presence of a stray dog on the road in front of his cavalcade; clearly the Tibetans feel this would be a grave dishonour. This farewell ritual for their beloved leader is of the utmost seriousness. Many of the Tibetans who live near the Dalai Lama do not like to be separated from him.

Finally, we hear the slamming of car doors from up the hill and the first of the white jeeps, red flags flying from its bonnet, is upon us. The second comes through, this one with a flashing red light on its roof, and also full of security personnel. Then comes a light brown saloon car and in the front seat, beaming out, is the man who is arguably the world's most famous religious leader. The Tibetans are bowing low, their hands joined in prayer at their foreheads. I, however, cannot resist breaking rank and waving as the Dalai Lama drives by and I am rewarded by an intense smile and a wave in return.

Even this briefest of encounters leaves me feeling blessed. The ability to reach strangers in that fleeting moment is one of the Dalai Lama's greatest attributes.

In the evening, I sit in the lounge room at Chonor House and watch some old videos of the Karmapa. One of the waiters from the quiet restaurant below comes to stand and watch, too. I ask him whether he himself has seen the Karmapa.

'Of course. Karmapa stayed here for a week when he first arrived in India, there in the Songsten suite.' He gestures towards the room right beside the lounge room. 'We had the honour of serving him.'

The waiter is a young Tibetan man, perhaps no older than the Karmapa. One day, the stories this man will pass on to his grandchildren will include memories of the week he spent serving tea to a bodhisattra.

For a moment, I can imagine myself in the Karmapa's shoes upon his arrival at Dharamsala and on being installed at Chonor House with its Tibetan paintings, furniture and carpets, and best of all its verdant terrace overlooking the Dalai Lama's own temple. Perhaps like me, Karmapa was woken by the chanting of monks when he stayed here on those first days, when he was still recovering from his journey and not strong enough to rise before dawn and chant himself. I like to imagine him on the lesser of the two thrones down there at the Dalai Lama's temple, surrounded by monks and Tibetans in their devotional practice. I realise that this image may have no grounding in reality, nonetheless, in the magical surroundings of Chonor House, the Karmapa must have felt something akin to boyish excitement.

LINEAGE:
THE ELEVENTH KARMAPA

The XIth Karmapa, Yeshe Dorje (1676–1702), was born in eastern Tibet while rainbow-coloured lights filled the sky. The young child enjoyed recounting his visionary experiences to his relatives, who soon deduced that the boy was not an ordinary child. Initially recognised by a master of both the Kagyu and Nyingma schools, it was Shamar Rinpoche and Gyalstab Rinpoche who sent their representatives to confirm that details of the boy's birth corresponded with those described by the previous Karmapa.

Although he lived only twenty-six years, he nonetheless fulfilled earlier predictions about his learning and lineage. He was responsible for the restoration of Tsurphu, which had been damaged – along with many other monasteries – by the

Mongols. When the great Vth Dalai Lama died, the regent who was appointed during the interregnum sought advice from Yeshe Dorje and became the latter's disciple.

The XIth Karmapa could reportedly manifest to different students in different places at the same time, and was said to have restored sight to a famous lama with blessed water. When he died, a number of his students claimed that they saw his form appear in front of the sun, accompanied by two other gurus.

THE BOY LAMA:
EYES OF THE WORLD

On Friday, the Chinese government confirmed that the lama had left China, citing a letter he had left at the monastery saying he was going abroad to retrieve musical instruments used by previous Karmapa lamas (sic). His departure was not meant 'to betray the State, the nation, the monastery or the leadership,' the government quoted the letter as saying.

The New York Times, 7 January 2000[58]

The fact that Beijing was grooming him [the Karmapa] as a pliable successor to the hated 64-year-old Dalai Lama only makes the pill more bitter. As recently as last year, he was feted by communist leaders and fawning documentaries on his life were broadcast on state-run television. Suddenly, there is no more mention of him in the Chinese media . . .

For India, the latest defection could not come at a worse time. Relations with China are still on the mend after New Delhi's 1998 nuclear tests, which senior ministers said publicly were aimed at countering the Chinese threat.

Christopher Kremmer, 'Free Spirited',
The Sydney Morning Herald, 15 January 2000

Western journalists repeatedly described the Karmapa's escape as an embarrassment to China, and a 'slap in the face of the Chinese, who are hypersensitive about the Buddhists'.[59] That the young lama had fled to 'the camp of the spiritual leader it [China] so bitterly denounced as traitor' made the blow all the more harsh.[60] The Karmapa's escape, what's more, was being touted as 'the most significant exodus' since that of the Dali Lama.[61]

Did the Indian government welcome the young footsore Karmapa with open arms? Alas not. Although journalists around the globe drew close comparisons between the flight of the Dalai Lama and that of the Karmapa, one fundamental difference would have an ongoing impact on the situation of the latest arrival. When the Dalai Lama first left Lhasa, en route to India, in 1959, his aides made absolutely certain that the Indian government was expecting him. A number of dispatches were sent from north to south, to ensure that the Tibetan leader would, at the very least, be officially received by Tibet's great southern neighbour.

Prior to or during the course of the Karmapa's flight, no such dispatches were issued. This omission is representative of a number of factors, the first being that the Karmapa was no head of state. He was, however, the Tibetan most highly prized by the Chinese government – as the Dalai Lama once was. What had changed most profoundly, over the forty years between the two high-profile escapes, was China's status. In 1959, the PRC was a significant regional force but by 1999 it had become one of the world's most valued trade partners and held a seat on the UN Security Council.

Would the Karmapa's official welcome have been any different, had the Indian government been warned of his arrival? It is almost impossible to say. Given India and China's strained relationship at the end of the millennium, it is not difficult to understand why the Karmapa's advisers might have chosen to keep his plans the best-kept secret in the Himalayas.

Official reports from Dharamsala, as quoted in the Western media, suggest that the Dalai Lama and his government had no knowledge of the Karmapa's planned exodus. While this might be technically correct in that details of his escape may only have been revealed to the exiled Tibetans upon the Karmapa's arrival at Dharamsala, a source close to the Karmapa reported that Tai Situ Rinpoche had been aware for some time of the Karmapa's desire to leave Tibet, and that he had personally conveyed this precious information to the Dalai Lama.[62]

After spending only four days at McLeod Ganj, the BBC reported that the young Karmapa had been mysteriously ferried away by a motor cavalcade under cover of pre-dawn. Although there was media speculation that Ogyen Trinley Dorje had been moved to a residence within the Dalai Lama's compound, or even to Tai Situ Rinpoche's monastery, Sherab Ling, a more reliable report from the local police suggested that he had been relocated to Gyuto Tantric University at Sidbhari, twenty-five kilometres away. Kalon Tashi Wangdi, minister for the exile government's Department of Religion and Cultural Affairs, was quoted a couple of times saying that the Karmapa was taken somewhere quiet and private so that he could recover from his ordeal. However, the Dharamsala superintendent of police was quoted in *The Hindustan Times* on 10 January 2000 as saying that the local authorities were taking precautions because of 'a serious threat to his [the Karmapa's] life . . .'

Already, speculation about the young Karmapa's motives was becoming colourful. Within ten days of Ogyen Trinley Dorje's arrival in India, *The Sydney Morning Herald* of 15 January 2000 quoted Shamar Rinpoche as saying, 'I believe he came here in agreement with the Chinese government, with their support,' and further suggested that Shamar Rinpoche feared the boy had come to India to steal the Karma Kagyu's most prized possession, the Karmapa's Black Hat. In the same article, journalist Christopher Kremmer mooted the possibility that the Karmapa may not be permitted to travel to his seat-in-exile, Rumtek Monastery in Sikkim.

Whether these views were widely held at the time, it was not long before rumours about the Karmapa's escape, and about those behind it, raged through the region. During my time in

India, I am repeatedly told that Shamar Rinpoche has excellent contacts in the Indian government.

TIBET: SMASHING THE 'THREE EVILS' OF THE PAST

Not even two months after the Dalai Lama's flight from Lhasa in 1959, the Chinese started to force Tibetans to participate in political rallies, condemning the recent revolt. Tibetans were divided into two groups, those who had participated in the rebellion and those who had not, and were treated accordingly. The aristocrats who had been involved in the revolt were arrested and subjected to *thamzing* (struggle sessions in which they were publicly criticised, humiliated and sometimes physically abused). Most of the Tibetan Army and many monks were arrested as counter-revolutionaries then incarcerated in labour camps in various parts of Tibet or China. In these camps, prisoners underwent the process of 're-education' and were used as cheap labour. They worked on large-scale projects such as building a hydroelectricity plant or working in the forestry industry. Many of the prisoners died or simply disappeared, never to return home.

In the absence of the Dalai Lama and the *Kashag*, the Chinese could proceed without restraint and went back on their promise of not introducing reforms prior to 1962. The Chinese used two Tibetans, the Xth Panchen Lama and Ngabo Ngawang Jigme (former Governor of Kham who was made first Governor of Tibet under the Chinese), to announce the reforms. The assumption on the part of the communists was that the promised material rewards alone (such as land and livestock ownership for the peasants) would not inspire the Tibetans to embrace reform, so they engineered an ideological campaign, also. The three evils of the past were identified as the Tibetan government, aristocratic estate holders and monasteries, while the Chinese were saviours.

The process of thought reform had commenced and the goal was that all Tibetans should think of Tibet as 'an inseparable part of the motherland'. For Tibetans in rural areas, this was their first real contact with the Chinese officials. Religion was targeted ruthlessly. Indeed, many of the Tibetans who left Tibet for exile in India – some 120,000 of them – did so as a direct result of this campaign.

While the reforms were supposed to have a thoroughly levelling effect that would end the delineation between rich and poor, the Chinese were careful to promise aristocrats that their own estates would remain intact and their systems unchanged if they adopted and supported communist ideals. For the monasteries, however, land reform would prove devastating; they relied on income from their estates in order to feed the thousands of monks within.

Although the Panchen Lama continued to act as something of a spokesperson for the Chinese in public, he was growing less supportive of Chinese initiatives. He began to criticise Chinese policy in Tibet and initially his comments were heard respectfully, in some instances even agreed with. Mao went as far as issuing a new six-point directive on the party's work in Tibet that took into account some of the Panchen Lama's criticism.

The somewhat relaxed, new policy was not enough to make a genuine improvement for Tibetans. During the Panchen Lama's travels in 1961, he witnessed his people's suffering, ranging from starvation to a widespread deterioration in their living standards and in the economy in general. These woes came as a direct result of communisation programs and PLA strictures.[63] While the situation was far worse in eastern Tibet, the Panchen Lama was certain that this fate would befall central Tibet, too, if reforms continued. He, along with most other Tibetans, was adamant that the monasteries and monks should retain the position they had enjoyed pre-1959.

In early 1962, the Communist Party held a meeting to discuss its 'nationalities policy' in which all in attendance, including non-party members, were encouraged to air their grievances without fear of reprisal. During the conference, the Panchen Lama started to write what became known as the 'Seventy Thousand Character Petition' to the Party's Central Committee about life in Tibet under the communists. Although the petition has never been published in full, some of its contents have been. It amounted to a fierce criticism of China's policy in Tibet and Tibetan regions, asserting that the rapid reforms endangered Tibetans as a people, that the Tibetan population had been reduced and Buddhism virtually destroyed. In some areas, the Panchen Lama alleged that all the young men had been arrested and there were only old people and women in the villages. As well as calling for the release of innocent people who'd been arrested during the anti-rebellion campaign, the petition called for the punishment of party cadres who had acted inappropriately.

Chinese cadres working in Tibet claimed the petition grossly exaggerated mistakes they had made there, but other party leaders seemed prepared to accept some of the Panchen Lama's assertions. The party cadres from Tibet were asked to come up with draft proposals to address the criticisms. The degree to which Beijing accepted the Panchen Lama's scathing criticism is indicative of his strategic importance to the Chinese. He was only twenty-four years old at the time.

6 OCTOBER 2003

LINEAGE: THE TWELFTH KARMAPA

THE BOY LAMA: THE LION BEGINS TO ROAR

TIBET: THE CARVE-UP

6 OCTOBER 2003

On my last day in McLeod Ganj, I am granted an interview with the Tibetan people's first democratically elected leader, Kalon Tripa Samdhong Rinpoche. Later, I will take the overnight train south to Delhi, and tomorrow I'll fly to Siliguri in West Bengal before driving on to Gangtok, near Rumtek Monastery in Sikkim.

Back in 2001, the Dalai Lama pushed through an initiative that many Tibetans found revolutionary. At his behest, Tibetans would directly elect the *Kalon Tripa* – Chairman of the Cabinet of the exile government. Tibetans outside Tibet went to polling booths across the world in July 2001 and overwhelmingly elected the sixty-two-year-old Professor Samdhong Rinpoche. From that moment forward, the Dalai Lama's role has been as the Tibetan's spiritual leader alone.

The monk who comes to sit with me in the airy meeting room at the offices of the exile government has the appearance of someone with the weight of the world on his shoulders. When I first laid eyes on Samdhong Rinpoche five years earlier in Sydney when he spoke at an Australia Tibet Council function, he genuinely seemed like the simple monk the Dalai Lama calls himself.

Samdhong Rinpoche happened to be in Delhi at the time of the Karmapa's arrival in India in 2000, and he explained the role he played then in his capacity as Speaker of the Assembly of the Tibetan People's Deputy.

'I was able to manage the first day possible crisis and able to establish contact with the Indian government and also speak to Dharamsala quite constantly.'

He confirms to me that members of India's government were suspicious about the escape but asserts that they were more dubious about those accompanying the Karmapa, and their possible connection with the Chinese government, than about the Karmapa himself. For those in Tibet, Samdhong Rinpoche tells me, the Karmapa's escape was more a source of inspiration than a blow, despite the fact that he was arguably their most senior religious figure.

On the subject of the PRC recognising *tulkus*, Samdhong Rinpoche gives a small, unamused laugh. 'That is a combination of political hypocrisy and the blackmailing of the Tibetan faith.'

In the past, the Chinese emperor had, himself, upon occasion, participated nominally in the selection of the Dalai Lama by drawing a name from the now fabled Golden Urn. Samdhong Rinpoche tells me that it's all very well for the Chinese to claim their tradition of using the Golden Urn gives them the right to recognise incarnate Tibetan lamas, but if they wish to honour this tradition then they should honour some others, as well. 'There are many other long-term Buddhist customs in which previous Chinese governments were involved: to offer various things to the monasteries; to protect the monasteries; to look after the welfare of the monasteries and the nunneries . . . and those traditions they have not respected.' Samdhong Rinpoche adds that out of fourteen Dalai Lamas, only four were recognised by the process of the Golden Urn, and only one Panchen Lama was recognised this way.

Further, he confirms that the threat against the Karmapa's life is indeed very high, and cites the Chinese and those supporting the other candidate for recognition as the XVIIth Karmapa, Thaye Dorje. Samdhong Rinpoche is confident, however, that the Karmapa will be permitted to travel to Sikkim, the exile seat of the Karma Kagyu, one day, once the legal proceedings surrounding him have ended.

As I leave the new leader's presence, I hear his opinion of the XVIIth Karmapa echoing in my ears. 'He is dynamic and intelligent . . . he might be able to play a very important role for the Tibetan people.' That's if he survives, I find myself adding silently.

The Department of Information and International Relations (DIIR) staff and I are driven up the hill into McLeod in a massive four-wheel-drive vehicle – oh that I could ride in such relative safety more often while in India! Now that my trip is already more than half over, I'm feeling pangs of anxiety lest I should not make it home safely. Despite the reassuring solidity of the vehicle, I comment that you need courage to drive on the

Dharamsala roads; the road on which we drive is horribly pot-holed and one side of it is crumbling down a steep ravine. One of the Tibetans grins and tells me that when Pierce Brosnan was in town recently he was almost sitting in his driver's lap in fear while travelling on these roads. This spectacular failure of nerve on the part of the current James Bond delights us all. I've heard that two other Hollywood Tibetophiles, Richard Gere and Goldie Hawn, have raised hundreds of thousands of dollars to rebuild the roads of Dharamsala; and not a moment too soon, I say.

The DIIR officials have invited me to lunch, in my capacity as both a writer researching a book on Tibetan affairs and as a director of a Tibet support group. I'm taken to the Hotel Tibet, a government-run enterprise that's clearly seen better days and is destined for privatisation, for lunch at the DIIR's invitation. Thubten Samphel, Sonam Norbu Dagpo and Tenzin Lekshey are all on their very best behaviour with me. They're encouraging and helpful about my book but no one's giving away any secrets, worse luck. I give them a rundown of the myriad rumours that are circulating regarding the escape and the reasons behind the Karmapa's present situation of virtual imprisonment. When I mention that one of the rumours suggests that the Karmapa's escape was backed by the CIA, Thubten laughs and feigns surprise. 'Just like the Dalai Lama's!'

As the lunch progresses and I realise that I am not going to be made party to any state secrets, I start to feel a little foolish for having ever imagined such a thing. What were these diplomats going to tell me? That the Dalai Lama had the Karmapa smuggled out of Tibet? That even the exile administration believe the Karmapa is a spy? Unlikely! Eventually, I remove my writer's hat and we speak of Sino-Tibetan politics and Chinese President Hu Jintao's forthcoming visit to Australia.

Early afternoon I begin my journey away from the comfort zone. As I am driven from the Himalayan foothills and onto the plains of the Punjab, I remember once again that I am in India. It is, indeed, possible to forget this up there among the Tibetans.

I try to store as many mental images now to compensate for

the photos I never took: contented, stray dogs lying in the dirt beside the road, oblivious to the traffic; children herding goats in the ditch as cars fly by; families of four on tiny mopeds; road-side Hindu shrines adorned with flashing, coloured discoesque lights; sweet-faced donkeys cruelly loaded with sacks of gravel and cement; deep river gorges with villagers' washing drying on the banks; and finally, children everywhere, curious and shyly smiling.

I board the Jammu Mail with a middle-class family from Calcutta who have adopted me, albeit briefly, for this part of my journey. In the relative comfort of my second-class, air-conditioned sleeper carriage, I am immediately drawn into the drama unfolding across the aisle from me: a middle-aged son leads his ailing, elderly father onto the train, the old man clearly approaching the end of his life and gasping loudly, painfully, for every breath. Can the fellow possibly survive the journey, I wonder, as I listen to his every groan, cough and wheeze. He is paralysed, explains the son. Perhaps, I think, but I'm certain that the old man is also tubercular. We all look away as he spits blood into small blue plastic bags. Sitting only two feet from the man is a skinny, pregnant girl.

LINEAGE:
THE TWELFTH KARMAPA

Changchub Dorje (1703–1732), who would be recognised as the XIIth Karmapa, was born, as predicted, beside the Golden River (the Yangtse) in Derge, eastern Tibet. At the age of only two months, the child announced that he was the Karmapa. Shamar Rinpoche dispatched a search party, which recognised the boy officially.

After his enthronement and the transmission of the lineage, Changchub Dorje travelled with a trio of prominent Kagyu *rin-poches* – Shamar, Tai Situ and Gyalstab – to Nepal and India on pilgrimage. In Nepal, the Karmapa is said to have conjured the rain that brought an end to a devastating drought, as well as ending an epidemic. Changchub Dorje accepted an invitation to travel to China and embarked on the journey with Shamar Rinpoche. En route, the Karmapa conducted ceremonies for world peace. During his travels in China, he contracted small-pox, to which he ultimately succumbed, aged only thirty. Before his death, he had already written and dispatched his Last Testament to Shamar Rinpoche, following the tradition adhered to by almost all his predecessors.

THE BOY LAMA:
THE LION BEGINS TO ROAR

In the weeks after the young Karmapa's arrival in Dharamsala, speculation was rife about whether he would ask for and be granted political asylum in India. Indian newspapers ran opinion polls on the question of what the Indian government should do with Tibet's newest, high-profile refugee and although popular consensus seemed to indicate that the Karmapa should be per-mitted to remain in India, the question was: on what terms? Although the Dalai Lama himself is said to have applied to the Indian government for asylum for Ogyen Trinley Dorje, one Indian official – reportedly 'close to the Dalai Lama' – was quoted in London's *Daily Telegraph* of 2 January 2000 as saying, 'I think you will find that within a week to 10 days that the application for political asylum will be withdrawn and an announcement made that the Karmapa is welcome to remain in India.'[64]

The issue of terminology here is crucial in India's relationship with China. India was the first nation to state publicly that it regarded Tibet as part of China; this attitude was cemented in the *Panch Sheela* agreement in 1954 that stated each country would refrain from tampering with the other's 'domestic affairs'. In the eyes of Chinese officials, India granting the young Karmapa political asylum would be akin to a reversal of its policy on Tibet as it would imply that there was genuinely something to flee from. While a Chinese Foreign Ministry spokesman did warn India to consider its relationship with China while handling the Karmapa, he did not mention the ramifications should India grant the boy political asylum.[65]

The Indian media promptly erupted over the suggestions, first made by Shamar Rinpoche, that the Chinese themselves might have orchestrated the Karmapa's flight into exile. Indian government ministries also questioned the Karmapa's story. Some journalists seemed to agree that this theory was plausible, because of the unlikelihood of the Karmapa's escape succeeding. Given the difficulty ordinary Tibetans have in exiting Tibet illegally, the chances of such a well-known Tibetan as the Karmapa succeeding were admittedly slim. Other analysts discounted the likelihood that the Chinese were behind the escape, claiming it highly unlikely that China – ever seen to be ensuring that she 'keeps face' internationally – would have willingly brought such ridicule on herself as that which was meted out by the international media following the Karmapa's arrival in India.

Shamar Rinpoche was widely quoted in the Indian press questioning Ogyen Trinley Dorje's motives after the young Tibetan's arrival in India.[66] There were also rumours circulating that the Dalai Lama had been involved in this curious play and that Ogyen Trinley Dorje had gone to India at China's request.

Once again, Shamar started touting his one-Karmapa-for-the-free-world-and-one-for-Chinese-occupied-Tibet proposal, suggesting that Thaye Dorje, whom he had started calling the Indian Karmapa, should have Rumtek Monastery and that the 'Chinese Karmapa', Ogyen Trinley Dorje, should have Tsurphu. In an interview with *The Indian Express* on 18 January, he threatened that it would be 'very embarrassing' if his own Karmapa was stopped from going to Rumtek, because all his papers were in order, unlike those of the 'Chinese Karmapa'. Shamar Rinpoche went on to state that Ogyen Trinley Dorje and those who travelled with him were, quite bluntly, Chinese citizens without visas for India. Should any spiritual leader be permitted to travel to India without a visa? He alleged that the

Karmapa had not been subjected to religious persecution and that he was a VIP in China so was in a comfortable position there.[67] This, he insisted, meant there could be no claim of human rights violation. This, it seems, is an extremely tough line of argument for a Tibetan who himself once travelled to India as a refugee.

Meanwhile, the supporters of Ogyen Trinley Dorje refrained from entering the media fray. What was not widely reported was that Tai Situ Rinpoche had been banned from commenting on the Karmapa's escape by an Indian government official. This left Kalon Tashi Wangdi to speak officially about the Karmapa's motives and needs. Wangdi's cool, diplomatic statements would never receive the sort of blanket coverage that Shamar Rinpoche's rhetoric would. With the story of the controversy all through the Indian media, the Indian government seemed to have had very good reason to delay making a decision on the Karmapa's status in its country.

In the first official comment from the exile government on the reasons behind the Karmapa's flight from Tibet, Kalon Tashi Wangdi cited 'the harsh conditions on religion, arrests of monks and nuns, serious violations of human rights and the indifferent attitude of Chinese vis-à-vis the Karmapa Rimpoche [sic] for the last few years . . . it is with that background he had to flee'.[68] As yet, the Karmapa himself had neither spoken publicly nor been quoted by journalists.

The first public speech the Karmapa made in exile was at the Tibetan Institute of Performing Arts in Dharamsala (TIPA). The Karmapa had been in India for a little over six weeks before attending the TIPA event that commemorated the sixtieth anniversary of the enthronement of the Dalai Lama. The institute's director, Jamyang Dorjee, invited the Karmapa to say a few words, explaining to him that those gathered did not even know in which Tibetan dialect the Karmapa spoke. Despite the fact that the Karmapa was clearly under pressure from both Indian and Tibetan officials to keep his silence, he eventually conceded.

The young Karmapa opened his speech in a fairly predictable

manner, noting the reason that they had all come together that day. He went on to offer his greetings to the Dalai Lama and named all the other groups gathered there. Then his speech turned political.

'Generally speaking, there are conflicts in many different regions of the world. Likewise, in some regions and places, due to the lack of freedom to enjoy the right to individual freedoms; and the lack of knowledge and understanding, conflicts occur in such regions and countries. To take the case of our own country Tibet – the Land of Snows – it used to be a land where the sacred faith [Buddhist] and all aspects of [Tibetan] intellectual and literary culture flourished. However, over [the last] twenty to thirty years, Tibet suffered a great loss whereby Tibetan religious traditions and culture is now facing the risk of total extinction.'[69]

These comments fly in the face of Chinese propaganda of the time. The very act of the communist government's recognition of the XVIIth Karmapa should, the Chinese asserted, prove to the world the PRC religious tolerance. These were courageous comments from a boy who had left behind his entire family in the hands of those who had wrought the 'extinction'. Kalon Tashi Wangdi, in relation to the reasons for the Karmapa's escape, had himself said that within Tibet things were as difficult now as they had been during the Cultural Revolution.

The Karmapa went on to say that he prays for the day that all Tibetans will be able to enjoy peace and happiness under the 'boundless kindness' of His Holiness the Dalai Lama. 'Generally speaking, I am an ordinary refugee from Tibet. However, due to the kindness of the government and people of India, His Holiness the Dalai Lama and the Tibet government [in exile], and the blessings of all the non-sectarian leaders and beholders of the various Buddhist traditions, I happen to have become a sort of prominent refugee here in India – the land of Arhats; likewise, Tibetans scattered in different parts of the world and a considerable number of journalists, too, have shown an interest in my case. Therefore, to you all, I express my sincere gratitude and "Thanks".'

Locals present at TIPA on this day tell of the exiled Tibetans' excitement over the Karmapa's arrival in India, and of their immense pride in him. On that day, apparently, some of the gathered Tibetans were calling the Karmapa 'our second Dalai Lama'. Most Tibetans, in the clear light of day, do not wish for anyone but a future incarnation of the XIVth Dalai Lama to replace their leader. This is not to say, though, that for many Tibetans, the XVIIth Karmapa's sheer charisma, along with the courage he displayed in defying the Chinese, might see him elevated to the status of their overall spiritual leader in years to come.

Perhaps the Karmapa saw this speech as a warm-up, anticipating many more opportunities to speak publicly about his people, his Tibet. From his rooftop terrace at Gyuto Tantric University, with rolling green hills of Himachal Pradesh before him and the Dahuldhar Mountains rising steeply behind him, the young Karmapa had good reason to believe that for him, freedom lay within easy reach.

TIBET: THE CARVE-UP

On Tibet's borders, the Sino-Indian War was set to ignite in early 1962 and the CIA was training guerillas and providing arms for a Tibetan resistance base in the Nepalese territory of Mustang. When, in November 1962, the Indians were decisively defeated by the PLA in border fighting, India was quick to seek support from the US. For the first time, the Americans informed India of their covert support for the Tibetan resistance movement. This moment proved a turning point in India's attitude to the Tibetan exiles. Within months of the defeat, there was genuine support and encouragement for the Dalai Lama at the highest level. The Indian government did not impede the establishment of a Tibetan government-in-exile, but nor did they encourage it.

In Tibet, things were about to take a dramatic turn for the worse for the Panchen Lama, who would be quickly singled out as one of the 'reactionaries' Mao had announced were obstructing the revolution. The proposals that had been drafted and approved as a result of his 'Seventy Thousand Character Petition' were to be rescinded. At a PCART meeting on 18 September 1964, the Panchen Lama was described as the 'most dangerous enemy' in all of Tibet. Among other heinous accusations, the Panchen Lama was accused of training a revolutionary cavalry.

The Chinese sought to discredit the Panchen Lama publicly in order to turn the Tibetans against him and mounted a damning exhibition about him and his clique. The display included a photograph of a jeep – supposedly a military vehicle – and a technical school he had set up, which was dubbed a counter-revolutionary headquarters. The communists even went as far as proclaiming that his dogs were for fighting. Genuine ill will was generated towards him by convincing the Tibetans that those in his inner circle led extravagant lives while the ordinary Tibetans had so little. His trial quickly turned into a struggle session at which he was subjected to physical assault by the Tibetans in attendance, including one of the incarnate lamas.

The Panchen Lama remained defiant. Although there was no proof to support the allegations that he was planning an armed rebellion, the Panchen Lama was given three hats to wear (resembling dunce hats), proclaiming his treachery: they were labelled anti-party, anti-people and splitting the motherland. In December 1964, the Panchen Lama was formally stripped of his titles as acting Chairman and permanent Vice-Chairman of PCART because of his 'counter-revolutionary activities'.

With the demise of the Panchen Lama, there was no longer a credible Tibetan leader in Tibet. Most notably, the monasteries suffered as there was no authoritative figure to protect them. What's more, Tibetans no longer sent the monasteries their sons. Not only had the communists promised Tibetans education – which had been one of the monastery's roles – but religious pursuits were eschewed by the new regime.[70]

In 1965, the Chinese established what was to be known as the Tibet Autonomous Region (TAR), which represented only a small part of the ethnically Tibetan area. Historian Warren Smith asserted in his book *Tibetan Nation* that the exclusion of Kham and Amdo from the TAR meant that more than half of the richest of Tibet's territory, in terms of physical resources, and two-thirds of its population, would not fall under the provisions of the 17-Point Agreement.[71] These areas became the Chinese provinces of Qinghai, and parts of Sichuan, Gansu and Yunnan. Rather than giving the Tibetans anything like genuine autonomy, the event marked an even more absolute integration.

The next radical change for Tibetans came with the implementation of the commune system. Not only did the ownership of land and animals become collective, but households were also forced to hand over all privately owned goods. The previous land reform, which had involved redistribution of land, had become quite popular with the Tibetan peasants, but now they were forced to relinquish the land that they'd only acquired so very recently. In economic terms, the commune system was a failure because of poor management and lack of motivation to work, meaning that the system had to be subsidised by Beijing. Even more disastrous was the process of transforming nomads into commune-dwellers. Their crops continually failed because of the climate and terrain. Shortages of butter, cooking oil and cooking fuel followed, and grain was no longer kept in sufficient reserves.

Tragically, the changes imposed by the Chinese that, in their eyes, offered so much often resulted in impoverishment, sometimes in starvation.

7 October 2003
Lineage: the thirteenth Karmapa
The boy lama: caged lion
Tibet: the Cultural Revolution

7 OCTOBER 2003

I toss and turn all night on my hard, narrow Indian Railways bed. I'm en route to Delhi before I fly east, towards Sikkim. My elderly travelling companion seems to sleep much better than I. Pre-dawn I wake on the outskirts of Delhi and watch the railway sidings turn from black to grey. I remember reading that over 1000 bodies are found annually on the railway tracks around Delhi and that most of these deaths go unreported to any authority. Along the tracks are small shantytowns, washing strung out to dry between the humpies. Children are born right here, by the tracks, and I've little doubt that many die here, having lived out their entire lives between the metal rails.

An Indian woman and fellow traveller takes me under her wing this time. I had asked her before we pulled into Old Delhi Station about getting from there to the airport and, with a distinctly motherly air, she tells me not to worry, I'm simply to follow her. And follow her I do as she pushes her way through the human river exiting the train and endeavouring to leave the station. Not only does she take me to the auto-rickshaw office and buy my ticket, but she pushes the two of us into the same rickshaw. The airport is on her way, she informs me briskly.

I learn that I am in the company of a scientist, who has a daughter in Michigan. Although I am selective in whom I confide in India, I tell the scientist exactly what brings me to her country and the nature of my research. She, in turn, tells me the nature of hers. The woman is extremely polite with me but on her face I can see that she is baffled that I should come all the way to India to write about a Tibetan when there are so many interesting, notable Indians around.

At Delhi Airport I strike up a conversation with an Austrian woman. She, like most Westerners in whom I have confided during my travels, is instantly captivated by my story. The woman lives her life between California and southern India, apparently inhabiting something of a religious supermarket – a bit of this, a bit of that. On the subject of Tibetan Buddhism and its idiosyncrasies, the woman part boasts, part confesses that she has visited Steven Seagal's home in Los Angeles. The scowl I try to control betrays my innate cynicism which is immediately triggered by this Western story of reincarnation. Seagal, a Hollywood actor and martial artist, was recognised a few years ago as an important incarnation by one of the hierarchy of the Nyinmga school. While I accept that the Tibet support movement attracts Hollywood actors who feel they are in a position to help, I find it hard to get my head around the notion of one of them being recognised as an incarnate lama. The woman, as if to assure me that Seagal is genuine, goes on to explain that being inside his house felt like being in the centre of a diamond.

Back to the Karmapa – to whom the woman confesses she is hopelessly drawn; did I know that he is deemed by the Indian government to be at the highest risk of assassination? 'The Chinese,' she whispers ominously. While I was all too aware that the Karmapa was being held very tightly, the detail about being an assassination risk causes me to shiver in the chill of the heavily air-conditioned airport. I recall my sense that the guards at Gyuto were more interested in what the Karmapa said than in his personal safety.

The woman goes on to tell me that I have an extraordinary clarity about me and that this will have made the Karmapa and his aides take me seriously and will illuminate the book. I can only ascribe this clarity – if it does indeed exist – to ten toddler-free days.

Rural India appears brown and flat as I watch it from the plane but I realise that the detail is totally obscured by a haze of pollution. I look out, constantly, for the Himalayas as if they were a close friend, despite the fact that I'm on the wrong side of the plane.

Bagdora Airport is the perfect introduction to West Bengal: it is stinking hot and displays a mighty military presence. I wonder what percentage of India's jet fighters are here, ready to strike at China should the day ever come. The nearby Siliguri is a mess of traffic and Bengali tourists; I have arrived in 'the season'. There's not a jeep to be had in which to travel to the hills, and taxis are scarce, too. A dozy official tries to commandeer me and promises to arrange transport for me within two hours, but that's two hours more than I can bear to spend here. I happen upon a young, urban Indian man, looking cool and unflustered in his black pressed cotton shirt and blue jeans. We agree to share a taxi to Gangtok and I am immensely relieved. Sundeep, on noting my reaction, asserts that he's helped me so much that one day he will come to Australia where I can look after him! Sundeep is in software, *yaar*, and is quite the dude in his silver-rimmed sunglasses. Within half an hour, Sundeep thinks he's taken over my itinerary for the coming days, dismissing all the plans I've made for my short time in Sikkim. He is all contra-dictions, claiming that he does not want to get married because it's too expensive, then going on to proclaim that he loves people who speak from the heart but hates people who speak from the mind. He is, I note, attractive in a long-legged, chubby-cheeked way and seems rather pleased when the driver asks him whether I am his wife.

The drive from Bagdora to Gangtok spins out from a man-ageable three hours to an agonising five. The van in which we are passengers screams around hairpin bends above deep ravines, overtakes gay, ornately painted trucks with only cen-timetres to spare and lunges perilously close to the road's edge. Below us, the turquoise waters of the River Teetsa churn; they are, at times, as many as a few hundred metres below us. A cheerful highway poet and aphorist has been hard at work composing ditties to keep the drivers on their toes. I chuckle as I read, clutching the ceiling handle in a white-knuckle grip: 'No time for whisky when the road is twisty' and 'Keep your nerves on the curves'.

At Rangpo, some four hours into the drive on the Sikkimese border, I am summarily issued a permit that makes my months of anguish over whether I'd be granted entry into Sikkim seem a little silly. (Having been told that it was difficult for foreigners to enter Sikkim, I had originally inquired about obtaining a permit at the Indian embassy in Canberra. When I was asked my reasons for travel, I naively mentioned researching a book on a Tibetan lama. The barrage of questions my reply triggered had made me certain that, no matter how I answered them, I would never be granted entry. The India experts I consulted on the subject of visas were astounded that I'd been foolish enough to even mention anything to do with Tibet while applying for permits or visas. Under the circumstances, I was rather surprised when I was issued a tourist visa for India, some months later.)

India proclaims this former kingdom to be the Switzerland of the East. What Sikkim lacks in cleanliness it (apparently) compensates for in mountains. With the descending dark comes mist that seems to hang like a shroud from the dense cloud above us. As we finally approach Gangtok, I feel myself to be truly in the mountains. Across deep valleys I see the lights of villages, perched on steep slopes. I clutch my naked arms, pleased to feel cold after ten days in the gentle heat of Dharamsala and the fierce heat of Delhi.

From my window at Gangtok's Hotel Tashi Delek, I would be able to see the world's third-highest mountain – Kanchenjunga – were it not indelibly lost in the mist and cloud.

LINEAGE:
THE THIRTEENTH KARMAPA

Dudul Dorje (1733–1797), the XIIIth Karmapa, is said to have been born with sacred marks on his body. As a very small child, he described details of the journeys to Nepal, India and China that he had made in his previous lifetime.

Recognised when he was four years old, Dudul Dorje became famous for his ability to communicate with animals and was said to be able to transmit *dharma* to the creatures that sat near him while he meditated. When Tibet's most sacred temple, the Jokhang in Lhasa, was threatened by flooding, the Karmapa was called upon for assistance. Guru Rinpoche had previously prophesised that only the Karmapa could save the temple and the sacred Jowo statue within from the flooding caused by a powerful serpent. Dudul Dorje called up the serpent's spirit, beseeching it to leave the precious statue unharmed. The waters immediately ceased to flow. When the Karmapa presented the revered Jowo with a prayer scarf, the statue's arms were said to have permanently changed position to receive it.

Dudul Dorje's death was greeted by a shower of flowers, and by clearly audible celestial music.

THE BOY LAMA: CAGED LION

By Tibetans, the Karmapa is considered a *bodhisattva* and, as such, his role is to liberate all sentient beings. From within the confines of Gyuto Tantric University, where the Karmapa's own liberty is confined to a few rooms and his rooftop terrace, this might seem a daunting task.

The notion of freedom, in the months after the Karmapa's arrival in India, must have been playing on the young man's mind. At Gyuto Tantric University, he had become the proverbial bird in the gilded cage. Early visitors to the Karmapa explain that security surrounding the newly arrived Tibetan was so tight that there was always an Indian Intelligence Bureau agent at his side, even sitting beside him on the sofa while his teacher sat at his feet, and that his room was always crowded with guards. Those few visitors who gained admittance to his audience room were carefully searched. Initially, the Indians had erected a rope in his audience room to separate the Karmapa and his devotees so that even the tradition of the lama touching his devotees' heads was denied him. Eventually, the rope was removed after a critical editorial in a local newspaper, but almost all the other security measures remained.

On the one hand, the young Karmapa was being protected from those – real or imagined – who might wish to do him harm. Followers of the challenger, Thaye Dorje, were seen as would-be assassins, as were the Chinese agents operating in India. The security, however, also served to gag the young refugee of whom so very much was expected. Not long after the

Karmapa's arrival in India, China's ambassador to that country made a direct request of the Indian government that the Karmapa not be permitted to engage in political activities while on Indian soil. While the Indian government had put the same restriction on the Dalai Lama, the constant surveillance under which the Karmapa lives suggests that the Indians really mean it.

Yes, the Karmapa now had access to his root gurus, Tai Situ Rinpoche and Gyalstab Rinpoche, but he was forbidden to travel to Tai Situ's monastery, only two hours from Gyuto, let alone even consider visiting Rumtek in Sikkim. The Indian government was clearly taking no chances. Yet despite the grave limitations under which the Karmapa was forced to live during that first year in India, his story had reverberated far and wide.

For instance, a group of young Tibetans in Delhi were quoted in *The Washington Post* of 29 May 2000 as claiming that their parents' struggle against the Chinese in Tibet felt distinctly removed from their reality and that the oft-repeated tales of Tibetans' flight to freedom across the Himalayas just seemed like stories from another age. The Karmapa's escape changed that for them. 'Karmapa's escape happened right in front of my eyes,' said young Tibetan Tenzin Dhondup. 'I thought, "Wow, this is cool stuff!"' Another in the group, Tenzin Pulchung, reported his profound dissatisfaction with the passivity of the Tibetans' freedom struggle, and himself envisaged the training of Tibetans to destroy Chinese military bases. As for the Karmapa, he regarded him as 'the wrathful manifestation of the Buddha', who may well inspire Tibetans to direct action.

At a press conference a little over a month after the Karmapa's arrival, Shamar Rinpoche argued that permitting the Karmapa to travel to Sikkim would turn the state into another Kashmir. One Indian journalist reported from the press conference that Shamar Rinpoche alleged that the Karmapa had come with an 'assurance' for the people of Sikkim that China would support their fight for independence if he was allowed to head Rumtek.[72]

Despite the Karmapa having effectively been gagged, in July

he made his second appearance on *Time* magazine's (Asia edition) front cover. In the photograph, the Dalai Lama is in the foreground and the Karmapa in the background. By mid-September, the Indian government was yet to make a decision on the Karmapa's status in India. The young man's fate was the subject of a meeting between the Indian Home Minister and the Dalai Lama on 16 September.

On a lighter note, during the same month, *The Hindustan Times* reported that the Karmapa had been permitted a meeting with one of his high-profile Western devotees, Pierce Brosnan. One Karmapa-watcher glibly suggested that perhaps this would bring MI5 to the young lama's aid.[73]

Back in Tibet, at Tsurphu Monastery, already those who had been prepared to sacrifice all for the Karmapa had paid a price. Two Tibetan security personnel from the monastery, one of whom was a monk, had been detained by the authorities, with no details on their safety or whereabouts available. Officials at the monastery had undergone rigorous questioning, while monks were counselled to improve their 'political attitudes' under threat of additional patriotic education sessions should they fail to do so. Lama Nyima, the Karmapa's tutor, had been detained by the Chinese authorities, although not until June 2002, for his involvement in the Karmapa's escape. He was released just over a year later.[74] The monastery, by mid-January, had been closed to the public.

The Karmapa's parents, Karma Döndrub and Loga, had been removed from their Lhasa house by authorities and returned to the Chamdo region. They were, reportedly, either being detained or, at the very least, kept under close surveillance. These same 'authorities', only a matter of weeks earlier, had claimed that the Karmapa was only going abroad to collect precious Kagyu items, such as the now infamous Black Hat, and would certainly be returning to Tibet. Interestingly, to this very day the Chinese government has not publicly criticised the Karmapa, claiming instead that he was just a boy who had been influenced by those in the anti-Chinese faction. They have been keeping the door open for his return.

As I ponder the apparent thwarting of my would-be hero, I recall the vague threat that was issued to the Dalai Lama by a Chinese bureaucrat during the Tibetan leader's visit to India in 1957. 'The snow lion looks dignified if he stays in his mountain abode, but if he comes down to the valleys he is treated like a dog.'[75]

TIBET: THE CULTURAL REVOLUTION

In early 1966, the banning of *Mönlam* (the Great Prayer Ceremony) in Lhasa marked the beginning of the Cultural Revolution in Tibet, although its official launch was not until August. The communists regarded it as the 'final battle before the coming of the new society'.[76] A few months later came the banning of the 'Four Olds' (old ideas, old culture, old customs and old habits) as well as pressure on the people to study the recently published Tibetan edition of *Quotations from Chairman Mao Tsetung*.

By late August, Tibetan students who formed the first group of Red Guards from the TAR, undertook the study of Mao's 16-Point Directives, something of a blueprint for the Revolution, which in particular advocated targeting those within the Communist Party who had taken the capitalist road. The Red Guards in Tibet published their own directions for the eradication of feudal culture. Religion was heavily targeted and the guidelines went as far as the banning of such 'feudal practices' as giving parties and exchanging gifts, and of keeping cats and dogs in the house,[77] while in every village, religious and cultural artifacts were destroyed. Religious figures were targeted mercilessly and subjected to the enforced public wearing of dunce's hats. In Tibet's monasteries, religious icons were smashed and those made of precious metals were sent off to China. Reports of indiscriminate violence against peasants detail beatings, imprisonment and an array of gruesome methods of torture.

The only former Tibetan leader spared the horrors of the Cultural Revolution was Ngabo Ngawang Jigme, who remained in Beijing and escaped its attacks on Tibetan aristocrats; he had been made Governor of Tibet when the TAR was established. The Panchen Lama was subjected to further struggle sessions and abuse.

Within Tibet, the Cultural Revolution was to transform Tibetan life in its entirety and would not go unanswered. In 1969, Tibetans began to revolt against the chaos and vindictiveness of the Cultural Revolution and its agents. In some areas, the PLA had to be called in to suppress the uprisings that the Chinese labelled separatist and reactionary.

Within three years, all of Tibet's monasteries had been vandalised, as had the Tibetan language, which had been stripped of words deemed classist. The Chinese started to believe that cultural difference between the Tibetans and the rest of China was no longer an issue. In addition, Tibet during the early seventies was becoming increasingly militarised. This factor was not unrelated to the modernisation of India's military and its road-building in the Himalayan foothills.

The commune system gradually became more effective, as far as the Chinese were concerned, with production slowly rising. Tibetans were forced to produce wheat instead of barley, and not only was it of exceedingly poor quality but the government took any excess. The Tibetans' standard of living had not improved, contrary to Chinese propaganda. Although some industrialisation had occurred in Tibet, including one small hydroelectric plant, the Chinese claims that they had industrialised the roof of the world were grossly exaggerated.

According to historian Melvyn C. Goldstein, forces set in motion by the Cultural Revolution 'in a decade of pain and suffering' virtually destroyed the nomads' way of life.[78] One nomad of western Tibet claimed that during the Cultural Revolution they were no more than 'servants of the commune'.[79] Goldstein goes on to claim that while some nomad households prospered under the system – those with many workers – for most, the quality of life deteriorated considerably as a result of high taxes, forced quota sales and because nomads' level of care for the commune's livestock was lower than for their own livestock.

Socially and culturally, the duration of the Cultural Revolution was a devastating time for nomads, as it was for other Tibetans. Nomads were forced to cut their hair, and women to slaughter animals. It has been argued that the Chinese wished to reduce the Tibetan identity to language alone.[80]

Of significance to Tibet, and to the Dalai Lama's status in India, was the 'normalisation' of the relationship between the US and China in 1972. China and the US had commenced diplomatic relations, first with Henry Kissinger's secret visit to China in July 1971 and then with President Richard Nixon's visit to China a year later. Meanwhile, the relationship between Presidents Indira Gandhi and Richard Nixon was exceedingly poor. Now isolated in her region, India sought to establish ties with the Soviet Union.

CIA aid to the Tibetan guerilla force based in Mustang had been gradually diminishing during the sixties and many Tibetan guerillas were co-opted into joining the Indian Army. In 1973, the Nepalese government – now trying to strengthen its relationship with China – demanded that the remaining Tibetan guerilla forces in Mustang surrender their arms. It was not until the Dalai Lama sent a recorded message to them that the last of the group was disbanded, most surrendering to the Nepalese Army. Some of the guerillas tried to flee to India; most were killed en route in skirmishes with the Nepalese forces.

In 1973, anti-Dalai Lama and Panchen Lama campaigns were launched within Tibet in which the Chinese described the Dalai Lama as a jackal whose 'hands are stained with the blood of the million serfs in Tibet'.[81] Conditions inside Tibet were more stable with education – predominantly in Chinese and with political aims – gaining more attention. Education was deemed necessary for 'ideological transformation'. Furthermore, the communists believed it would foster 'successors to the proletarian revolutionaries'.[82]

8 October 2003
Lineage: the fourteenth Karmapa
The boy lama: dance of diplomacy
Tibet: Hu Yaobang and liberalisation

8 OCTOBER 2003

Gangtok is a sprawling, charmless town of some 90,000 people, with a somewhat staggering 500 hotels. At an elevation of 2200 metres, it gives the impression of being of the clouds themselves. I am told that in 1975 there were no buildings of more than a single storey; now Gangtok buildings rise – or drop down the slope from road level – four to eight storeys. All looks hastily and cheaply built and I find myself feeling distinctly uneasy on this Sikkimese slope.

It is Rumtek Monastery, only twenty-four kilometres from Gangtok, which has brought me to this former kingdom bordered by Nepal and Bhutan. At the monastery I hope to speak to one of the XVIth Karmapa's four regents, Gyalstab Rinpoche. The meeting has been arranged for me by Lama Phuntsok but, like all our arrangements, this one is vague. I am simply to arrive at Rumtek some time this morning and find the high lama. As much as I hope to learn something, anything, new about the Karmapa from Gyalstab Rinpoche, here in Sikkim the main attraction for me is the monastery itself. Its magnetic pull has drawn me from one end of the Himalayas to the other, via Delhi, for the ridiculously short period of two days.

From my window, I look out on a construction site. A great concrete tower is being built, the modern skyscraper somewhat incongruously being capped by the Chinese-style tent roof that's so common here. The building will steal Tashi Delek's charm, the hotel manager tells me, and I try not to look too sceptical. *Tashi Delek* are the words Tibetans use to greet and farewell each other and they convey a sense of goodwill and auspicious tidings. My room is alive with ugly switches and exposed wires and its red felt carpet has rotted through in places . . . but the water is hot and the bed is clean. From about six in the morning, my room hums with the sound of construction. Later in the day, and somehow more ominously, it thrums with the music of deep, resonant horns and cymbals so large that one imagines it would take two men to play them. Right below my window, I learn, is the town cinema.

Twenty-seven kilometres up the valley lies Nathu-la, the high mountain pass that was once the most commonly used route between Tibet and India. How I hanker for a look at Tibet, but I will get no closer to it than I am now, here in Gangtok. Not only is the pass and its environs entirely closed to foreigners because the Indian government deems this border region so sensitive, but Indians may only visit it four out of seven days per week and only if they're in a group and in possession of permits themselves. My first impressions of the area – that there are more military personnel in Gangtok than anywhere else in India – do not change. Sikkim is disputed territory. Resolutions taken in the Sikkim Assembly in 1973–74 supported the merger of the former Indian Protectorate with India proper. A referendum followed that seemed to confirm this merge was, indeed, the genuine wish of the Sikkimese people. Sikkim needed developmental aid and India, should the merge go ahead, was poised to provide it. China refused, however, to recognise Indian sovereignty over the border territory.

I am reminded that one of the theories about Rumtek and the Karmapa is that if he is permitted to reside in Sikkim the Chinese will be inspired to come and claim both him and the territory. One can almost imagine the Chinese marching in, telling the Sikkimese that they have come to liberate them from the Indian imperialists and her Western allies. China's influence is already tangible around Gangtok: everywhere are peaked roofs; Chinese food appears on almost every menu; Chinese products abound at the markets and in the shops; and hotels boast names like The Golden Pagoda. Although I am told that this place of mixed population – Indians, Sikkimese, Nepalese and Tibetans – does not support a Chinese population, many of Gangtok's residents look distinctly Chinese.

I set off for Rumtek by taxi at eight-thirty. To reach the monastery, we drive on some of the worst roads I've yet encountered in India. One road seems at risk of being washed away by the next light rain. The four-wheel-drives and taxis passing us from the opposite direction tell me that the Bengali tourists have started early and have already ticked Rumtek Monastery off their itineraries before nine o'clock. A new Sikkimese senior minister who is particularly sympathetic to the Karmapa is campaigning for his prompt instalment at Rumtek in the interests of boosting tourism to the state. It takes an hour to travel the twenty-seven kilometres from Gangtok to Rumtek and I can well imagine Tai Situ Rinpoche, as a boy, revelling in the adventure of the seven-hour journey by horse.

We drive through an arch welcoming us to Rumtek, but still there is a long climb ahead of us between rice paddies and jungle, bamboo and vine-covered trees vying for light on the shady slope. Out on the roads of northern India I have seen the whole world and here is no exception. A young man washes his enormous silver four-wheel-drive in a muddy roadside stream. Whole families work repairing roads: the women carrying baskets of gravel and stone on their heads; the men smashing the rocks with sledgehammers and digging; and the tiny, half-naked children playing in the mud, no more than a metre from the passing traffic. A man walks along the road with two huge, dirty pigs, both on leads, and the smell of cow dung rather than the invisible mountain is the only thing that evokes Switzerland for me. For only a moment, the mist parts and I can see Gangtok, way across the other side of the valley.

My pulse starts to race as a policeman flags my taxi. I try to suppress the crazy thought that he is the one who's been waiting for the Australian woman, illegally researching a book. All he wants is a lift to Rumtek yet I cannot shake a sense of foreboding. He pays not a jot of attention to me but, nonetheless, I am determined that he will not see my notebook or tape recorder.

As we drive ever higher into the clouds, I am transfixed by the avenues of white prayer flags on their vertical bamboo masts. Discoloured as they are, there is something ethereal and majestic about them. Finally, we arrive at the true gates of Rumtek and, once again, the details of my passport are transcribed into yet another ledger that I doubt anyone will ever read. Police use a metal detector in a desultory fashion to scan the arrivals. When a beep sounds, the policeman simply asks the visitor what they're carrying, and when the answer is a camera he simply waves them on. Surely this can only be for show? The guards, having recorded my passport details, simply wave me on without the charade of checking my commodious red shoulder bag.

Before I reach the monastery itself, I pass a couple of teashops. Most of them proudly display stickers featuring the Dalai Lama and Karmapa, posing almost cheek to cheek. I start to see copies of a black-and-white poster sporting a photo of the Karmapa and the slogan 'Karmapa to Rumtek, We've waited long enough!' I go on to see copies of the poster and sticker all over Gangtok and make it my mission to own a copy of both of them. To the locals, or so it seems, the Karmapa is the closest thing to a local hero cum Hollywood star they have.

Once again, at the entrance to the monastery's main courtyard there is the security sham. We are all asked to step through a metal detector and asked the same casual question about the contents of our bags. I could be carrying a sawn-off shotgun and the half-dozen guards would be none the wiser.

That Rumtek is an active, living monastery is immediately apparent. The three walls of the central courtyard comprise two storeys of monks' accommodation, all the doorways and windows painted in traditional Tibetan style with lots of red, and detailed in blue and yellow. Everywhere are Karmapa stickers and posters and I am left in no doubt as to which candidate for Karmapa that the monks of Rumtek support. This is Ogyen Trinley Dorje's territory.

For some unfathomable reason several Bengali tourists request again and again to appear in photographs with me. At first I'm confused, certain that they're asking me to photograph them . . . But no, they genuinely wish to gather around me – and the closer the better – to be in a holiday snap with this tall, pale, frizzy-haired Western woman. All my aspirations of being inconspicuous amount to nothing. Curiously, the Bengalis do not ask to photograph the dozens of cute boy-monks.

In the Shrine hall, fifty-odd monks sit cross-legged on low benches covered in carpets and cushions. They are chanting their prayers and even the youngest of them, aged around five, is not distracted by the constant flow of tourists around the edges of the room. The monks are notably young; at a guess, the oldest among them is about forty. One of the boy-monks goes from row to row, pouring *chai* into his fellow monks' bowls. Some of the younger monks, positioned in the back row, steal glances at the tourists but do not smile at us and I am certain that they are under instructions not to engage with us during prayers.

While the visiting Bengalis show respect towards the images and statues of the deities in the temple – indeed, they make money offerings and bow their heads before the great, gold-painted Buddha – I am a little disconcerted that their presence (up to fifty of them in the temple at once) gives the holy room the air of a tourist attraction. Atop a throne before the altar is perched a rather less glamorous photograph of the Karmapa. A young monk stands to the throne's side, keeping his eyes both on it and on the nearby *mandala*, the intricate, circular design in coloured sand of which would be ruined by a tourist's sneeze. I smile at him and pull my red blessing cord from beneath my collar. I finger the thread and look up at the Karmapa's portrait. 'You've seen him?' the boy asks, and from the longing in his voice I gauge that he has not. I tell the boy I'm looking for Drupon Rinpoche and he offers to lead me to him once he's found someone else to take up the post at the throne.

Drupon Rinpoche is a twenty-something monk who tells me that Gyalstab Rinpoche is not at the monastery at that time. Rinpoche seems unmoved by my claims that there must be some mistake. I explain that Lama Phuntsok had arranged a meeting for me with the former regent but my voice, no doubt, registers my uncertainty. Even as I speak, I know how pathetic I sound when I say, 'But I've travelled all the way from Dharamsala.' Drupon Rinpoche subsequently tells me that he has also just come from Dharamsala but that, unlike me, he took the bus all the way.

In one of the teashops outside Rumtek's gates, I use a public telephone to contact Lama Phuntsok. He is most apologetic, telling me that he had not been able to reach Gyalstab Rinpoche by telephone but had tried many times. He insists that he will sort something out for me and instructs me to go and wait at the monastery office.

Eventually Drupon Rinpoche reappears, clearly not as willing to assume the role of my fixer as Lama Phuntsok was. He tells me that he can arrange a very large jeep to take me to Gyalstab Rinpoche's monastery, which is only four hours away but over very bad roads. Every fibre in my body tells me that this is a very bad idea. For no sensible reason I am overcome by a sense of foreboding about this journey, pretty sure that I've already used almost all my allocation of luck on India's roads over the last fortnight. What's more, my return flight to Sydney leaves the following evening. When I tell Drupon Rinpoche that I will travel no further, he makes some attempt at consoling me by telling me that Gyalstab barely speaks a word of English anyway. I laugh, shrilly, at the thought of having undertaken yet another mad drive only to find that my interviewee cannot converse with me.

The younger *rinpoche* agrees to guide me on a tour of Rumtek Monastery and the adjoining Nalanda University. We visit the Shrine room in which the XVIth Karmapa's remains are interred and I see for myself a piece of bone that was found among his ashes. Looking at the thing, I am queasy; it is quite clearly in the form of the Buddha.

Within the Nalanda University, I visit the room in which the students practise their prayer rituals. There is a gallery of photographs; a number of the previous Karmapas are featured, as well as the image of the young Jamgon Kangtrol Rinpoche, whose predecessor was killed in the car crash before he could lead the search for the XVIIth Karmapa.

Drupon Rinpoche locates some boy-monks with a set of important keys and leads us up flights and flights of stairs to what must, I am sure, be the highest point of the monastery. We emerge onto a terrace and one of the boy-monks struggles with a locked door that is clearly rarely opened. Inside is yet another throne with a Karmapa portrait but this smallish room has a palpable energy of its own. I am told that it is here that the XVIth Karmapa conducted his private audiences. The floor is of an amber-coloured timber, polished to a high gloss and as smooth as satin beneath my sock-covered feet. The throne is flanked by a pair of elephant's tusks standing as tall as me, a gift from a Bhutanese king. On either side of the tusks sit row upon golden row of buddhas in ornate carved cabinets. With the Karmapa himself upon the throne, even a cynic might feel to be in the presence of a being from another realm. This room is a far cry from the near-clinical room at Gyuto, off to the west, in which Ogyen Trinley Dorje conducts his strictly controlled audiences atop his Perspex throne.

Behind us, the two boy-monks are gliding around, polishing cloths beneath their feet. Now the reason for the floor's incredible shine becomes apparent. They are polishing away the imprint of our feet only moments after we've left them there. Rinpoche and I leave the room and in our wake the boy-monks continue to glide in unison, removing all trace of our visit and leaving the room to its memories. I hope that they are also, symbolically, cleansing the room for a future that will feature the presence of the XVIIth Karmapa.

I am led out onto the terrace and ushered towards a vantagepoint from which I can see a pavilion atop the audience room. This is the monastery's highest point, crowning the temple's roof. Those rooms, I am told, were once the XVIth Karmapa's and will one day be inhabited by the XVIIth. I have a memory flash, like a sudden pain, of Ogyen Trinley Dorje being ushered from his room; the concrete walls of Gyuto Tantric University were unadorned and he had been flanked by his bored, impatient Indian protectors cum jailers. Rinpoche and I turn our backs on the uninhabited rooms, up there in the sky, and look out across the mist-shrouded valley. Gangtok is there, he says, pointing northwest. And beyond it, I think, tantalisingly close, not even thirty kilometres away, lies Tibet.

I spend a long time standing outside the main buildings of Rumtek Monastery, gazing back at it through the gentle rain. To the monastery's right, jungle rises steeply, a tangle of vines competing with string upon string of coloured Tibetan prayer flags for their place in the trees. It is almost impossible to imagine the clash of monks with the Indian Army in this otherworldly place.

The Karmapa posters at the monastery and back at Gangtok remind me that the castle is without a king. The image of the boy-monks, however, skating across the Karmapa's audience room does not leave me. They're young, bright-eyed and have a tendency to giggle. I fear for what their future will hold should they never get to serve the young Ogyen Trinley Dorje.

As much as I am eager to leave Gangtok for my return journey to Sydney and my family, I am already planning a return to Sikkim. One day I wish to visit that audience room in the clouds and to experience the future there, not the memory of an increasingly distant past. One day, I vow, I will meet the XVIIth Karmapa there.

LINEAGE:
THE FOURTEENTH KARMAPA

The birth of the XIVth Karmapa, Tegchog Dorje (1798-1868), was said to have been heralded by the blossoming of flowers in the middle of winter and by the appearance of rainbows overhead. As a baby, the XIVth Karmapa recited the Sanskrit alphabet. Like some of his predecessors, he studied at Karma Gön Monastery in Kham before proceeding to Tsurphu in central Tibet.

Tegchog Dorje is said to have saved numerous lives by prompting the release of prisoners, banning hunting, and protecting domestic animals from slaughter. Known as a great teacher, Tegchog Dorje was responsible for a profound *dharma* renaissance in Tibet.

The XIVth Karmapa's death was heralded by a sweet perfume in the area, while the sky was alive with rainbows and myriad coloured flowers.

THE BOY LAMA:
DANCE OF DIPLOMACY

Twelve months from the Karmapa's arrival in India and he was still walking towards freedom, although symbolically so, and only within the walls of the Gyuto Tantric University. He had spent the entire year there at Gyuto, studying and receiving visitors and devotees. He had not been permitted to speak to journalists. If it weren't for the contact the young Karmapa had been granted with his teachers and with the Dalai Lama, he would arguably have been better off at Tsurphu. At least there he could walk from the monastery grounds to the mountains behind, albeit with a troupe of minders.

For the most part, the restrictions placed on Ogyen Trinley Dorje seem, in particular, designed to protect India's fragile relationship with China. If the young man's safety was the prime concern, there is no reason to have banned him from speaking to the press.

'The position is that the Karmapa can stay in India. It is not correct to say that he needs a legal status; the government is allowing him to stay,' Kalon Tashi Wangdi was reported as saying in early 2001. 'However, the government of India does not wish his stay in India to be high profile and it seems that they wish things to move cautiously, particularly in terms of diplomatic exchange and in the light of forthcoming visits by senior figures in the Chinese Communist Party to India . . . But we are optimistic that the Karmapa will go to Rumtek sooner rather than later – possibly within the next six months.'[83]

Since the moment of the Karmapa's arrival at Dharamsala, detailed preparations were being made for his reception at Tai Situ Rinpoche's monastery, Sherab Ling. A year on and the preparations, including the rehearsal of the traditional Tibetan Lion Dance, had been for nothing. The Karmapa had not yet been allowed to visit.

The young Karmapa took his case to the very top, writing his own letter of explanation and clarification to the Prime Minister of India, Atal Bihari Vajpayee.[84] In the letter, the Karmapa is said to have given concise details of his escape and the reasons for it. In particular, he requested permission to travel to Rumtek in Sikkim. Other submissions had been made to the the Indian government to permit Ogyen Trinley Dorje to travel to important Buddhist religious sites in India such as Bodh Gaya and Varanasi. (Visiting these places and giving blessings there are considered part of a high incarnate lama's core work.)

Meanwhile, the Dalai Lama had been paving the way for the future. Since his time in exile, he has spoken strongly of breaking down the sectarianism between the different schools of Tibetan Buddhism. While he has clearly made progress, certain Tibetans continue to believe that the Gelug school would never allow the other schools to become too powerful.

When he addressed a Kagyu conference in August 2000, the Dalai Lama stressed the importance of the younger generation of leaders such as the young Karmapa and also the son of Sakya Trinzin, head of the Sakya school. 'When I met [the Karmapa] I told him that the present generation is getting old and I am already sixty-five years old. We have always prayed for the indestructible life, but in reality, everyone has to leave [die] sooner or later . . . In the near future . . . the new lineage holders of the Sakyapas, Gelugpas, Kagyupas and Nyingmpas will be very important'.[85]

While the exile Tibetans now have a democratically elected prime minister, the Dalai Lama undisputedly remains the public face of Tibet. As almost no Western government – at the insistence of the Chinese and under threat of reprisal – recognises the Tibetans' exile government, the Dalai Lama's solely spiritual role provides a loophole for Western politicians to validate their meetings with the high-profile Tibetan. If the Tibetan situation does not change and Tibet remains China's colony, another high Tibetan monk will one day need to fill this role until the XVth Dalai Lama attains his majority.

TIBET: HU YAOBANG
AND LIBERALISATION

Chairman Mao died in September 1976 and, soon after, his widow and her allies – known as The Gang of Four – were arrested and blamed for the horrors of the Cultural Revolution. The death of China's great helmsman would trigger tremendous change in Tibet. Meanwhile, the Chinese were allowing some controlled visits to Tibet by sympathetic Westerners. They were attempting to generate propaganda in support of their claims that they had transformed Tibet into a glowing new society.

The party, under new leadership, sought to improve its relations with Tibetans and identified the Dalai Lama – only recently vilified within Tibet – as the key to this issue. In 1977, Reuters reported that Ngabo Ngawang Jigme had told a visiting Japanese delegation that the Dalai Lama may return to Tibet under certain conditions.

A 1979 census showed that despite two decades of party propaganda to the contrary, economic and social development in Tibet was well behind that of the rest of China, including the other so-called minority regions. The communist directives stipulating that Tibetans should cultivate wheat, combined with the trauma of the class struggle, resulted in terrible impoverishment.[86] In order to address these development issues, the party decided to adopt some tenets of capitalism and to open certain territories to outside investment. In doing this, these regions were to be given some cultural and religious freedom. The Panchen Lama, now released from prison, was once again given an official role in 1978. For a time, it appeared that policy had come full circle.

Not only were Tibetan government officials who had been imprisoned during the Cultural Revolution released, but many who had been involved in the 1959 uprising were, too. Tibetans, however, remained sceptical about China's motives. For the first time, some Tibetans were allowed to travel abroad to visit their relatives in India but were expected to give them a glowing report on developments within Tibet and to urge the exiles to return. The Chinese wanted the Dalai Lama back and were placing pressure on the Indians over this. A serious dialogue between the Dalai Lama and the new Chinese leadership, headed by Deng Xiaoping, commenced by way of intermediaries. The Chinese leadership never recognised the exile government, and so if there was to be any official contact between the exile Tibetans and the Chinese government, it would have to be with the Dalai Lama and his envoys.

In August 1979, at Deng's invitation, a fact-finding delegation travelled from Dharamsala to Beijing. It would visit all the Tibetan areas, not just the TAR. The Chinese leadership, for the most part, felt confidence about the plentiful benefits of development and progress that the exile Tibetans would see in their homeland. Contrary to Chinese expectations, the delegation was mobbed by thousands of Tibetans in the former Amdo and Kham regions who wished only to recount their sufferings. Throughout the six months of the tour, the delegation received the same overwhelming welcome and was burdened with hundreds of similar stories of loss.

A second exile delegation visited Tibet in May 1980, and a month later a third was dispatched. The visits to Lhasa triggered major anti-China demonstrations accompanied by public demands for Tibetan independence. The Chinese had badly miscalculated the situation and cancelled future delegations. A fourth delegation was, however, permitted to travel to eastern Tibet in 1985. After all of the party's efforts at smashing religion and diminishing the status of the Dalai Lama, Tibetans saw him as their only hope for freedom. They complained to the delegations that their economic situation had only worsened under Chinese occupation. The message conveyed loud and clear to the delegations seemed to suggest that instead of smashing the Tibetan people's devotion to the Dalai Lama and old Tibet, in many cases the Chinese had fuelled it. According to historian Warren Smith, China's occupation of Tibet was profoundly destructive, and yet it actually created Tibetan nationalism.[87]

Indeed, a visit to Tibet in 1980, by newly ascendant Party Secretary Hu Yaobang, confirmed that for many within Tibet living standards had declined since the communist invasion. This, after three decades of ceaseless propaganda, was a radical statement. In his speech to party members, he spoke of having 'let the Tibetan people down'. He further compared the situation in Tibet with colonialism.[88] Hu Yaobang announced a new liberal policy on Tibet that promised autonomy, short-term freedom from tax, increased agricultural subsidy and the development of Tibetan language, culture and religion. While the policy did not meet the Tibetans' demands for the respect of their basic human rights, it was welcomed nonetheless. Many of the new policies, however, were resisted by local leaders and party cadres.

In 1981, the hated commune system was ended and, virtually overnight, the communes' animals were equally divided among their members. Households regained complete responsibility. It was decided that Tibet's nomads and so-called peasants would not have to pay tax for a decade so as to counter the poverty of the TAR. Monetary restitution was even made to some of the former wealthy nomads for the animals and belongings that had been confiscated.

Hu Yaobang now began in earnest the process of trying to entice the Dalai Lama home. While Hu's invitation promised the Dalai Lama a return to his pre-1959 status, its terms effectively prevented him from assuming any power in Tibet by insisting he live in Beijing and hold only a nominal role. The offer was rejected on the grounds that it reduced the Tibet issue to the status of the Dalai Lama alone.

Within Tibet, improvements were made and the Tibetans were starting returning to their traditional clothes and agricultural practices. Religion, once again, was practised overtly and resumed its integral place in Tibetan society.[89] While the Tibetans' standard of living had risen dramatically over the last few years since the end of the Cultural Revolution, it had now only reached a level commensurate to that of pre-occupation Tibet.

The XVIth Karmapa had not yet been dead a year before the Chinese permitted the Panchen Lama to visit Tibet in July 1982.

This was the first time since 1964 that the Panchen Lama had been home. Despite the Party's earlier attempts to vilify him, many Tibetans remained devoted to him. Even the Panchen Lama, it is reported, was shocked at the degree to which his country's culture had been destroyed.

Some Tibetans believe it is no coincidence that the period during which the Karmapa was preparing for rebirth was also a period of hope and regeneration in Tibet. Such is his monks and followers' belief in the Karmapa's power that one *rinpoche* from Rumtek Monastery told me the Karmapa himself had been responsible for the softening of party policy within Tibet.[90]

9 OCTOBER 2003

LINEAGE: THE FIFTEENTH KARMAPA

THE BOY LAMA: REFUGE?

TIBET: FROM RENAISSANCE TO MARTIAL LAW

9 OCTOBER 2003

It's just before three on the morning of my last day in India. I have woken to the sound of soft rain falling outside which means that I will not glimpse Kanchenjunga before I leave this kingdom in the clouds. Nonetheless, I feel a deep sense of privilege. During this trip I have been in conversation with a deity, with someone who will, I believe, one day play a significant role in the destiny of his people.

Tai Situ Rinpoche said that the Karmapa himself has manifested my book. While my initial reaction to this claim was bemused scepticism, which I probably did not hide by nodding smilingly, politely, I've been pondering the notion ever since. That scepticism has been carried away by the shifting clouds and is probably gradually dissolving somewhere over Tibet by now. I remain unable to fully rationalise my attraction to the Karmapa and his story.

Outside, in pre-dawn Gangtok, the dogs are barking furiously, determinedly, and I'm intrigued by the possible cause of the fracas. Could it be that some wild animal – tiger or snow leopard – wandered into town in search of an easy meal, only to be bailed up in a dingy alleyway by a pack of stray dogs?

In part, my insomnia is caused by a near-palpable need to hold my daughter and smell her soft skin, now that my nose is turned towards home. I also feel an anxiety about the journey itself that is new to me since Isla's birth. Now that I'm a mother, I travel neither easily nor readily, yet somehow my dreams have grown wilder.

It's raining in earnest by the time I'm due to leave and the prospect of driving for at least three hours in a small, white minivan without a seat belt is less and less attractive by the moment. My driver, the same man who drove me yesterday in a most moderate and even-mannered way, seems to have sensed my intense desire to be home now and is driving accordingly. There comes a point, while the rain is hitting the windscreen in sheets and we're heading downhill at speed with no apparent use of the brakes, that I just give in to the perils of the drive and relax.

I fumble in my now damp shoulder bag for my notebook and set myself the challenge of recording the road poet's finest efforts; the distraction posed by this feat of determination makes the drive less onerous. In a spidery yet legible script, I copy the following:

Sinking area ahead, inconvenience regretted
If married, divorce speed
Drive don't fly
Faster will see disaster
Reach home in peace, not in pieces
Mountains are pleasure, only if you drive with leisure

As I write, it occurs to me that the slogans are probably more of a distraction to the tired drivers than a saviour.

We drive down out of the Sikkimese Himalayas and onto the plains of West Bengal. I quickly feel nostalgic for the drama of the terrain we've left behind us. Later, when there's a small explosion in an overhead light on my Air India flight, which the Indian passengers and crew treat as very much the everyday occurrence, I decide that I have had enough drama, after all.

LINEAGE:
THE FIFTEENTH KARMAPA

Khakhyab Dorje (1871–1922), the XVth Karmapa, was born with a small white tuft of hair between his eyebrows, as was Shakyamuni (the buddha who had been born as Prince Siddhartha). The infant showed great intelligence, and by the age of four was composing prayers.

Several great masters experienced prophetic visions about Khakhyab Dorje, prompting a search party to seek out the child. He was recognised in accordance with details from the XIVth Karmapa's prediction letter. Enthroned at Tsurphu Monastery when he was six years old, an atmosphere of miracles apparently

221

surrounded Khakhyab Dorje. On one occasion he was asked to consecrate a distant temple, so he drew an image of it on paper then poured scented rice onto the page at the time of the ceremony. At the temple itself, scented rain was said to have poured from the sky. While in meditative retreat, the Karmapa displayed the ability to pass through solid rock.

In 1898, Khakhyab Dorje travelled to Bhutan, bestowing transmissions on numerous followers. Upon his return to Tibet, he took several consorts (just as his guru had predicted) and went on to recognise his own son as the incarnation of the previous Jamgon Kongtrul Rinpoche. Khakhyab Dorje died aged fifty-one.

THE BOY LAMA: REFUGE?

Almost thirteen months after the Karmapa's arrival in Dharamsala, and hot on the heels of Chinese Premier Li Peng's visit to India, the Voice of America reported on a leak that the Karmapa had been granted refugee status in India.[91] Himachal Pradesh's *Tribune* also covered this story, adding that restrictions on the Karmapa's travel had been lifted.

During the early days of February 2001, the story of the granting of the Karmapa's refugee status was covered in newspapers around the world. On 3 February, Kalon Tashi Wangdi confirmed the report on the Karmapa's status, adding that the five Tibetans who had escaped with the Karmapa had also 'been granted asylum by the Indian government'.

Followers of the Karmapa globally greeted the news with jubilation. One can almost imagine the symbolic portents that would have been seen to accompany it by older Tibetan devotees: multiple rainbows, sun showers, snow, blessed rice falling from the heavens.

Kalon Tashi Wangdi went on to report that still no permission had been granted for the Karmapa to travel to Rumtek in Sikkim. His comments suggest that he and his colleagues anticipated that the Karmapa would be told, imminently, that he may travel to his seat in exile. In the days following the official announcement, other details about the Karmapa's purported liberty were released. The news that the Karmapa was free to travel was qualified by the detail that this freedom was only granted within India. The Indian government, it transpired, was still intent on keeping the Karmapa from Tai Situ Rinpoche's monastery, Sherab Ling, either as a visitor or as a resident. The first reported comments from China were along the lines of what the communists had been saying all along: India must not allow the Karmapa to engage in anti-Chinese activities.[92]

World media was divided over India's grand gesture to the Karmapa. A guest writer for the *Bangkok Post*[93] opined that India had used the Karmapa as leverage against China over the previous twelve months, and that Beijing was only grateful for India's sensitive handling of the Karmapa affair. Italy's *La Stampa* said that China's silence on Indian policy over the previous year had been because India was holding the Karmapa. The Italian newspaper also asserted India's handling of the Karmapa affair had impacted positively on the two countries' attempts to resolve their longstanding border dispute, which had triggered the Sino-Indian war of 1962. During this period, maps detailing a proposed border had been exchanged between India and China. Although no mutually agreeable border was decided upon, these exchanges represented considerable progress.

At the other end of the spectrum, *The Scotsman* of 1 February 2001 purported that India's granting of refugee status to the Karmapa was 'a move strenuously opposed by China's communist government'.[94] The same journalist went on to report that the official line on the Karmapa's disappearance within Tibet remained that he was only temporarily absent.

Such a divergence of commentary on the matter could well leave the discerning reader rather undecided on whether or not the Karmapa had indeed been granted his freedom. Comments from a Chinese Foreign Ministry spokesman, Sun Yuxi, are, however, ominously clarifying. *The Hindustan Times* of 6 February reported that the spokesman claimed that

China was not overly concerned about India granting the Karmapa refugee status because of her 'explicit comments' on limitations over the Karmapa's activities in India. The newspaper went on to report the already well-publicised statement that the Indian government would not permit the Karmapa to engage in any anti-Chinese activities. More alarmingly, it asserted that the Indian government would prevent 'foreign forces' from using him for the same purpose.[95]

The Indian government appears to have a diplomatic coup on its hands. Not only has it pleased its citizens (or the majority of them) by giving haven to the revered Buddhist leader, but it has effectively won itself an ongoing bargaining tool over its great northern neighbour. By this time, the United States, in its Country Reports, had already twice cited the Karmapa's escape as proof that human rights abuse, by way of religious persecution, was endemic in China.[96] One can only imagine the stir that might be caused were the Karmapa to testify, as other Tibetan refugees have done, before the United States Congress. To this day, the Indian government has not granted the Karmapa permission to leave the country.

TIBET: FROM RENAISSANCE TO MARTIAL LAW

In early 1984, one of the changes announced by Hu Yaobang was for 'the opening of Tibet', both to other Chinese and to tourism. While tourists, particularly those travelling independently, would bring the sympathetic focus of the international media to Tibet, the growing numbers of Chinese entering Tibet would prove ultimately devastating for the Tibetans and would make them second-class citizens in their own country.

The decision to once again allow Tibetans to celebrate New Year with the *Mönlam* ceremony convinced Tibetans that they really could practise their religion again. Full of hope, they began to display photographs of the Dalai Lama, to rebuild monasteries and temples (although technically this required a permit that was often overlooked) and young boys started to join monasteries again.

While the early eighties were symbolised by a time of religious flowering, the period also marked the commencement of large-scale immigration by Chinese. It did not take long before the more highly skilled Chinese dominated Tibet's economy. The administration in Tibet, however, was gradually being Tibetanised, with party positions going to Tibetans for all but the highest roles. Pressure was also exerted to Tibetanise education and to revive the teaching of the Tibetan language.

The removal of Hu Yaobang from his position in 1987 was very bad news for Tibet, heralding a move against liberalisation in the party. While liberalisation looked as though it might be halted within Tibet, Tibet was becoming something of a cause célèbre in the West. Concerns about human rights abuse, the environment and the preservation of Tibet's culture were selectively promoted at a time when these issues were generally topical. Western parliaments, such as those of the United States (Congress) and the Federal Republic of Germany (Lower House), discussed the Tibet issue. In 1987, US Congress went as far as labelling Tibet an occupied country, many Congress members having already requested direct dialogue between the Chinese president and the Dalai Lama.

In September 1987, the Dalai Lama addressed the US Congressional Human Rights Caucus and issued his 'five-point peace' proposal that called for, among other things, the abandonment of China's population transfer, respect for the Tibetan people's human rights, environmental protection and negotiations on the future status of Tibet. While the Chinese rejected the Dalai Lama's proposal outright, the means of its delivery was of grave concern to them. Three days later, in Lhasa, the Chinese publicly executed two Tibetans whom the authorities dubbed 'criminals' but who were more likely political prisoners.

The Dalai Lama's speech in Washington prompted the first anti-China demonstrations in Tibet since the visits of the exile Tibetans. Monks from Drepung Monastery who staged the demonstration were arrested and beaten by the Chinese police. A second demonstration was staged that was again suppressed, and this time Western tourists were witnesses. A much larger public demonstration ensued and non-Chinese reports confirm that police fired straight into the crowd, killing eight to ten bystanders, in order to disperse it.

In June 1988, the Dalai Lama visited the European Parliament and there he clarified the proposals he'd laid down the previous year in Washington. Notably, in what was termed the Strasbourg Proposal, the Dalai Lama announced that he would relinquish his claim for Tibet's independence, but now called for genuine autonomy and a 'voluntary association with China'. While he reiterated that Tibet should be a zone of peace, the Dalai Lama agreed that China would remain responsible for foreign policy and could retain a small military presence in Tibet for defence purposes. For many Tibetans, the Dalai Lama's relinquishment of the demand for Tibet's independence was extremely problematic, and remains so today.

Analysts suggest that the notion of Tibet as a zone of peace was quite likely an Indian-inspired initiative as that situation would have recreated the status of Tibet as a buffer zone between herself and China. Regardless of the origins of the 'zone of peace' proposal, more than fifteen years later the words 'Tibet' and 'peace' are regarded in the West as synonymous. At the gathering of the World Social Forum in January 2004, convened in Mumbai and dubbed a reply to the institution of the World Economic Forum, one of the many slogans that emerged from the forum was 'Tibet is peace is Tibet'. While Tibet's history is as bloody as that of any other nation, the contemporary 'Tibet struggle' is characterised by non-violence.

For the first time since 1954, an Indian leader made a formal visit to China in 1989. During this visit, Prime Minister Rajiv Gandhi confirmed that India recognised Tibet as part of China. Another blow for Tibet came with the unexpected death of the Panchen Lama in January 1989. In the days prior to his death, he had told the Chinese press that Tibet had lost more than it had gained under Chinese occupation. While Chinese authorities claimed he had died of natural causes, many Tibetans assumed that he had been murdered (by poison) because of these and similar publicly stated views.

In early March 1989, in the lead-up to what has become known as National Uprising Day, Tibetans demonstrated in Lhasa in the largest numbers since 1959. Despite all manner of ideological coercion imposed upon them by the authorities during the crackdown of the previous months, Tibetans proved extremely resilient, most refusing to denounce the Dalai Lama. Martial law was imposed by the new Party Secretary in Tibet, Hu Jintao (currently China's president). Tibet's brief period of liberalisation had come to an end.

In the same year as the imposition of martial law in Lhasa and the ill-fated demonstrations in Tiananmen Square, the Dalai Lama was awarded the Nobel Peace Prize. The award gave a tremendous boost to Tibetans; to them it was synonymous with Western support. Tsering Shakya in *Dragon in the Land of Snows* claims they regarded it as second only to independence. The timing of the award, in the wake of the Tiananmen Square bloodletting, was particularly symbolic and clearly proclaimed the world's attitude towards China.[97]

Tibet was no longer to be seen as an exception by the Chinese leadership, where allowances would be made for cultural and economic reasons. Hu Jintao announced a new policy that was described as 'grasping with both hands', which would involve immediate police or military oppression of unrest, accompanied by accelerated economic development. The UN Sub-Commission on Human Rights formally censured China. Western diplomatic delegations began to visit Tibetan prisons and called for the release of political prisoners (with little result). China dismissed this censure as politically motivated and an extension of other nations' foreign policy. She was able to gain the support of other Asian nations in asserting that human rights concerns were internal affairs of the state in question.

It was, of course, during this period of crackdown in Tibet that the XVIIth Karmapa, Ogyen Trinley Dorje, was enthroned at Tsurphu Monastery. Endorsed not only by the Dalai Lama, the XVIIth Karmapa was also officially acknowledged by the stridently secular Chinese government. It is unlikely that the Karmapa's enthronement heralded a sign that the party supported the blossoming of Tibetan Buddhism that had been a feature of the eighties. More likely, in the wake of the Panchen Lama's death, the Chinese government was seeking a Tibetan religious leader who they could indoctrinate. It needed a highly respected Tibetan, trusted by his people, who might argue its case among ordinary Tibetans and who might even help the government break the Tibetans' loyalty to the Dalai Lama.

PART TWO

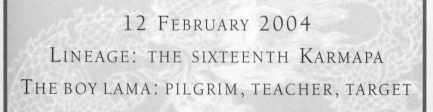

12 FEBRUARY 2004

LINEAGE: THE SIXTEENTH KARMAPA

THE BOY LAMA: PILGRIM, TEACHER, TARGET

12 FEBRUARY 2004

SQ 222. I am returning to India. Over the past months, the Karmapa's impact on my life has been subtle yet profound. I have thought of him constantly and the sense of privilege I carried from my meetings with him has not left me.

In early November, during *savasana*, the meditation period at the end of a yoga class, I had a very strange experience. Normally, I am queen of the monkey mind – the chattering in one's head so aptly named by Buddhist teachers – and the only time I feel stillness or a meditative state is when my body can convince my mind to give it all a rest. That day, I lay back in a particular relaxation pose – a blanket covering my body and a silky, weighted bag covering my eyes – and left the noise of the neighbourhood behind. I had the Indian Himalayas on my mind and, as time passed, I felt lodged in that familiar landscape, in those foothills rising behind the Norbulingka Institute, and in the rolling green hills to the south. The sense of place was gradually superseded by the clean lines of the young Karmapa's face: his smooth, glowing skin; his high cheekbones; and his knowing, dark eyes. Had I tried to, I could not have cleared my mind of the Karmapa's presence.

When I opened my eyes, once my teacher had sounded her chime, I knew that I had been summonsed.

I have heeded Lama Phuntsok's command to return. This time, I vow to myself, I will sit at the Karmapa's feet every day for a fortnight, my notebook on my knees and my gaze on his face. I still imagine that I can truly know him.

This longing to return is not the only seed that was sown during my time near the Karmapa that has come to fruition. The question that mysteriously plagued me on entering the Karmapa's presence the first time has been answered. Paul and I have conceived a second child.

Here I sit, flying to Singapore and then Delhi. It is only four-and-a-half months since my other departure and I am just a little bit pregnant. Despite my glib protestations of October past about being too work-focused to have another child, my response to this pregnancy is as simple as they come. Joy. I feel joy and happy anticipation. Now, when I return to the Karmapa, my questions to him about his life will be disturbed only by the thought of the new life inside me.

Over a dinner with my publisher and two writer friends, only a day before departure, I find myself spluttering about the privilege that I feel. It has been a privilege to immerse myself in Tibetan history and religion and, in particular, to spend time with a young Tibetan who already commands audiences in the tens of thousands.

I delight to myself that this new life inside me will be in the presence of one of Tibet's great lamas. His or her sister, after all, received an intimate blessing from the Dalai Lama (on a trip to Australia to give teachings) when she was not yet six months old. I and my ATC colleagues had been standing in line to welcome him to an official function. I was wearing a suit for the first time in many months, with baby Isla in a sling at my chest beneath the jacket. When the Dalai Lama reached us, he stopped. Carefully, he touched each one of Isla's fingers as the cameras clicked and flashes popped behind him. Isla, for her part, remained utterly sanguine. Her mother, however, announced 'Isla met the Dalai Lama, Isla met the Dalai Lama' to friends and strangers for weeks afterwards.

I find myself returning to thoughts of the Karmapa's mother over the months. Her name appeared as Lolaga in the XVIth Karmapa's prediction letter, in his Last Testament, and I, in my fanciful, writer's mind, call her Lolaga as well. When she and her husband went to their lama, seeking blessings for a son, they would have known that the master might one day call for more payment than their offering of butter and milk. Perhaps it is this part of the Karmapa's story that made me hesitate about seeking advice from him about a second child . . .

Yes, the master told Lolaga that he would pray that a son would be born to them. I can almost imagine Lolaga's thrill of certainty, the excitement of a pregnancy's first confirmation. With one certainty for Lolaga would have come another more troubling one. The boy would not be hers for long. When the master's words confirmed this, it would have been as though Lolaga had already heard the message in a dream.

In Tibet at that time, under Deng Xiaoping, there had been a thaw that must have felt as pregnant with promise as spring itself. Monasteries were being rebuilt from both within and without. Walls were being patched and roofs raised, but, even more significantly, after nearly three decades, families were bringing their children to the monasteries once again. There would be – or so everybody fervently wished to believe – great monasteries once again.

Perhaps Amdo Palden identified in the Karmapa's parents some gleam of hope, of brilliant, pure faith, that made him certain that one day they would produce a special child. Or perhaps, quite simply, his monastery needed building from within and children weren't being brought to him quickly enough. Whatever he knew or did not know, the boy who would soon be born to Lolaga had already been chosen.

This moment in the Karmapa's story makes me think, once again, about free will and destiny. Some would say – perhaps we of lesser faith – that for the first time during his current incarnation, the XVIIth Karmapa's destiny had been thrust into someone else's hands. Others – those devout and of faith – would say that the Karmapa's own will was the only force at play. According to one of the Karmapa's monks who has not yet even met his master when I speak to him in Sydney, the Karmapa manifested the softening in Tibet during the early eighties. Anyone believing this would also believe he chose his parents and directed them to Amdo Palden, as well.

LINEAGE:
THE SIXTEENTH KARMAPA

Rangjung Rigpe Dorje, the XVIth Karmapa, was born in 1924 to a noble family. Like many of the other Karmapas, he was born in Tibet's east. Rumour has it that towards the end of his mother's pregnancy, the baby disappeared from her womb for the entire day. Upon the baby's return to the womb, those nearby could clearly hear him chanting. His mother had learned from different Buddhist teachers and masters that she would give birth to a great, enlightened being and chose to go and stay in a cave called Lion Sky Castle that had been used by one of Guru Rinpoche's emanations in the past. When the baby was born, he apparently stood up and said that he would be leaving his mother soon.

Rangjung Rigpe Dorje was quickly located in the traditional method. His predecessor's prediction letter led the searchers to the child. At the age of seven, the boy was taken to Tai Situ Rinpoche's monastery where he was ordained as a novice.

After the XVIth Karmapa's arrival at Tsurphu Monastery, he was received in Lhasa by the Great XIIIth Dalai Lama who performed the sacred hair-cutting ceremony on him. During the course of the ceremony, the Dalai Lama apparently had a vision of the Vajra crown above the young boy's head. Ultimately, the boy was installed on the sumptuous throne at Tsurphu that was supported by eight great lions in the presence of official representatives from Tibet, Bhutan, Nepal, Sikkim, India, Ladakh and China. The XVIth Karmapa would go on to receive the majority of his teachings from Tai Situ Rinpoche, but also received transmissions from the heads of all the lineages. When the boy was only nine years old, he formally recognised his first reincarnation, foretelling things such as the place where the child had been born, the direction in which the family's door faced, and the existence of a red watchdog.

As a young boy, the XVIth Karmapa is rumoured to have danced with snakes, declaring himself their king. On one occasion, he stayed at a monastery with a critical water shortage and ordered his bath water to be poured onto the grass. Spontaneously, a spring erupted there and water was never again a scarcity in the area. When a smallpox epidemic broke out at Tsurphu, Rangjung Rigpe Dorje is said to have performed a religious ceremony that caused the epidemic to quickly subside, with those affected recovering.

At the age of twelve, Rangjung Rigpe Dorje embarked on a journey to Kham and on the way left his footprint in some ice. Even when the ice had melted, it was said that his footprint clearly remained visible in the water. This was not the first time the imprint of his foot would remain to be seen by others for posterity. On another occasion, the boy joked about 'the ability to transform material reality'. He then drew a sword from his attendant's sheath and tied it into a knot. Another report has him riding a deer along the ropes that ran from tent to tent, high above his travelling monastery.

In 1940, when he was only seventeen years old, he wrote a song that suggested he could see into the future to the time when he and many of his countrymen would leave their homes for exile. Its last line said, 'There is nowhere to turn but to India, to the east.' Four years later he went on to write:

> I will not stay, but go to uncertain places
> To experience the fruit of the karma of my previous lives.
> The cuckoo will come to Tibet in the Spring,
> The day the saddening song is sung,
> You will wonder where the man Rig grol is.
> O! Dependent ones! Don't you realise you will feel distressed?

In addition to his scholarly and meditative pursuits, the XVIth Karmapa forged strong relationships with other Buddhist states and accepted an invitation to Bhutan in 1944. He travelled on pilgrimage to Nepal, India and Sikkim in 1947, visiting the holy sites of Buddhim, Lumbini, Sarnath and Bodh Gaya.

In 1954, four years after China's invasion of Tibet, the Karmapa travelled to China with the Dalai Lama and other high lamas. As the representative of the Dalai Lama, he visited a number of monasteries in southeastern Kham, giving both teachings and secular advice. The Dalai Lama and Karmapa returned to central Tibet together at which time the Tibetan leader was invited to Tsurphu. Clearly, this was a time that saw great strengthening of the pair's relationship.

By 1956, Chinese persecution in Kham had intensified and in the hope of securing some temporary peace, the Karmapa, under the auspices of the Tibetan government, travelled to Chamdo in Kham where he emphasised the need for peace between Tibet and China and negotiated the delay of reforms for a five-year period.[98] The promised truce that was to accompany the delay in reforms was not upheld. Upon his return to Lhasa, he gave a detailed report of the circumstances in the east to the Dalai Lama.

In late 1956, the Karmapa, the Dalai Lama and the Panchen Lama all travelled to India on a pilgrimage at the invitation of the Mahabodhi Society of India to celebrate the 2500th invitation of Buddhism. Notably during this period, the Rangjung Rigpe Dorje spent time with the Sikkimese king and the Bhutanese Buddhist princess. While he turned down invitations from both the king and the monks to visit Rumtek Monastery, the XVIth Karmapa apparently said that he would go there in the future, when it was necessary. He returned to Tsurphu safely in early 1957.

Reports from eastern Tibet about the PLA's tightening controls over monasteries to the east had by now reached Rangjung Rigpe Dorje. Important *rinpoches* were fleeing Kham for temporary sanctuary in central Tibet. Among them was the young Tai Situ Rinpoche, whose previous incarnation had been the one to formally recognise the XVIth Karmapa and whose own lineage can be traced back to Drogen Rechen, to whom the first Karmapa handed his Last Testament.

By 1959, the PLA had entered Lhasa and controlled western Tibet, also. Monasteries, along with aristocratic families, came under particularly harsh repression. While Rangjung Rigpe Dorje sent a number of the young Kagyu lamas into exile in India and Bhutan, he was determined to remain in Tibet until the last possible moment to render assistance to those who needed it. Ultimately, though, the Karmapa informed the Dalai Lama of his intentions to leave Tibet in early 1959. Rangjung Rigpe Dorje – dressed in lay clothing – and his retinue of 160 lamas, monks and laymen left Tsurphu Monastery and Tibet, taking with them various sacred and precious objects belonging to the Karma Kagyu.

The escape route took the party through southern Tibet, where the local people gave the travellers every assistance. They were heading to Bhutan, which they could only reach by crossing a border pass of over 6000 metres. Before they reached the pass, the Karmapa apparently urged his people on, telling them that it was crucial they cross the pass that day. The night after they arrived in Bhutan, a blizzard blocked all passes for a couple of days. The Chinese military, in close pursuit behind the party, were prevented by the storm from capturing them.

In Bhutan, the Karmapa and his people were warmly received, yet ultimately he decided to extend his journey to Sikkim. When the Sikkimese king invited the Karmapa to establish his seat in Sikkim, the party travelled on to Gangtok. It was 1960. Of the various sites offered to him by King Tashi Namgyal, the Karmapa chose Rumtek – at the time, almost in ruins – as his seat in exile. It had been founded by his predecessor, the IXth Karmapa. As a testament to their friendship, the king and his sons offered the Karmapa legal title to seventy-five acres of land there. It was another three years before construction of the new monastery began, funded by the Sikkimese royal family and the Indian government.

Over the coming years, the Karmapa travelled widely in the region: to Dharamsala for a five-day religious conference presided over by the Dalai Lama; to Ladakh to give teachings; back to Dharamsala to receive an empowerment from the Dalai Lama; and to Bir and Dalhousie to visit the Tibetan monk and lay communities there.

The sacred objects brought from Tibet were installed at Rumtek and the Karmapa officially inaugurated the seat on Tibetan New Year's Day, 1966. It was named 'The Dharmachakra Centre, a place of erudition and spiritual accomplishment, the seat of the glorious Karmapa'.

In 1968 he made consecrated pills or Karmapa pills there and was said to have distributed them miraculously throughout Kham. From within Tibet came stories of addressed packages of these pills being found mysteriously in remote, wild places. (Making these pills is part of the Karmapa's enlightened activity and they are reputed to bring extraordinary blessing to those who receive them. They may simply be worn around the neck or on the body in a relic box, but may also be ingested either as a support during illness or at the time of death, to assist with rebirth. Chinese doctors, it is said, have been stunned by results achieved when patients have reported using the pills. One of the pills' miraculous properties is their ability to reproduce themselves.[99])

In 1974, the Karmapa travelled to the United States where, for the first time, the Black Crown Ceremony was performed in the Western hemisphere. Again, in 1976 the Karmapa visited the US and then travelled on to Europe where he had a meeting with the pope in Rome. Over the following years, he worked ceaselessly towards the building of new meditation and *dharma* centres, expanding and educating the monk community, and publishing rare Buddhist texts. He is said to have given novice vows and full ordination to more supplicants than any other Karmapa.

During his final illness, the Karmapa is reported to have told two of his associates, 'I see Tibet, and there I clearly see my father and mother of the future.'[100] The Western doctors who tended the XVIth Karmapa were clearly deeply affected by him. One commented that as the Karmapa lay dying he was more concerned with the way those around him felt than how he felt himself.[101] In November 1981, he died in Zion, Illinois, and the doctors there reported their astonishment over the fact that his heart remained warm for many days after his death. This, according to Tibetan Buddhism, is a sign of his realisation. The Karmapa's body was flown back to India for cremation at Rumtek Monastery. The ceremony was attended by thousands of disciples from around the world and a host of Indian dignitaries. Above Rumtek, a rainbow appeared in the clear blue sky.

THE BOY LAMA:
PILGRIM, TEACHER, TARGET

In little more than a fortnight of the Indian government's announcement of the Karmapa's official status and its granting him limited permission to travel, it was reported in the Indian media that he was expected to be absent from Gyuto between 19 February and 18 March 2001. Although reports suggested that he would travel to Chandigarh, Delhi, Varanasi and Bodh Gaya, no itinerary was released for security reasons. Given the planning that would have been involved in mounting such a journey, one must assume that the Karmapa's people had been forewarned of India's impending announcement on the young lama's status.

Upon his arrival in Delhi, Agence France Press reported that the roads were lined with thousands of flag-waving Tibetans. School teacher, Dicky Topden, said, 'I am dying to catch a glimpse of the Karmapa. We love him because he is so brave to have escaped from the Chinese authorities. In him we see hope for our future and the future of Tibet.'[102]

Another reporter claimed that when Ogyen Trinley Dorje toured the area of Delhi that is home to many of India's Tibetan refugees, Tibetans lined the streets seven-deep.

Security concerns would, to a large extent, dictate the parameters of the visit and the Karmapa was said to be travelling with a large retinue of security personnel from both the Indian government and the Tibetan government-in-exile. His public appearances were strictly limited but this, apparently, did not diminish the enthusiastic admiration of those who had gathered to pay homage to the six-foot-tall Tibetan.

During his time in Delhi, the Karmapa apparently met various Sikkimese officials, former Indian government officials and representatives of the National Commission for Minorities (while the Chinese regard the Tibetans as a minority group in China, this term accurately describes their status in India) and the National Commission for Scheduled Castes and Scheduled Tribes. Although the young Tibetan is reported to have waved to the gathered press and public, he did not speak. The fact that the Karmapa met the Sikkimese ministers echoes repeated suggestions that the wishes of the federal and state governments were at odds over the Karmapa's return to Rumtek. Factionalism among Tibetan Buddhists aside, the Karmapa's presence there would most certainly generate a tourist bonanza for the north-eastern state.

From Delhi, the Karmapa travelled to Sarnath, near Varanasi, where Buddha gave his first teachings. Here, he was greeted by scores of maroon-clad monks and remained for almost two weeks, giving teachings and conferring blessings. He presided over Tibetan New Year celebrations on 24 February and, at this moment, might have felt more optimism about his future than he had during the preceding twelve months.

Not two days later, Agence France Presse and *The Times of India* reported that an armed intruder had been apprehended trying to forcibly enter the Vajra Vidhya Institute where the Karmapa was staying. The man, who was travelling on a German passport, alleged that he was carrying the knife for his own safety. Questioning would continue.

From Sarnath, the Karmapa travelled on the pilgrim's path to Bodh Gaya, where Siddhartha gained enlightenment and became Buddha. At the same time as the young Tibetan was leading prayers for tolerance, sanity and peace, the Taliban was destroying Afghanistan's massive sandstone statues of Buddha which were believed to date back to the third century.

13 FEBRUARY 2004

This time I will take a taxi from Delhi to Dharamsala, reluctant to sit on an Indian train with the close press of humanity and perhaps suffer an early onset of morning sickness. Although the journey ahead of me will take twelve hours, I am confident that I will be in safe hands, as the person arranging the car has stressed that it is for an Australian Chairman. I am currently chair of the Australia Tibet Council's Board.

The car, when it arrives, is a dusty white Ambassador taxi, but without any of the features – such as seat belts or springs in its seats – that one might hope for in a so-called deluxe edition. My driver, whose name I never learn despite my numerous inquiries, has only a few words of English, such as 'Madam, fifty rupees for toll.' When I ask him whether anybody has explained where I am going, he simply shakes his head in incomprehension. He keeps repeating Dharamsala, Dharamsala, as though to him – like the thousands of Tibetans who flee Tibet for the place each year – the word itself represents refuge and salvation. Dharamsala, in fact, means safe haven or resting place.

We drive through suburban Delhi. One moment there are shantytowns and half-naked children in the cold of an early winter's morning, and the next there are fine houses and apartment blocks, secure behind high, glass-topped walls. Here are stray dogs, with patches of naked skin decorating their mangy coats, and there a glossy black Labrador on a lead, wearing a furry, leopard-skin coat.

The fog that encompassed Delhi when I flew in last night still covers the city like thick, white gauze. We turn to the east and, for a few minutes, a fat, orange sun hangs low in the sky, burning through layers of fog and promising blue skies ahead. The blue skies do not materialise and, at times, the fog we drive through is so thick that this land I think of as so full of life feels, instead, like the world of the dead. I can see only two metres ahead of us on the road – cannot discern the lights of the car in front of us.

While my driver proves skilled at navigating us around car

crashes and traffic jams, he falls down badly in another area. He has never before driven from Delhi to Dharamsala and his only clue as to how to find this fabled town of the northwest is to first find Chandigarh, then to ask directions to Rupar. Indeed, even before we reach Chandigarh, he is stopping by the way, seeking directions. The groups of men from whom he solicits information eye me with unconcealed curiosity. 'Do you have a map?' I ask him again and again, thinking that I can navigate for him. Whether or not he understands what I am asking, he dismisses it out of hand. My map, very usefully, is packed safely at the bottom of my suitcase and I do not relish the spectacle of my underwear, books, shampoo, yoga mat and tape recorder attracting the scrutiny of a group of Indian men while I search for it.

Three hours into the trip I am pleased to leave the state of Haryana – the only distinguishing feature of which is, from my perspective, a roadside hotel curiously named Cassowary – and enter the Punjab. I have a soft spot for turbans, even the deep purple and orange ones worn by the rifle-wielding police. It is on the roads of the Punjab that I truly start to fear for my life. It's not for fear of the turban-clad policemen; the road has become considerably narrower and it is now more pothole than macadam. I finger the card Paul gave me as I left home that reads: 'Please return safely to us.' Under my breath, I alternate mantras, one after the other: *'Om mani padme hung'* and 'Please return safely to us.'

I am surprised to see, when I read my map later and when it's of no use whatsoever, that Chandigarh has been dubbed a Model City and bears the influence of le Corbusier. To the weary traveller on the poorly sprung back seat of an Ambassador taxi, it simply looks crowded, concrete and distinctly lacking in character. A large regional centre, Chandigarh boasts infrastructure, not charm.

Beyond Chandigarh, the concrete subsides and we pass painstakingly constructed, onion-shaped grass huts. Whether inhabited by humans or not, they sport circular doorways and hollowed-out interiors. Now come the frantic requests from my driver to roadside malingerers for Rupar, and beyond that unmemorable town my driver asks for Dharamsala itself. I raise myself in keen anticipation from the heap into which I have slumped. Some eight hours after we left Delhi, I am heartened as the flat plains become rolling hummocks and the dusty fields are softened by the delicious colour green.

At the town of Una, just over the border into Himachal Pradesh, I feel a thrill of familiarity. It reminds me of the larger, lower Himalayan towns through which I passed on my drive to Tai Situ Rinpoche's monastery last October. I see a sign that puts Dharamsala 146 kilometres away. Then I see it again and again . . . somehow, now that we are so close, we are simply not getting any closer. Nonetheless, I imagine arriving at the haven that is the Norbulingka Institute in the pink of dusk and in time for a leisurely shower before dinner.

Some three hours later and in the dead of night, I direct my driver up a narrow laneway, past the famous 'Sacredheartschool', to the Tibetan compound. We have been on the road for twelve hours exactly and my driver has the look of someone who has come to a foreign place and wishes only to return home. I, by contrast, feel I have returned to my home from home.

THE BOY LAMA:
IN HIS OWN WORDS

With the Karmapa's refugee status came a significant first for the young Tibetan: a press conference at which he would, quite plainly, put his extraordinary story into his own words. At it, he would face a tremendous challenge: that of presenting his case with sincerity, yet without engaging in the forbidden anti-China rhetoric. Sixteen months had elapsed since his arrival in India.

On 27 April 2001, the young Karmapa issued a press statement to accompany the press conference in which he outlined his reasons for leaving Tibet, stating simply his wish to give and receive teachings. He also gave clear details of the story of his escape, most of which had already appeared in media reports over the past year. Of the most difficult part of the journey, the trek through Mustang, the Karmapa said 'despite the difficulties, I was completely determined to reach my goal'.

When asked about his momentous meeting with the other great Tibetan, the Dalai Lama, the Karmapa said simply, 'My joy knew no bounds.' He went on to acknowledge the Dalai Lama's 'continual and generous assistance'. The Karmapa also reported that he was receiving the empowerment and transmissions of the Kagyu lineage from Situ and Gyalstab Rinpoches, as well as other Kagyu masters. 'In this way, I am preparing for my life's work: to teach and study Buddhism and to encourage compassion and wisdom within the hearts of all beings.'

He went on to explain the necessity of his return to Rumtek. 'From my point of view, going to Rumtek Monastery would be like returning home to continue the activity of my predecessor.' In perhaps the only political point in his speech, the Karmapa said, 'I am fully confident that I will be able to go there [Rumtek] since Sikkim is a state of India.' While supporting his new patron, politically the young Tibetan was inviting the wrath of his former patron, China, who was yet to accept India's claims over Sikkim. The Karmapa further expressed confidence that soon he would be able to travel abroad 'to meet my numerous disciples and fulfil their spiritual needs'.

As if to quash media speculation over whether he was the heir apparent to the Dalai Lama, the Karmapa said, 'In the past, the Gyalwa Karmapas did not engage in political activity and I can do nothing but follow in their footsteps. Concerning the future path of Tibet and the Tibetan people, I endorse and fully support everything that His Holiness the XIVth Dalai Lama stands for.' While the young man clearly wished to deny having leadership aspirations, his very support of the Dalai Lama's stance on Tibet is political.

Although many felt that permitting the fifteen-year-old Karmapa to answer journalists' questions at the press conference was akin to throwing him to the sharks, the floor was nonetheless opened to questions from the gathered media.

Upon being asked about whether the Karmapa would return to Tibet, he replied that he would not return to his homeland until the Dalai Lama did so. 'I will go back with him.'

On the heavily reported subject of China's allegation that the Karmapa had gone to India to reclaim the infamous Black Hat, he declared, 'It is true that I left a letter behind me, but as I wrote the letter myself, I'm perfectly aware of what was in it and what wasn't. I said in the letter that I left because, although I had for a long time, persistently and repeatedly, requested permission to travel internationally, I had never received it and so I had to leave. I did not, in the letter, mention the Black Crown, the Black Hat. Why would I want to retrieve that from India and bring it back to China, anyway? The only thing that would be served or accomplished by doing so would be to place that hat on [President] Jiang Zemin's head.'

One journalist wanted to know whether Tai Situ Rinpoche was a Chinese agent. In answer to this loaded question, the young Karmapa explained that he had repeatedly asked the Chinese government for permission to invite Tai Situ Rinpoche to Tsurphu for teachings. 'But they refused to allow Tai Situ Rinpoche to enter China, saying that he could not come because he had a close connection to His Holiness the Dalai Lama and was, therefore, inadmissible to the country of China. I think that, if what you said were true, they would have been delighted to let him in.'

When asked whether he would support the Dalai Lama in promoting 'awareness of Tibet and in the cause of Tibetan independence or autonomy', the Karmapa diplomatically explained that it was his responsibility to support the religion and culture of Tibet. 'I think that by doing this I will benefit Tibetans and the people in Tibet, and benefit the situation in Tibet as well. In that sense, in the sense of supporting Tibetan religion and culture, I will assist His Holiness the Dalai Lama as much as I can.'

One journalist wanted to know whether the Karmapa felt that he was being 'reared by China for a political purpose' and, if so, what that purpose might have been. 'I have heard it said that, in a sense, the government of China was planning to make use of me. I was certainly treated as someone very special. For example, when I was taken on tour in China to Beijing, I was well treated. But I came to suspect that there might be a plan to use me to separate the people within Tibet from His Holiness the Dalai Lama.'

The final thorny question of the press conference was on the subject of Thaye Dorje and the Karmapa's reaction to the assertion by some Karma Kagyu Buddhists that it is Shamar's candidate, and not Ogyen Trinley Dorje, who is the real Karmapa. 'The identity of the Karmapa is not decided by a popular vote or a debate between groups. It is decided by the prediction of the previous Karmapa,' he responded.

Those who feared that the young Karmapa would be shark bait at the hands of the assembled media were proven wrong. Clearly, the Karmapa's years of monastic debating training, as well as centuries of accrued wisdom, stood him in good stead for this twenty-first-century media scrum.

14 FEBRUARY 2004

The reflection of the sun on the bright snow of the mountains behind the Norbulingka compound dazzles me. As it's too cold for my longed-for shower and yoga session, just as it was last night, I comb the dust of the highway from my hair and dress myself in layers of clothing. With my stomach empty and threatening queasiness, I head for the temple to resume the ritual of my previous stay here at Norbulingka.

On the temple's roof I look south, taking in the rolling hills and the bright, white domes of a grand home in the haze of the distance. To the north, behind the temple, the Himalayan foothills rise with great pomp, scrub giving way to snow beyond the green-tinged slopes of the foreground.

Just as before, my monk friend with his large, roundly smiling face, emerges from his quarters on the temple's roof as though he has sensed my arrival. We smile and nod and bow to each other, two old friends with barely a word in common between us. I gesture towards the mountains and he gives me the two Tibetan words for snow. After more nodding and smiling, we turn to part and then, as though acting on impulse, he calls me back and invites me behind the curtained doorway and into his room.

Geshe's dwelling is simple and bright, with a bed, a desk and a chair. His wall of windows – which I think must let in the biting cold – also gives him a view of the Dalai Lama's home, although I cannot discern it myself. I imagine that he can see it even from his bed. Geshe delightedly shows me his Norbulingka identity card so I can truly know his name – Palden Chodrak – and then presents me with his certificate from Drepung University at Karnataka in southern India. The original Drepung, in Tibet, is still operating albeit in reduced circumstances, more of a museum than a thriving monastery. Geshe, as his title suggests, is a master of philosophy, and he teaches the subject to the students at the institute. I long for him to be my teacher, also, but it is not to be.

Back in my own room, I resume the endless process of redialling the Karmapa's private secretary's mobile phone number. I can imagine the sleepy way he'll say, 'Ah, Gaby, where are you?', knowing all the while that I am just down the road and bursting to ask when I might see his master. I have such high hopes, so many expectations.

Eventually, I try the main monastery number although I know that Lama Phuntsok avoids speaking there, in the monastery's office, where there is no privacy from the everlistening Indian security personnel. Soon the phone is answered, but when I ask for Lama Phuntsok I am told he is gone. Dharamsala or Delhi, the Tibetan at the other end offers, but he has no idea when he will return. I don't know what's more disappointing: to no longer have Lama Phuntsok as an ally on this journey, or the fact that it is unlikely I'll ever be able to present him with the 'Dharamsala red' fleece jacket I have carried with me all the way from the boiling summer of Sydney.

The Karmapa's new man has only some vague knowledge of me and offers me an audience with his master in two weeks' time.

'No, no, this is not possible,' I plead, and I start talking fast, quoting Lama Phuntsok's last email to me stating 'all appointments after January 15th confirmed'. Eventually, I wangle myself an audience in three days' time, on Tuesday, but this secretary will not agree to see me beforehand – he is far too busy. I bite my tongue lest I start to whine, 'But I've come all the way from Australia.'

Early afternoon, I take a taxi to Gyuto to attend one of the Karmapa's public audiences. As before, there are scores of Tibetans awaiting Karmapa's blessing, ranging in age from the newborn to the elderly women with their steel-grey plaits. There are numerous monks in the forecourt and lingering in the temple surrounds. It quickly becomes clear to me that the once-deserted monastery is now inhabited by more than the Karmapa's own small retinue. I chat to one of the young monks, who tells me that there are about 450 Gyuto monks of the Dalai Lama's Gelug school in residence now. They are the same Gyuto monks who regularly tour the world, giving performances. Indeed, the monk to whom I speak tells me casually that he has performed at the Sydney Opera House. The Karmapa's men, by contrast, now number only fifteen.

The Kagyu monk with whom I speak, with his youthful, angular limbs and timid manner, tells me that he has come from Rumtek and will remain here at Gyuto with his master for a year. This, of course, is an ingenious and necessary system. While the Karmapa cannot go to his monks at Rumtek, they may come to him for their teachings, but in very small numbers. I cannot help but wonder whether, out of context and under the guard of the Indian police, their master and leader, for them, has lost some of his lustre.

There are easily as many Westerners awaiting the Karmapa as there are Tibetans. I imagine that in northwestern India, even if you're not a Western Buddhist, seeking blessings is a compulsory tourist activity. And the Westerners present range from those who appear to be everyday tourists with their hiking boots, backpacks and plastic water bottles, to young Western nuns and monks who look as though they've dropped out of college on the west coast of the United States for a season. I am particularly taken by a young American couple, standing just ahead of me in a queue. She has badly bleached blonde hair, wears white pancake make-up, chunky black boots and a full-length Tibetan *chupa* with striped apron denoting her status – or probably not – as a married woman. He wears baggy, multi-pocketed trousers, a loose, pale T-shirt and enough metal on his head – through his nose, lip and ears – to send the dodgy-looking metal detector into red alert.

I recruit a Ladakhi man, who has travelled from the north of Jammu and Kashmir for the audience, to help me fold my suit-case-crushed *khatag*. It's the same white greeting scarf that I bought at the Norbulingka temple some months earlier. Actually, for all its white, silky glory, it's a bit of an embarrassment. It's so long that I cannot wear it around my neck without it touching the floor – and it must not be allowed to come into contact with the ground under any circumstances – and its fringed ends are so hairy that it's awkward both to fold and unfold. The Ladakhi man, nonetheless, comments on the scarf's beauty and together we embark on the serious business of folding the thing. I am reminded, happily, of the ceremony of folding crisp white sheets with my smiling Swiss aunt. The scarf must be folded like a Roman blind so that as it is unfolded all the good wishes inside shower onto the recipient. In my case, these wishes seem destined to fall in a heap at the Karmapa's feet.

There is an uneasy air of competition hanging over the waiting crowd. Both Tibetans and tourists alike start to jockey for position the moment there's any indication that anything is about to happen. First comes the process of registering – Tibetans in one place and Westerners in another – and the waiting hordes rush to queue so as not to be the last to have one's passport number recorded. On everybody's mind, or so it seems, is the desperate need to position themselves as close to the Karmapa as possible, when the moment comes. There's some confusion, however, because soon those of us who are waiting on the balcony outside the temple are ushered away by the Indian guards and asked to form two lines on the concrete steps. This mob clearly has no queuing mentality and two sloppy, sprawling masses are formed to the temple's right, on the steep steps. I am halfway up the steps in one of the two lines when the pushing starts. The Karmapa has not even appeared yet and already there's an insistent pressure from behind to move forward. Soon we are about twenty-strong across the steps, quite simply a mob of people, hustling for position. I am starting to feel distinctly uneasy, a fall down steps is not what I need, nor do I relish being trampled by a group of *khatag*-wielding devotees. I make a very poor guru-chaser.

When the Karmapa finally appears, not that I can see him from where I stand, the pushing from behind starts to get serious. I would not like to be a small person standing on these steps, nor would I like to be the Tibetan man nearby with his tiny baby strapped to his chest. Without explanation, it has been decided that there will be no teachings today, simply a 'file past' on the terrace outside the temple and blessings. The Kagyu monks have placed a red, floral carpet outside the temple and on it sits an ornate, brocade armchair. Before the chair lies a low table on which devotees may place their offerings. There's a system, of sorts, whereby the Karmapa's monks unfurl our *khatags*, place them around our necks and usher us forward. When my turn comes, I sense a communal grumble behind me as it takes the young monk so long to unfurl my carefully folded prayer scarf. In other circumstances, I'd be chuckling.

I say there's a system but really there's barely controlled mayhem. I'm not sure whether people are afraid that if they don't rush forward as one of the first then the Karmapa's blessings will run out, or whether they simply cannot bear to wait another moment. Whatever the case, the sudden movement forward smacks of herd mentality. By the time I reach the Karmapa, he is standing, trying to keep up with the flow in front of him and to distribute his red blessing cords to devotees and curious tourists alike. I pass before him quickly and cannot catch his eye. His face is set in a fixed expression that seems to read, 'Lord Buddha, get me through this ordeal.' The Karmapa's monks not only have to keep the crowds from him, but also keep them moving. Some people try to stop and ask him something, and from the vantagepoint I assume to his right I see that he is trying to hear and understand their requests but the circumstances make it nigh on impossible. For a moment, I am reminded of my usual feelings of inadequacy in trying to meet the needs of my daughter, my husband, my dog and extended family members. How must this eighteen-year-old feel in this situation?

I am left feeling anything but blessed. I feel, instead, a little sullied by my participation in this group activity of very uncertain motives. To the Tibetans, the Karmapa is an emanation of all the buddhas and, traditionally, they have believed that their lives will benefit insurmountably from this contact. Indeed, folk belief states that seeing the Karmapa only once in a lifetime will ensure that one is reborn in human, not animal, form for the next seven lifetimes. As for the Westerners, I imagine that some feel like that also, or think that they do. For others, perhaps this strange, uncomfortable gathering is simply about being in the presence of the other famous Tibetan, the one who is not the Dalai Lama. As such, it is an end in itself. And why not? As for myself, I am hard pressed to say why I find the whole gathering so disturbing. Perhaps it's the way Indian security personnel push everybody around – the tourists and the Tibetans alike. Or is it the feeling that somehow another people's culture is being cashed in upon and distorted?

As much as the writer in me wishes to stay and observe, I find myself fleeing the scene without a backward glance. I can't help but feel cross for allowing myself to get caught in a near stampede. I clearly lack something that I can only describe as blind devotion to this man whose story I have given so much to tell . . .

THE BOY LAMA: CELEBRITY

I have yet to read a single negative report from the young Karmapa's press conference held in April 2001. Indeed, Rahul Bedhi for *The Daily Telegraph* (London) claimed that the fifteen-year-old 'completely dominated' the meeting with the hundred gathered journalists and photographers.[103] Luke Harding, for *The Guardian*, described Ogyen Trinley Dorje as 'serious and exceptionally gifted', and suggested that it would be 'nice' if the Indian government gave him 'the benefit of the doubt' and allowed him to move to Rumtek in Sikkim.[104]

Reporters from around the world continued to flock to the deserted grounds of Gyuto Tantric University. Their reactions to the young Karmapa were at times quite extreme. One described his eyes as 'beautiful, dark and hypnotic like horizontal teardrops that hold the secrets of the past 1000 years.'[105] The same journalist went on to write, 'Cloaked in flowing maroon and saffron, his copper skin shining with adolescence, Ugyen Trinley Dorje exudes a spiritual opulence that belies his modest surroundings.'

Clearly, 2001 was a time of great optimism for the Karmapa and his followers. Angus McDonald interviewed the Karmapa for the Associated Press, and quoted the young Tibetan as saying 'it's as though the sun of my freedom is starting to rise'.[106]

The Karmapa's celebrity was rising to dizzying, even ditzy, heights. A few months after the Karmapa's press conference, the September 2001 edition of American *Elle Magazine* named the young lama as one of its 'Elle 25'; that is, one of the twenty-five people who just everybody would be talking about over the next few months. The XVIIth Karmapa's name, incidentally, appeared above that of Madonna.

Also in September, the Karmapa appeared – with the slightest of smiles on his face – on the cover of an Indian magazine, *First City* and was featured in a story called 'The Chosen One'. He was quoted as saying, 'I don't think I am any different from people my age. I have never considered myself special or different. I have my weaknesses, my faults. I also experience joy and sorrow and suffering. I pray and work for the well-being of all sentient beings. It is my duty to be concerned about the welfare of all. My life is devoted to the cause of universal well-being, maybe I differ from other 17-year-olds in that aspect, [though] there are several people who work selflessly for the welfare of others.'

In April 2002, *Time* magazine (Asia), selected the young Karmapa as one of the twenty-five Asian heroes of all times. His name appeared alongside that of Burma's Aung Sung Suu Kyi and Hong Kong action star Jackie Chan. Tibetan Tenzing Sonam wrote the *Time* essay that featured the Gyalwa Karmapa. In it he referred to the Karmapa's escape as 'a reviving gust of fresh air' for the Tibetan freedom struggle. The escaped, he asserted, made a mockery of China's claim that Tibetans inside Tibet could freely practise their religion and were content with their lot. He claimed that the Karmapa's escape proved that the Tibetans' struggle was 'as desperate as ever'.

> To me, a Tibetan born and brought up in exile in India, news of [the Karmapa's] escape came like a reviving gust of fresh air that blew away the cloud of confusion and inertia that seemed to have descended upon our decades-old freedom struggle. With that one act of desperation and courage, the Karmapa exposed the Chinese lie that Tibetans were happy and prospering under their rule and that they were free to practise their religion. . . . The Karmapa's escape was a loud wake-up call to those of us who have spent a lifetime in exile. It reminded us forcefully that the cause we are fighting for is alive and just and as desperate as ever.[107]
>
> 'Out of the Red', *Time* (Asia) 29 April 2001

With the Karmapa's growing fame there came, also, increased threat, or so it was alleged. In April, the Indian media reported on a group of Kashmiri militants at large in northern

India with a kidnapping agenda. Among the names of VIP targets on the group's list was that of the XVIIth Karmapa.

For the boy who was said to like to travel, 2001 held some real excitement by way of a second journey in September to Ladakh, a region rich in Tibetan Buddhism. Come December and the Karmapa was, once again, in Bodh Gaya, leading prayers for world peace. After the terrorist attack on the Indian parliament on 13 December (in which Pakistani nationals killed nine policemen and parliamentary staff), security surrounding the Karmapa had been increased once again. Despite the Indian government's decree that the young Karmapa was free to travel within India, reports suggest that all his travel plans had to receive government clearance beforehand. Sikkim and Tai Situ Rinpoche's monastery, Sherab Ling, remained firmly out of bounds.

15 FEBRUARY 2004

My two days' travel have caught up with me today and although I sleep for longer than I've slept for weeks, I wake with sore eyes and little energy. It's bitterly cold in my room and I force myself from my bed and into my thermal underwear for a yoga session before striking out for the temple's roof.

This morning, I have brought Geshe an envelope of photos of my daughter. In it, there is also one of Paul and my friend seems delighted to know that I am married to a former student of philosophy who also wears his head shaved of its hair. He calls Isla '*ninje*', using one of the few Tibetan words that comes to my own lips without prompting. It means compassion, and is used as a term of endearment.

Geshe, in turn, has found a large English-Tibetan dictionary and together we struggle to try to translate the title of my last book. I have brought him a copy, although we both know that he will never be able to read it. Once we have painstakingly translated the title, *The Truth About My Fathers*, what follows is the even more painstaking process of explaining it. In our halting way, we swap stories about our families and seem, somehow, to have arrived at the same place. Despite loss and sadness, his on a very different scale to my own, we agree that we are happy people, both of us, leading fortunate lives.

I tell Geshe that I wish he could be my teacher, knowing it's not possible. 'Why?', he asks me, as though a Western woman like me, travelling the world, could have no need for such a thing. Reincarnation, I tell him; I want him to explain it to me in a way that I will truly understand. He studies the word in his dictionary and eventually laughs and laughs. 'Not possible, not possible,' he mutters.

Finally, we speak of the Karmapa. Geshe is a Gelug monk and does not get that faraway look of devotion on his face – that is clearly reserved for the Dalai Lama – when he speaks of the Karmapa. He is careful about what he says on the subject of the Karmapa, but categorically dismisses the possibility that he is a spy. He agrees with me, a little sadly himself, when I tell him I think Karmapa is an unhappy man.

Throughout the day, I float between my laptop computer, the telephone and the beautiful stone paths and flowerbeds in the Norbulingka's grounds. I drift in and out of conversation with those Tibetans I already know, and learn that very little prompting brings their stories pouring from them.

I ask Pema, one of the staff at the guesthouse, about what she will do at *Losar*, and quickly see that I've touched a nerve. Tibetan New Year will fall at the end of the week and Pema has been baking – she and some others. Between them, they've made some twenty kilos of *kapsi*, the biscuit that Tibetans traditionally offer at New Year. Actually, it's a sad time for her, she tells me, because she is alone here in India and without family. Born near Shigatse in central Tibet, Pema was sent from her rural home at seven to work for relatives in Lhasa. There she was badly treated, forced to pull great loads in a hand cart from the market when she was only small and weak, and beaten when she could not carry out the work to an acceptable standard. By fourteen, she was travelling by foot to India, with two other girls, via Nepal. With no schools accessible to her in the area where her family lived, and unable to pay for an education in Lhasa (where it is free to Chinese children), at the age of fourteen she walked into exile. Like so many other young Tibetans, she was chasing the promise of a free education courtesy of the Tibetan Children's Village.

Back in Pema's village, her mother leads a difficult life. Her husband is dead and she has only girl children to perform the difficult, manual labour that is necessary for survival. When her daughter phones from exile in India, her mother begs her to come home, just once for a visit. And Pema used to have grand plans herself of returning to her village and starting a small school there, but here in India she failed her maths exams again and again, and eventually contented herself with a job in which she could at least use the English she had so recently learned. Now, should she return to Tibet, she fears she will be under constant surveillance by the Chinese authorities. She would lose her job at the institute and should she ever return, if she could manage to leave Tibet a second time, she would have to start all over again.

As *Losar* approaches, I imagine that the Karmapa and his sister pine for their family, too. Last time I spoke to Ngodup Palzom, she told me that they could not even speak to their parents, to Loga and Karma Döndrub, on the telephone. I miss my own family, having been away only for a few days, and send an email home saying 'please phone, I'm lonely'. I doubt that I even know the meaning of the word.

The Boy Lama: 'The Lama Wars'

The young Karmapa's growing following seemed to only fuel those who opposed him to try to discredit him and his supporters. Once Ogyen Trinley Dorje was safely arrived in India, Shamar Rinpoche is quoted in *The Indian Express* on 28 January 2000 as saying that he only ever supported Tai Situ Rinpoche's candidate 'because I did not want to create trouble'.

In 1996, Shree Narayan Singh, reportedly a former monk, filed a petition in the Patna High Court using a different name. In it, he alleged that Tai Situ Rinpoche, Gyalstab Rinpoche and the Dalai Lama were engaged in anti-India activities and were agents for China. This extraordinary charge was also dismissed the following year. Singh went on to file a civil suit against the trio under the same charges.

Shree Narayan Singh filed a similar criminal complaint against the three high lamas in the office of the Chief Metropolitan Magistrate in Delhi in 1998 but the case was dismissed in January of the following year. It is worth noting that back in 1994 Tai Situ Rinpoche had been banned from entering India. The ban was revoked in July 1998, but Tai Situ Rinpoche would no longer be permitted to visit northeast India and Sikkim. Dugo Bhutia, one of the pair who filed the initial writ in Gangtok, challenged the government's revocation of the ban and Tai Situ Rinpoche's return to India, but his writ was quickly dismissed.

Shamar Rinpoche, along with two other trustees from The Karmapa Charitable Trust and the trust itself, filed a case before the High Court of Sikkim in July 1998, claiming that the state of Sikkim and Gyalstab Rinpoche had illegally dispossessed them of the trust's property, including Rumtek itself, at the incident at the monastery in August 1993. It was widely reported, around the time of Shamar filing the claim, that the trust controlled all moveable and immoveable properties of the XVIth Karmapa. The year before, Shamar Rinpoche had failed in his second attempt to get the Dalai Lama to review his decision on the recognition of Ogyen Trinley Dorje as the XVIth Karmapa's reincarnation.

Shamar was the only one of the four Rumtek regents who did not have his own monastery in Tibet and the associated wealth and power, this as a result of the actions of his predecessor (deemed treason by the Tibetan government) way back in 1793. He was, however, the nephew of the XVIth Karmapa and received many gifts from his uncle, including a monastery in Mehrauli, India. Now a wealthy man in his own right, he owns property across India and Nepal, including the substantial Galangka House in Kalimpong.

By mid-2002, Shamar Rinpoche's case was progressing somewhat, with the court upholding his demands that an inventory should be made of all the moveable properties at Rumtek Monastery. This, however, would prove somewhat controversial as many of the sacred items were in closed boxes – and had been since the death of the XVIth Karmapa – whose seals should not be broken by anyone but the XVIIth Karmapa. In 2002, Ogyen Trinley Dorje was still being denied permission to enter Sikkim. After his intervention, the inventory was able to proceed, overseen by a bank official and three representatives of both parties (that is, Shamar's people and the Karmapa's people). Shamar, despite his insistence that he should be present, was barred from the proceedings and the court deemed that certain sacred objects, such as the Karmapa's fabled, sapphire-adorned Black Hat, should not be removed from their boxes nor have the seals on those boxes broken.

On 28 September 2003, a court ruled in favour of Shamar Rinpoche's claim that the assets of Rumtek Monastery did, in fact, belong to the Karmapa Charitable Trust. The Karmapa's legal representatives contested this and the appeal was scheduled for mid-2004.

The next in the now impressive list of legal challenges came, once again, from Shree Narayan Singh, at this time known as Lama S. N. Singh. In December 2003, this suit saw the Delhi High Court issuing summonses to the Dalai Lama and the Indian government over the alleged illegal recognition of Ogyen Trinley Dorje as the Karmapa, and called for his deportation. The suit also sought a restraint upon the Dalai Lama from interfering in matters of the Karma Kagyu school. Singh alleged that Ogyen Trinley Dorje was a Chinese citizen and, as such, was being used by China as an instrument to influence the people of Sikkim. Shamar Rinpoche, in January 2004, is reported to have distanced himself from the ubiquitous Singh and the case before the courts as a result of rumours that he and Singh were somehow affiliated.

Singh further asserted that a report from a medical examination of Ogyen Trinley Dorje when he arrived in India claimed that he was much older than his 1985 birth date suggested. All bar one report in *The Hindi* newspaper (dating back to April 2000 when the Karmapa was examined by five doctors at Chandigarh) announced that the doctors pronounced the young Tibetan's health quite normal. Mick Brown, for his book, *The Dance of the 17 Lives*, himself spoke to doctors at the Chandigarh hospital and learned there was no basis for the claim.

While, to an outsider, the claims attempting to discredit Ogyen Trinley Dorje's recognition as Karmapa seem to become more shrill and less credible, they cannot have done anything to diminish the air of controversy that was created around him when he first arrived in India. What's more, they seemed to have no notable impact in terms of elevating the standing of the other 'candidate', Thaye Dorje.

16 FEBRUARY 2004

By dawn, I am finished on my yoga mat. When I look out my window, I see a fat brown owl staring in at me from the tree that is only two metres away. I don't know what the Tibetans say about owls but to me they are auspicious creatures. A couple of years ago I was determined to start a book with the words 'I saw an owl in the cheese tree and mistook truth for hope.' Now, I am more in the 'hope for truth' camp. I have such great hopes for the Karmapa; are they grounded in reality?

A beautiful young woman, Rinchen, who comes from a part of Kham close to the Karmapa's own birthplace, tells me her story. Like Pema, her parents sent her from her homeland for a Tibetan education that was not available to her in her own rural community and now she, too, works at the Norbulingka Institute. Of her seven siblings, only the two youngest of them received any schooling locally. For the first time since her arrival in India some five years ago, Rinchen has spoken to her mother on the telephone. She tells me that the woman cried constantly. Rinchen's two youngest siblings are on their way to India, currently passing through Kathmandu. Soon she will hold them in her arms; they are ten and seven years old, and they, like her, may never see their parents again. They'll go to Bir, some fifty kilometres east of Dharamsala, for schooling there. Their mother, although the children leave with her blessing and at her prompting, says she can hardly bear the loss of her three children.

I confess that I struggle with the widely accepted premise that Tibetans feel only honour, and not even a jot of regret, when a child in their family is recognised as a *tulku*. In Clemens Kuby's documentary on the Karmapa, *Living Buddha* (1996), we are told that, 'The family feels the Karmapa would have been too precious to keep for themselves and they gladly give him up for the benefit of others'.[108] We even see the family's final symbolic separation from their boy, after his enthronement as Karmapa. Far from looking glad, Loga appears bereft and bewildered.

Out in the field beyond my window, a group of Indian men squat over a day-old game of cards. Inside my room, a strange humming sound reminds me of the celestial sound of a conch shell, but it is only a bee trapped between the glass and the fly screen. I assure myself that the foetus in my womb is safely ours – mine and Paul and Isla's – for now.

THE BOY LAMA: COMING OF AGE

In June 2003, the concrete grounds of Gyuto Tantric University quickly filled with the usual crew of Tibetan and Western devotees and ogling tourists. The day was hot and the wait, for the Karmapa, was long. The temple was nearly full and the Karmapa's devotees fussed with all manner of offerings to him, in addition to the hundreds of *khatags* that had been brought for him.

When, eventually, the young Karmapa strode onto the raised dais and approached his throne, some of those who had become familiar with him noticed that his bearing was even more serious, more intent than was customary. It was his eighteenth birthday, or his nineteenth in the Tibetan reckoning (to Tibetans, during the first year of a child's life he or she is deemed to be already one). The young Tibetan attached the small microphone to his robe and cleared his throat. The room was impossibly quiet, given the great number of people it contained.

'It's my birthday today,' announced the Karmapa, as if anyone in the room needed to be told. 'For this reason, instead of giving teachings, I'd like to share a few thoughts with you.'

The Karmapa's translator repeated his master's words in English, only moments after they had been spoken in Tibetan.

'I understand that in the West one celebrates birthdays, but I cannot see anything to celebrate,' he announced. 'Birth is full of pain and life is full of pain.'

The Karmapa's devotees may have been surprised to be reminded that their master also suffered pain, despite the fact that suffering is one of Buddhist teaching's Four Noble Truths.

'I understand that it is also customary [in the West] to give birthday presents,' he continued. 'The best gift you could give me is to stop indulging in hypocrisy and deception.'

Apart from a few sharp intakes of breath, the room remained eerily silent. His Western devotees anxiously fingered the cards and trinkets they'd brought for the Karmapa.

The young man in whom the Chinese had invested so much, and in whom Tibetans now place so much hope, went on to say something along the lines of 'This is what I am surrounded by', but eyewitnesses have not been able to agree upon the exact words he used.

'For me, this is a time to remember my beloved homeland and family,' said the Karmapa.

After a few moments' silence, when all in the room remembered that so many among them had left families behind in Tibet, the Karmapa continued. 'The story is not all bad, because I have had the opportunity to know the Dalai Lama, and to see the way he has turned difficult situations to his advantage, and the way he deals with all situations with such patience.'

And thus the young Tibetan, so revered, so feted, gave his followers a rare, vivid snapshot of his life in exile. For those who like to pretend that the Karmapa's confinement to a Gelug monastery is necessary for the progress of his studies or for his own safety, the young man's words would have caused at least a moment of discomfort. For others, the feeling of sadness that had already seemed apparent around the young man became something quite tangible.[109]

17 FEBRUARY 2004

This morning I am to see the Karmapa for a so-called private audience. In reality, I expect that there will be at least half a dozen others present. With Lama Phuntsok away, I am anxious about this meeting. I have no idea whether the secretary has any idea why I wish to see his master.

As before, I shall wear the guise of a *dharma* student. I am, however, a poor semblance of such a person because I do not prostrate and nor do I bow my head sufficiently low in reverence. Of course, I could do those things; I could have my Tibetan friends rehearsing me in these rituals, but I'm not keen on taking the masquerade to such lengths for the benefit of the security personnel. Such a charade would be insulting to both the Karmapa and to his devotees who bestow these honours on their master as if by instinct.

As I failed to sleep last night, I imagined different scenarios for the audience ahead. In the first, I am ushered into the Karmapa's audience room with a whole queue of other supplicants in front of and behind me. I am permitted to present my *khatag* and to bow low, and am immediately ushered away again. The second scenario is even more troubling: in it, Indian security guards take offence to my line of questioning and eject me from the Karmapa's presence. They detain me in a cold, urine-smelling room and finally deport me. Actually, I don't mind the sound of being deported but fret over how the police will transport me from Dharamsala to Delhi. Would they drive me all the way and, if so, would they let me stop to pee (this subject is on my mind increasingly as my pregnancy progresses)? Would they confiscate my laptop with its fifty-odd thousand words about the Karmapa upon it? Would they find the letter in my room from my publisher (that I show to some of my interviewees), which makes my status as a tourist in India a sham? And so the night went on and sleep did not come . . .

When I open the curtains at dawn, my owl friend is staring back at me. She is, I have learned, an Asian Bart Owlet. I imagine the wise one is counselling me to be calm and to trust in myself. This is what I choose to take from her.

I place an early-morning call to the exile government's Department of Information and International Relations. I ask the Protocol Officer, to whom I'd been assigned during email correspondence with his department, whether he can make sure the Karmapa's secretary is aware of the work I'm doing and of the interviews I hope to undertake over the next ten days. Far from reassuring me, the Tibetan tells me what I already know: the Karmapa's office is extremely difficult – even for them – to communicate with and operates in some isolation. They, like me, phone and phone and phone and cannot reach the person in power, cannot even be certain who it is. He will try, he tells me, but is not hopeful. I wonder whether the Karmapa will have to be in exile for forty-five years before his office works as professionally as that of the Dalai Lama.

With this knot of anxiety in my chest, I think of how life must be in India for Tibetans. For me, deportation means, in essence, a fast trip home. Tibetan refugees residing in India may at best possess a Registration Certificate (RC) that has been in use since the days of the British during the Second World War; since 1980, however, the Indian government has been reluctant to issue these to Tibetans. Those who hold a cherished RC have refugee status, but may not own land or vote; essentially, they remain foreigners in India. Falling foul of the Indian authorities, if you're a Tibetan, might prompt all manner of frightening scenarios: return to Tibet and to the Chinese authorities; or a trip across the border into Nepal and to the chance of being handed over to the Chinese. While the Nepalese government hosts a Reception Centre run by the exile government for Tibetan refugees and allows many Tibetans to live in Nepal as refugees, in recent years it has appeared to bow to increasing pressure from China. Not only has Nepal banned celebrations of 10 March – Tibetan Uprising Day – in Nepal, but Tibetans have been handed over to the Chinese authorities from the Reception Centre (in one instance) and by regional Nepali police.

Even Tibetans returning to their country of their own free will may face detention upon return. I can only guess that the exile Tibetans have become just a little accustomed to the precariousness of their lives here in India. How else can I account for the refugees' easy smiles and ready laughter?

Gyuto Tantric University is bustling with activity when I arrive, the monks clearly preparing for *Losar* celebrations. There are other foreign tourists milling in the courtyard but I no longer size them up as competitors for my time with the Karmapa. I no longer have any expectations. Indeed, in the room of the grubby white sofas there are already eight people awaiting their sought-after private audiences. There's a young Ladakhi couple who look for all the world as though they're seeking a blessing for their marriage; a Tibetan mother and son, dressed in their finest, who take turns to work a set of ornate prayer beads; two Tibetan monks; and three Westerners. Yes, it is better to come without expectations. I take my gift for the Karmapa from my bag: a beautiful illustrated book on Australian art from the Art Gallery of New South Wales which I have lugged across the world with me. I would be pleased to have it on my own shelves but, at this moment, I will be even more pleased to be able to leave it with the Karmapa and carry it no further.

When we are finally invited to be searched – always a pleasure – I see that there are about two dozen Ladakhis who have been waiting outside and who will also accompany us on the seedy walk through the monastery's kitchens and up to the

Karmapa's audience room. We Westerners are asked to wait until last to step behind the golden curtain and into the Karmapa's room. The man ahead of me turns in indignation after he's taken a glimpse beyond the curtain. 'They're not prostrating!' he informs me. He then turns to ask the Tibetan monk at the door whether he, himself, might prostrate before the master. I'm only sorry that I don't manage to witness the spectacle of this extremely tall, broad-shouldered American flinging himself into full prostrations before the all-seeing young Tibetan.

When I finally walk into the Karmapa's audience room, I try not to allow myself to be too distracted by my *khatag*. The Karmapa, discerning my problem, takes it from my hands to unfurl it himself. The gift of the art book is met with only mild interest, but not complete dismissal either. The only moment of genuine contact between us today is when I ask for a blessing for my baby, pointing at my stomach where the only bump is a money belt. The Karmapa smiles almost sadly at this request, as though babies are from a world of which he is no longer a part. My request granted, I am ushered away and the next supplicant is brought before the young man.

I feel surprisingly content with my visit. While I did not win a precious interview, I was granted a blessing that will resonate long after the final copy of the book I am writing has disintegrated.

In the Gyuto grounds, I take a seat in the sun beside my favourite policewoman, the one with the baby boy. She looks at me curiously, trying to remember, before I hand her an envelope containing recent photos of Isla. She softens immediately, lingering over each image and returning to the one in which Isla's face is being licked by her dog. Her own boy is now eleven months old and she insists that she has no plans for another. After some hesitation, she confesses shyly that she will think of another baby when her son is two. I confess, also shyly, that my second child is already growing inside me. For the first time, she tells me her name, Sarna, and says she would like me to sit with her, there in the sun, and chat, but I know we've already exhausted our area of interest. As I leave she implores me, earnestly, to take care. I promise that I will.

18 FEBRUARY 2004

I am woken before six by the eerie combination of devotional music and howling wind. Rain is driving at my window with such force that I imagine it is gradually loosening the glass in its wooden frames. I wonder where my owl friend is perched this morning. Beneath the covers piled high above me, I struggle in vain to return to the mental quiet of sleep. My mind is abuzz with all the stories, snippets and rumours about the Karmapa that waft around this Himalayan domain.

With the Karmapa inaccessible to me, I know it's time to head south, back to Delhi, to try my luck there. In Lama Phuntsok's absence, I clearly need to start all over again by making new, personal contact with whoever controls the Karmapa's schedule now. *Losar*, though, is one of the busiest times in the year. I had asked Lama Phuntsok more than once whether *Losar* was a bad time to interview the Karmapa, only to receive the same, encouraging yet vague replies. I can only assume that had Lama Phuntsok been here, he would have ensured that I was granted a good proportion of the Karmapa's private audience time, of that measly one hour per day.

Yet there is still a slim chance of an audience with the Dalai Lama. In earlier correspondence with the Dalai Lama's private secretary, I had been told that the Dalai Lama had to break his winter retreat to travel briefly to Delhi. Upon his return to Dharamsala, there would be an opportunity for me to speak to the Dalai Lama before he re-entered that retreat. Our scheduled meeting has already been postponed once because his flight from Delhi was cancelled. One of the resident Westerners insists that it is he, above all others, who will speak frankly to me about his young protégé. The Dalai Lama, however, remains in Delhi, his return prevented by the very same storm that has just woken me.

In the quiet after the storm, six new guests arrive, pre-dawn, at my haven. Although I will not see any of them for nearly forty-eight hours because they remain sequestered in one room meditating, their shoes, all neatly spaced outside the room opposite mine, and their constant chanting, declare their presence.

19 FEBRUARY 2004

Today I am told by the Dalai Lama's private secretary, when I visit him in his office in the Dalai Lama's compound, that the Tibetan leader has re-entered his retreat after the interruption of the lengthened trip to Delhi. This means no private audience for me and no *Losar* photo opportunity for the film crew that has arrived from Europe with the specific purpose of capturing the Dalai Lama in action as he presides over the Tibetans' New Year celebrations.

'There are many disappointed people,' Tenzin Geyche tells me, shaking his head in concern.

Although I too am disappointed, I think 'Good on you.' I have long been concerned for the Dalai Lama's health (only because he carries such a weight of responsibility on his shoulders) and am pleased to know that he will remain in seclusion for a little longer. His well-being, both spiritual and physical, is of importance to millions of people, not only to Tibetans.

Tenzin Geyche, the Dalai Lama's long-term private secretary, is a picture of sartorial grace. With his carefully cut dark hair and his silk cravat tucked into the open neck of his shirt, he has a sophistication that is at odds with his simple office and its pot-bellied stove.

As with all conversations, I steer the one we are having towards the subject of the Karmapa. I volunteer my usual observation, that the Karmapa appears a very unhappy young man.

'Yes, His Holiness is very worried about him,' Tenzin Geyche tells me straight out.

I picture the two together, the Dalai Lama and the Karmapa,

more than forty years' age difference between the two. In every photo of the two high lamas I've seen, the tall, well-built Karmapa is hunching forward so his head is not higher than that of the Dalai Lama. Usually the Dalai Lama is clutching the younger man's hand protectively. I sigh to think that even the protection of one of the most revered spiritual figures in the world cannot bring happiness, not to mention liberty, to the boy lama.

In the evening, I talk to a pair of the guests, whom I have dubbed the chanters, while Rinchen adeptly trims their *khatags* to modest, manageable lengths for them. Does my flamboyant, hairy version of same say something about my ego, I wonder?

I ask to whom the *khatags* are to be presented, although the group's presence here at the Norbulingka Institute, only ten minutes from Gyuto Tantric University, is a clue. The Taiwanese-American woman assumes the role of spokesperson for the pair and informs me that the group has been granted an audience with the Karmapa for the following morning. 'Have you seen him?' the woman asks, somewhat proprietorially.

'Yes,' I reply. 'A couple of times.'

I try not to sound proprietorial about him myself and hesitate to offer her information about her master that she may not wish to hear.

'What was your impression of him?' the woman asks me, deftly folding *khatags*.

'He comes across as unhappy,' I offer, wincing a little at the way my words must sound to her, and saving the drop-dead-gorgeous bit for someone who'll appreciate it. 'He's also extremely impressive, clearly highly intelligent and fully realised.'

The woman looks at me quizzically; wants to know why on earth the Karmapa would be unhappy.

'He's under house arrest over there,' I tell her bluntly. 'He's like a bird in a cage . . . can't leave his quarters without asking permission first.'

She looks at me agog, as though I must be making up this outlandish story.

'He would have foreseen all this,' she tells me knowingly and after some thought, as though this somehow makes the situation all right. 'And Buddhists would say that this life is merely a brief, passing moment. All is illusion, anyway, you know.'

I will not agree with her. In fact, I'm starting to feel annoyed by her attitude. It's all very well to know the Buddhist terminology for everything, but all of those moderate, measured words don't change reality, and don't make a bad situation better.

I volunteer the woman some extra information: I am not a practitioner but a writer. The expression on her face changes immediately and she says 'oh' in a way that makes me certain that my opinion no longer counts.

Actually, when I embarked on the journey that turned into this book I thought it likely that somewhere, along the way, I would genuinely metamorphose into a *dharma* student. Oddly, Buddhism now seems less accessible to me than it did at the outset, less easily digested by the Western mind and adaptable to the Western lifestyle. I have, I understand, come to realise that while you can swot on Himalayan history and politics, and on the intricacies of a Tibetan Buddhist lineage, you cannot swot on Buddhism itself. While I have made time in my life for the XVIIth Karmapa, I remain too goal-oriented to wholeheartedly practise Buddhism.

20 FEBRUARY 2004

Today I will turn my back on the Himalayas and go to Delhi . . . I have no idea when I will return but it will be in some years, not months. At dawn, I clutch Rinchen's hand outside the Norbulingka Institute's guesthouse. I press rupees upon her, telling her to buy something for her brother and sister when they finally arrive from the Reception Centre in Kathmandu. I want to say so much more than this: that I desperately hope it is a happy reunion for her and her two youngest siblings; that I very much hope they find in India what their parents believed they would; and, finally, that Rinchen gets to hold her mother in her arms again one day.

The three-hour taxi journey from the Norbulingka Institute to Chakki Bank station (some one hundred kilometres west of Dharamsala) does not bode well for the rest of the journey. I am queasy from the very outset and the maniacal way the driver, Sheshi, propels his mini-van past any vehicle before us on the road makes me grit my teeth until I get a headache. Even when we are ten minutes from the station, with a full one-and-a-half hours to spare, Sheshi takes every single risk to get us there just that little bit sooner.

Today I ride the Malwa Express down to Delhi. I have been dreading the journey. As during my pregnancy with Isla that saw me vomiting all through Umbria where Paul and I were on a walking holiday, early morning sickness is triggered by motion. I am relieved to have a whole compartment to myself but the general filth of the train only enhances my feeling of queasiness. I lie down to read the last 300 pages of Rohinton Mistry's unspeakably sad novel, *A Fine Balance,* and the book, combined with my delicate physical state, fill me with dread about my forthcoming days in the city.

A railway official in a perfectly fitted pink turban boards the train in Jalandhar and immediately shows a paternal concern towards me. When he learns that I am from Australia, it is as though we are family; his own brother went to settle in Sydney. My protector keeps all the single men away from me – chases them off when they come to loll on the long, empty bench opposite me to scratch their balls and stare. I feel extremely ill and pray that it is not today that the vomiting starts. The train's toilets are so rancid that the thought of leaning over one of them to vomit is almost enough to set me off. If I just keep reading, I tell myself, all will be well – and, as it turns out, this is the case.

I stare out the train's window unhappily as we reach the outskirts of Delhi. The shantytowns between the tracks make me heavy with melancholy. In these final minutes of my journey, all my doubts about my project, and about the XVIIth Karmapa, come crashing in. Do I still believe in him? Can he lead his people into the future? I hold my aching head in my hands and concede that I no longer know.

If anything, my two recent glimpses of the man conjure the impression of someone who has lost control of his destiny. So much for sitting at his feet for a fortnight!

Once the train pulls into New Delhi Station and I disembark, I follow the instructions I've been given closely. I do not leave the platform, despite the rat that scuttles past my feet and the fact that all my fellow passengers are quickly striking out for the exits at either end of the platform. As directed, I hold my ground right before the carriage in which I've ridden so unhappily. A group of Western businessmen pass me and one turns back, suggesting kindly that I should come with them. I thank the man and tell him that I am to be collected but, even from a metre away, he must hear the doubt in my voice. Red-clad porters approach me again and again, and single men, loitering, eye me with undisguised fascination. Nearly half an hour after my train arrived, and with night having settled around me as I wait, a man arrives bearing a sign saying 'Ms Goby Naher, Malwa Express'. I want to kiss him and will not hear his apologies about being late. He then takes my suitcase and sets off down the platform at breakneck speed. That's fine, I can keep up on the clear platform. Once we leave the platform, however, I have to push against the great human tide to even keep him in sight. I notice that my solicitous driver does not look back for me once.

At Mr Nath's Hotel, on the prestigious Prithviraj Road, I try to relax. Although I cannot see the grounds properly in the dark, I catch a glimpse of a painstakingly laid-out vegetable garden. There is no sign of the promised swimming pool, although later I learn it is discreetly enclosed, making it, perhaps, the only place in India where one might dare to swim nude. Mr Nath introduces me to his five dogs, although I will only remember one of their names: that of Jackie, the old German shepherd. My room is at the very front of the sprawling bungalow built by Mr Nath's father in 1934, and, to my mind, somehow open to the world with the road only twenty metres away. Having already asked to be moved from the noisy room next to the kitchen, I return to Mr Nath to ask him, in a timid, young girl's voice that I barely recognise, whether it's safe out there, at the front of his great big house near the road.

'Oh yes,' he tells me in a wise-old-man-of-the-sea tone, 'it's very, very safe. There's a night-watchman and then, of course, there are all my doggies.'

Feeling very, very reassured, I return to my room, with my stomach growling and my head pounding, to wash away the grime of the journey.

21 FEBRUARY 2004

Deepak Thakur, Deepak Thakur. I heard this name again and again in connection with the Karmapa while I was in Dharamsala. In the absence of a frank conversation with the Dalai Lama – which never eventuated – about the Karmapa's situation, I become convinced that it is only Deepak Thakur, the Karmapa's lawyer, who might be able to explain to me exactly why the eighteen-year-old lama is trapped up there in the Himalayan foothills. Thakur started working for the XVIIth Karmapa back in August 2002, leaving the firm at which he'd been an associate in order to do so. I believe that it is only Thakur – whose own connection with the Karmapa is said to date back to his student days when he met the XVIth Karmapa in Sikkim – who might tell me what lies ahead for his client. What I really want to know is when the Karmapa will be free . . .

When I phoned Deepak Thakur from my room at the Norbulingka Institute, I was surprised that he agreed, almost immediately, to see me during my time in Delhi. I have, it seems, come to expect obstacles during my time in India. I will later learn that while Thakur rarely speaks to journalists he's willing to speak to writers in the belief that their research is serious, methodical and sound. I'm glad that I'm unaware of these expectations before our meeting, to which I come clutching a handful of wild rumours regarding the Karmapa's legal situation.

Speculation surrounding the Karmapa's legal battle is as follows: that it concerns control of the Karmapa Charitable Trust, which takes in all of the XVIth Karmapa's property worth millions of US dollars; that it is only about control of Rumtek Monastery; that it seeks to establish the 'true identity' of the XVIIth Karmapa; that it will establish whether Ogyen Trinley Dorje is or is not a spy working for China; that it will decide upon whether the Dalai Lama has interfered in the internal workings of another Tibetan Buddhist school; and, finally, that it will establish whether Ogyen Trinley Dorje is eighteen or twenty-eight.

Deepak Thakur comes to speak with me in the grounds of Mr Nath's hotel. We sit on a lawn out the back, surrounded by flowering shrubs and Mr Nath's roses, far from the noise of Prithviraj Road. Only the antics of the old dogs can distract me from the lawyer's riveting tale.

The lawyer, I have been told, comes from India's ruling class, his white-flecked black moustache turned up at the ends accordingly. His voice is deeply resonant, his speech moderate and assured. For all this, he is relaxed, courteous and friendly, granting me a chunk of his Saturday afternoon that must be precious time away from his two daughters.

We start with small talk, Thakur telling me about his meeting with the previous Karmapa in October 1978. He describes the XVIth as 'very profound' and a man of 'many great qualities', most of which he did not display because of his own sense of discretion.

As my line of questioning is along the tell-me-everything theme, I'm grateful that Thakur knows exactly where we should start. He launches into an explanation of the Tsurphu *labrang*, the Karmapa's administration, saying that it has continued since the time of the first Karmapa in the twelfth century. I sense that each word is weighed before it is spoken.

'In 1959, when the previous Karmapa came out of Tibet, he came out not just himself but along with his *labrang*, his officers. This *labrang* continued to function while they were in India at Rumtek Monastery.' He goes on to explain that the Karmapa, or the institution of the Karmapa, is regarded in the common law system as a corporation 'to avoid the necessity of transferring property from one Karmapa to the next successive Karmapa'. I am bemused that lawyers in India are arguing to apply the law of corporations to the inscrutable domain of reincarnation.

We go on to discuss the now somewhat infamous Karmapa Charitable Trust, Thakur telling me that it had been established in 1961 by a total of fourteen settlers in Sikkim. These included twelve individuals living in Sikkim as well as the Karmapa in two different guises. Not only was he a party to the trust deed in his personal capacity, but also in his capacity as head of the Tsurphu *labrang*. The trust established a fund 'for the benefit of the followers of the Karmapa and the Karmapa himself' that might be used in funding schools, retreat centres, libraries, health care and so on. Thakur stresses that the only property ever conveyed to the trust by the fourteen parties to the deed was just over 250,000 rupees back in 1961. Presently, the trustees include Shamar and Tai Situ Rinpoches. On his twenty-first birthday, the Karmapa himself will become sole trustee.

Over raucous birdcalls and the slightly removed roar of the Delhi traffic, Thakur explains that when the Karmapa died in 1981 there was no document that conveyed any additional funds or property to the Charitable Trust. And this, I come to see, is at the heart of the fierce legal battle. The seventy-five acres of land, for instance, on which Rumtek Monastery stands, given to the Karmapa by the King of Sikkim in 1961, was never conveyed to the trust. In his status as a corporation, land owned by one Karmapa, and his other assets too, should automatically transfer to the next Karmapa.

'The claim of the Karmapa Charitable Trust – that they have the right to possess and control all the properties of the Karmapa simply because he was one of the settlers of the trust – is really far-fetched,' Thakur contends. He tells me that the only document on which those of the trustees who have become the plaintiffs rely to substantiate their claim is the initial trust deed of 1961.

I find myself agreeing with the lawyer. The way he's explained things, the claim – being made by a couple of the trustees, including Shamar – certainly seems far-fetched. Clearly, however, the claimants made the case sound quite different because they won a preliminary hearing, the outcome of which is still to be challenged by the Karmapa and his *labrang*.

Our conversation is interrupted by the spectacle of the feeding of Mr Nath's five dogs. One of Mr Nath's employees strides onto the lawn on which we are sitting, closely attended by the excited hounds. He carries large plates of meaty gruel. The lawyer's finessed account is drowned out by the clamour of hungrily yapping dogs and then by Mr Nath's booming proclamation that 'Dinner has been served!' It is only once the dogs settle contentedly to their meals – albeit closely watched by a small flock of glossy black crows – that Deepak Thakur and I can return to the tale in which we have both become enmeshed.

Thakur goes on to explain that the claimants assert that they were dispossessed of all the properties controlled by the trust by the Sikkimese government and Gyalstab Rinpoche on 2 August 1993. He adds that none of the trustees who form the group of claimants was even present at Rumtek – where the alleged dispossession took place – on the date in question when Tai Situ and Gyalstab Rinpoches attended Rumtek to conduct the ceremony for the rainy season retreat and were denied entry to the main Shrine Hall. The only trustee present was Tai Situ Rinpoche, who is not one of the claimants.

The claimants do not explain, Thakur tells me, how removing the key for the Shrine hall from one monk and giving it to another could possibly entail the dispossession of a whole parcel of immoveable and moveable properties, but this is what they assert, nonetheless. In fact, a Sikkimese government official took the key from one monk of the Tsurphu *labrang* and gave it to Gyalstab and Tai Situ, who in turn gave it to another monk of the Tsurphu *labrang*. Clearly the moment represents a watershed in the power struggle that had already been bubbling away between the regents since their master's death, some twelve years beforehand.

Another battle over assets is playing out before me as Deepak Thakur speaks. The German shepherd, Jackie, has set aside the large bone that was in her gruel. No doubt she will get to this later, perhaps burying it first and waiting until it is particularly ripe. A large black crow, however, is sidling towards the trophy that clearly, rightfully, belongs to the noble Jackie.

Thakur now explains to me, at some length, the series of events that led to the recognition of Ogyen Trinley Dorje as Karmapa. He also describes Shamar Rinpoche's attempts to have the Dalai Lama recognise his own candidate.

What Shamar and others who oppose Ogyen Trinley Dorje's candidacy seemed to want but could not get from the Dalai Lama was legitimacy for their own 'candidate' for Karmapa. Presumably with that legitimacy would have come control of the Karmapa's personal assets, thus rendering the issue of temporary control of the Karmapa Charitable Trust an irrelevance. Thakur explains that what they require is judicial recognition for the claims of the trust, not only over these properties, but over their claim of Thaye Dorje's title.

'I say this because their desire is to perpetuate their control over all these properties . . . They are the ones to say that Thaye Dorje is the Karmapa. Even though when he comes of age at twenty-one years he would assume his status of sole trustee of the trust once again, in reality, since he would be in their control and under their influence, they would continue to have control over the properties even after that.

Thakur goes on to tell me that Shamar Rinpoche and his associates only pursued their suit actively once the Karmapa was granted refugee status in India. No longer could they divide the claims of the two candidates between occupied Tibet and the so-called free world.

Thakur wishes to clear up a commonly held misapprehension. 'The suit doesn't talk about the identity or status of the XVIIth Karmapa. Nor is there any claim in the suit that the court should decide as to the identity of the XVIIth Karmapa. We don't say that the court should decide; for us, the Dalai Lama's sanction is the final word and the recognition and acceptance of the XVIIth Karmapa by all the high *rinpoches* of the Kagyu lineage.'

When I inquire about what happens should the Karmapa win

the case vis-à-vis travelling to Rumtek, Thakur explains that as the restrictions on Ogyen Trinley Dorje are political the outcome of the case will have no real impact. As a foreigner in India, the Karmapa's movements may always be restricted. He also tells me, they have been advised, although not in writing, that the Karmapa should not seek the Indian government's permission to travel abroad. 'Until such a time as this unverifiable direction has changed, we won't make any approach to the government to ask them to allow him to leave again.'

My mind is reeling at the complexity of the Karmapa's situation and the lawyer has clearly given me a very full account. Once our interview has concluded and I've switched off the tape recorder, Deepak Thakur relaxes a little and is now prepared to chat less formally about his client. When I mention that many see leadership potential in the young Karmapa, the worldly lawyer beams delight at me. He clearly agrees.

We leave our seats on Mr Nath's idyllic rose-bordered lawn and I walk to Deepak's car. The Karmapa's case seems a great responsibility for just one person but this beautifully spoken lawyer does not appear in the slightest bit daunted.

After his departure, I return to the lawn where the dogs now recline in full-bellied contentment. I wish I could feel such simple contentment. Although Deepak Thakur is utterly convincing, there are clearly so many factors keeping Ogyen Trinley Dorje from truly living as Karmapa and fulfilling his destiny to spread the *dharma*. Not only are there those who will employ every measure in order to ensure that the assets of the previous Karmapa will not fall easily into his hands, but a favourable decision in the courts may only change his status marginally.

22 FEBRUARY 2004

True to my method, bowerbird style, I travel all over Delhi in search of snippets about the Karmapa. These usually take the form of anecdotes and wise insights, but the way I gather them, almost haphazardly, makes me feel like a bird swooping.

Today I will visit a former exile government employee who, I've been told by one of my Dharamsala contacts, knows the Karmapa well. Mr Nath's driver takes me out to Lajpat Nagar, one of Delhi's suburbs, in fierce mid-morning heat. After the drive of some half an hour from Prithviraj Road, we make numerous sweeps around blocks identified only by a single letter. The roads are pot-holed and dusty and I wonder whether lying across the back seat will make me less queasy.

Jamyang Dorjee's apartment is up a couple of flights of stairs from the street, its interior all cool white stone. A vast bowl of *kapsi* on the coffee table before me reminds me that I've interrupted the family's New Year holiday.

I am given sweet, milky Tibetan tea by Jamyang Dorjee's teenaged daughter, who does not need to be asked to perform this courtesy. A Tibetan with some white in his longish hair, Jamyang Dorjee wears a Free Tibet T-shirt and jeans, and immediately puts me at my ease. His career has seen him in the employ of the Sikkimese government and the exile (Tibetan) government's Department of Religion. At the time of the Karmapa's arrival in India, Dorjee was director of the Dharamsala-based Tibetan Institute of Performing Arts (TIPA). In his directorial capacity, while at TIPA, he hosted the event at which the Karmapa first spoke publicly.

Dorjee tells me of one of his earliest meetings with the Karmapa, when the young lama asked him whether TIPA might create a musical score for some poetry he had written while fleeing Tibet.

'The Karmapa said that we must take into consideration – when we make the music – that it must have an element of sadness and happiness to it, because he wrote this poem sitting under a tree, en route to Mustang when he was trekking, under a very sad situation,' Dorjee tells me. 'It was the reflection of a dream he'd had the previous night. He said that this poem had been told to him by a white goddess who came from a cloud with a lot of music.'

The Karmapa had explained to Jamyang Dorjee that the music must have an element of sadness because the situation under which he was writing the poem was 'really pathetic'. It should have an element of happiness because every step that he was taking was towards freedom. And towards the Dalai Lama.

Apparently the director and a group of musicians went to Gyuto, not long afterwards, to play the music they had composed for the Karmapa.

'I was surprised that as he was listening he was writing musical notes,' Dorjee muses. 'He gave my musician this musical note and said, "This is for the flute." He said that when people have tension, this music would be good for relieving it. Those who came with him from Tibet, they were equally surprised because they said he never practised these musical notes. There are a few people in TIPA itself who can read these musical notes, but he wrote these musical notes which our musicians played on the flute.'

Some would insist that the Karmapa writing a musical score when he had never been taught music clearly indicated that he was displaying a skill from one of his previous incarnations. Others might argue that it indicated, quite simply, an exceptional aptitude for music. Whichever the case, it is difficult not to be deeply impressed.

Jamyang Dorjee speaks of his growing admiration for the young man, saying that he used to go to visit him regularly. 'Every time I saw him, every time I met him, I felt, here is this man who's got so much commitment for his nation, because when he talks about Tibet – "My Tibet!" – he becomes very emotional; I've seen it.'

I feel a pang of regret that I myself have not seen this passionate, political side of the Karmapa and I tell Jamyang Dorjee as much. He goes on to recount another anecdote to me.

'Tashi Tsering [of Amnye Machen Institute, Tibetan Centre for Advanced Studies] and myself were with him once and Tashi Tsering showed him a Tibetan Children's Village magazine.' A pained expression crosses Dorjee's face. 'They had dedicated this magazine to the flight of His Holiness the Karmapa. This magazine also talked about saving the white crane in Tibet. Since it was in English, Tashi explained this to His Holiness. The Karmapa said, "They are trying to save the white crane in Tibet?" He then tossed the magazine aside in disgust.

"'They can't save human beings," the Karmapa said. "Why would they save white cranes? There's not freedom for human beings. What's the use of talking about freedom for white cranes?"'

I imagine the force behind these words as that of the concentrated rage of a caged lion.

Jamyang Dorjee goes on to tell me with the zeal of a visionary about the new NGO he has recently created and will run himself. He has set up as something of a vocational guidance officer for young Tibetans and will try to help them find work in their chosen field, even before they have commenced their tertiary studies. This is not Dorjee's only endeavour. He also works for the Karmapa.

Before I leave, Jamyang Dorjee gives me copies of the Karma Kagyu magazine that he edits, *Dharma Nectar*, and instructs his son, Thupten, to offer me a copy of his novel. Thupten wrote *Anything for Tibet, My Beloved Country* when he was only a high school student. Jamyang Dorjee's apartment seems to crackle with the passion of his causes.

As I am driven back to Mr Nath's guesthouse, I find myself overwhelmed by sadness. I cannot shake the image of the Karmapa, aged only fourteen, on his self-proclaimed walk 'towards freedom'. That journey, for him, has not yet reached an end.

23 FEBRUARY 2004

On my last day in Delhi, I meet the man who became the Karmapa's spokesperson on his arrival in India, and who continues to act as conduit between the young Tibetan and the exile government. Tashi Wangdi is now the Dalai Lama's representative in Delhi, but at the time of the Karmapa's arrival in India was a *Kalon*, or minister, for the exile government's Department of Religion and Cultural Affairs.

I was to have interviewed Tashi Wangdi on my previous trip, also on my last day in India, but when my flight from Bagdora was delayed I ran out of time. Over the interim months, we have exchanged emails. I had harboured some notion of seeking clarification of the Karmapa's situation, vis-à-vis security, from the Indian government and was advised that Tashi Wangdi might direct me to the appropriate official. In reply to my initial query, he advised me that all security surrounding the Karmapa was for his own safety and counselled me not to read any other motive into it. Wangdi further advised me to correspond with the Joint Secretary of the East Asia Division of the Indian Ministry of External Affairs on the subject. The fact that he gave me neither a name nor an address made me certain he felt this was not a good idea. Conversations I had subsequently with those who know a good deal more than I about Indian bureaucracy, led me to believe that not only would such an inquiry mean no return Indian visa for me, but it would bear no fruit.

Wangdi agrees to see me on the third day of the Tibetan year, one of the *Losar* holidays. On the basis of our brief email correspondence, I am convinced that he will adhere to the most diplomatic of lines on the Karmapa. I arrive at his office at Lajpat Nagar on a hot, dusty afternoon, nursing many reservations and expecting – I admit! – to disbelieve him.

Wangdi has come from an official function and is wearing his grey *chupa* over his business trousers and shirt, but he has released his arms from the coat so the whole thing hangs loosely from the belt at his waist. I cannot help but think of the adaptations, of the compromises, Tibetans living in India make every day. Despite this casual gesture, he still appears elegant; he is long and lean and wears a carefully groomed goatee and moustache. I am feeling ill and am extremely grateful for the glass of Coke that appears before me. We sit in a pair of armchairs in a simple, cool office. We are far from the madding crowd that is Delhi and I am surprised to find that every fibre in my body wants to relax in this man's fatherly presence. Above the diplomat's desk is a delightful photo of the youthful XIVth Dalai Lama, taken around the time he came into exile. The youthful hope that is so apparent on the Tibetan leader's face in the photograph can, remarkably, still be seen there today.

The diplomat dives straight into the discussion from where we left off in our emails, telling me that he really doesn't think that the things that have happened to the Karmapa since his arrival – whether the Karmapa is allowed to visit Rumtek or not, for instance – are terribly important.

'There are other things about his own views, about Buddhism and Buddhist culture, about what he hopes to achieve as a religious leader – as a Tibetan and his visions about the world and humanity,' Tashi Wangdi tells me. 'I think those are the things that are important.'

I find myself nodding inadvertently in agreement and disarmed by such simple wisdom.

'Of course, these last few have been rather difficult years but I'm quite sure that things will work out . . .' Wangdi smiles and, for a moment, I think that's all he's prepared to say about the Karmapa.

I comment, a little too pointedly, that he's just made a most diplomatic statement. Wangdi argues against this assessment, insisting that his sentiments are genuine. I prompt him by commenting that despite the prospect of problems resolving themselves in the future, what exists now is a binding controversy.

'Who's Karmapa or who's not Karmapa is not the question, because it's for the Tibetans,' he emphasises, and I'm the first to agree with him. 'On a larger scale, there is no dispute. No other government has the right or power into this affair. This is beyond their constitutional authority. It's a religious matter – so no government can do that [intervene], except that unfortunately the Chinese try to. So there are no external factors in it. Then, on a larger scale, Buddhists, particularly Tibetans, basically follow what His Holiness [the Dalai Lama] says. And lastly, in the long run, the person himself has to prove it.'

This last comment echoes what I've heard from other

Tibetans. That is, that the real Karmapa's virtues and talents will become so apparent that nobody will doubt his identity.

Tashi Wangdi goes on to tell me that he doesn't think many of the Tibetans in Delhi support Shamar Rinpoche's candidate and he certainly doesn't know any who attended Thaye Dorje's enthronement. He is, though, careful to explain that the same Tibetans have nothing against Shamar Rinpoche. Wangdi himself treats Shamar Rinpoche just like any other Tibetan lama – with respect – and asserts that Shamar Rinpoche is well within his rights to believe that somebody else is Karmapa.

Why then, if all this is so clear-cut, may the Karmapa not go to Rumtek, in Sikkim? I suggest to Wangdi that the restriction indicates, in fact, that the Indian government has taken a side in the 'Lama Wars'. Wangdi tells me quite firmly that the Indian government is not influenced by different factions in the Tibetan community, but that it is motivated by larger issues. It does not, he stresses, have an unsympathetic attitude towards Tibetans or the Karmapa.

I decide to mine the spy-theory vein, asking the diplomat whether there's any chance the Indian government harbours suspicions about the Karmapa's motives. Wangdi remains utterly unphased by my line of questioning. His calm features give no hint that he might be annoyed.

'I don't think so. Him being a spy or him being this or that . . . I don't think so. How can a fifteen-year-old be a spy? If you were to search in the world for those who were the best informed about Tibet – the Tibetan situation, Tibetan people – the Indian government would be the best government.'

Wangdi goes on to tell me that he does not believe that the Karmapa feels personal frustration at his circumstances and, once again, I feel myself squinting a little in disbelief. The diplomat's theory is that any unhappiness the Karmapa might feel is for the people around him who are worried and disheartened. He's referring to the people who left Tibet with the Karmapa and who have sacrificed so much. I cannot disregard this suggestion, nor can I disregard Wangdi's assertion that the Karmapa has the ability to see the bigger picture.

I venture one last political question, wanting to know

whether most of the Indian government's decisions surrounding the Karmapa were made with a view of protecting its relationship with China.

Tashi Wangdi argues that this is far from the case, asserting that India's decision to give refugee status to the Karmapa would have been more annoying to China than just about any other course of action the Indian government could have chosen. Allowing the Karmapa such proximity to the Dalai Lama would have been all the more galling to China. The Indians, Wangdi argues, could have been complicit with China's claims that the Karmapa was still theirs, that he had only come to India to get his Black Hat.

I am too tired to argue subterfuge with the diplomat and am convinced that he's confident about everybody's good faith. So, what of the future, I want to know; what does Wangdi make of the Karmapa's potential?

The diplomat visibly relaxes. He beams as he tells me that he thinks the Karmapa is an extraordinary person and has always been impressed by him. Wangdi had expected that when the Karmapa arrived in India he would have needed an enormous amount of guidance, having come from such a sheltered background. Clearly, though, this was not the case. The Karmapa, apparently, consistently arrived at deep, far-sighted and mature decisions.

Tashi Wangdi explains that he has a son who is about the same age as the Karmapa, and that he often wondered how the boy would cope in a similar situation.

'It's been very difficult for him. I'm not a very religious man. I mean, I'm a Buddhist and for me it's the most important philosophy of life,' he confides, and I cannot help but look up at the Dalai Lama's photo as he says this, before he goes on to tell me that he's not 'that into' reincarnation, but just takes people for what they are. 'So I react at a personal level. And, in that way, because of my reaction to the Karmapa, I'm very impressed and have very high hopes.'

I turn off my tape recorder and tell Tashi Wangdi, as something of an afterthought, that I too have the highest hopes for the Karmapa. This comment produces a winning smile and I realise that Wangdi must have been wondering all along exactly where my sympathies lay.

When I leave the diplomat's office, I mull over his words during the course of the slow drive through the afternoon heat. The Tibetan diplomats responsible for the exile community's relationship with the Indian government have an unenviable role. They are charged with maintaining good relations with the country who was the first to sell out on Tibet (when India signed the *Panch Sheela* agreement with China) and yet which hosts the largest number of exile Tibetans, by far, anywhere in the world.

I dearly want to believe that the Indian government has only good intentions towards the courageous young Tibetan. I desperately want to believe that the Karmapa has not, in his dramatic flight from Tibet, merely become someone else's pawn. Like my views on the subject of reincarnation, however, I'm going to need an awful lot of convincing.

24 FEBRUARY 2004

Dear reader, I had hoped to give you a different ending. I had hoped that by the end of my own journey the Karmapa's would also have reached some sort of conclusion. This, alas, is not the case. As I, with my largely unappreciated freedom to come and go, fly into and out of Delhi (I'm currently flying in darkness, a couple of hours after take-off), the XVIIth Gyalwa Karmapa sits in his rooms atop Gyuto Tantric University, watching for the winds of change.

I, neither political analyst nor forecaster, cannot predict what will precipitate this change. Perhaps, as Kalon Tripa Samdhong Rinpoche told me, it is only a matter of time. I wait, with keen anticipation, for the signs that will herald some semblance of freedom for the Karmapa: permission to travel to Rumtek, or even to travel beyond India. I long to know that he has reached the destination, freedom, for which the Karmapa was headed when he left Tibet.

In the coming months, I will watch for those winds myself with such hope. Three days after my return home, I will read that the Karmapa has publicly stated that 'Tibet is India's problem'. When he is further quoted as saying that India, 'a big and powerful nation can do much more for the Tibetan cause',[110] I give a muted cheer. Brave, brave man.

What of my own journey and this strange endpoint? Yes, I am frustrated that I've travelled to India to sit at the guru's feet and have not done so this time. Yes, I'm annoyed, disappointed and very humbled but, at a certain level, I wonder what else one can expect. Ogyen Trinley Dorje is on a meteoric trajectory, yet, all the while, his physical journey is utterly stalled. Many of those who know the Karmapa personally share my awe for him. Each of them seems to happily grasp the words 'future leader' when I prompt them.

In writing of the XVIIth Karmapa, I have had to rely more than I'd ever hoped upon stories that others have told about Ogyen Trinley Dorje. I have a vision, however, of how the story of the XVIIth Karmapa will spread through the world and is already doing so. It comes from moments of footage from his enthronement, images that will never leave me.

The camera takes its vantagepoint from high above the gathered crowd, at the rear of the main courtyard of Tsurphu Monastery. In the footage, Tibetans and visitors alike are throwing their *khatags* high into the air, in the direction of the monastery's entrance. Each time a *khatag* falls towards the earth, it is grasped by another pair of hands, further forward in the crowd, and flung heavenwards again. Seen in fast motion, this scene might look like a cloud of celestial matter, passing hand to hand towards the monastery and the young Karmapa. Run in reverse, the footage might resemble the way the XVIIth Karmapa's story is being told. Passed from hand to hand, snippets from his life, stories of his visions and his fearless words might be disseminated as majestically, as poignantly, out into the world.

If the story I have told serves as yet another vehicle for the extraordinary tale of this courageous young Tibetan, I shall feel some satisfaction. Whatever happens, on the birth of my second child, I shall look into his or her eyes and remember Loga and her baby Apo Gaga in their yak-hair tent in Kham. And I will also remember all the other Tibetans who have been separated from their families during the last fifty years. I will hope, fervently, for the reunion of those who remain.

TIBET: TOWARDS THE FUTURE

For those Tibetans who might have taken hope from the enthronement of the Karmapa in 1992, newly held notions that the current Chinese government was genuinely supportive of their faith might have been smashed as early as 1993. It was in autumn of that year that the communists held their Third National Forum on Work in Tibet, at which a whole new anti-Dalai Lama campaign was launched. The 'cultural containment' policies that emerged from the Forum were, alas, reminiscent of the Cultural Revolution. It was around this time that it became clear that the Karmapa's teachers, Tai Situ and Gyalstab Rinpoches, would not have the access to him that they had been promised.

Late 1993 also saw the end of formal contact, for the time being, between Beijing and the exiled Tibetans. Indeed, it was on 4 September that the Dalai Lama published the correspondence associated with that contact, claiming that all hope for future discussion had now been extinguished.

In ongoing modernisation policies affecting Tibetan nomads that commenced in the late eighties, the Chinese authorities demanded the fencing and distribution of nomad pastures in a bid to raise production. After the settlement of some 56,000 of the 100,000 nomad households in the TAR's Qinghai Province and the fencing of 600,000 hectares of grassland, a Xinhua report called the living style of the nomads 'outdated' and asserted that it was inefficient, in terms of land usage, could not cope with natural disasters, nor aid 'social' modernisation.[111] This attitude is very much in keeping with that of Chinese scientists who assert that traditional nomadic pastoralism causes environmental degradation and devastation to livelihoods in the wake of natural disasters.[112] Indeed, another Xinhua report saw one Chinese official predicting the end to nomadic life in China by the end of the twentieth century.[113] There are persuasive arguments to suggest, however, that the nomads' grazing techniques – developed over centuries – are perfectly suited to the survival of both their stock and delicate pastures.

The next great threat to Tibetans' way of life came by way of the launch of China's Western Development Plan by Jiang Zemin in 1999. It called for 32,000 kilometres worth of new roads, thousands of kilometres of new railways, and a swathe of dams, factories, mining facilities, power plants, and oil and gas pipelines in China's western provinces, which include Tibet. Under the Western Development Plan, foreign investors have been lured to the region with various perks, including tax incentives and customs exemptions.

Not only does the Western Development Plan aim to bring development and prosperity to the regions in question – some three-fifths of China's territory – but it also strives to 'stabilise local society and contribute to China's unity'.[114] Another Chinese official described the Plan as having 'extremely high importance in solving China's current nationality problem'.[115] This so-called problem includes the Tibetans' ongoing struggle for self-determination.

To Tibetans, the Western Development Plan will only enhance China's colonial control over Tibet by building infrastructure and facilitating the migration of more Chinese. Rather than benefiting those in the affected regions, this type of development will transport Tibet's wealth to the east.

Despite sentiments expressed by the Dalai Lama in 1993, all hope of dialogue between Beijing and the exile Tibetans has not ended, after all. In September 2002, four exile Tibetans, including two of the Dalai Lama's envoys, travelled to China and Tibet in what was seen at the time as a significant development. In a statement released after the envoys' return to Dharamsala, Lodi Gyari, Special Envoy of the Dalai Lama to the US, described the trip as an attempt to 'create a conducive atmosphere enabling direct face-to-face meetings on a regular basis in the future'.[116] The goal is to arrive at a 'mutually acceptable solution' to the Tibet issue by way of the Dalai Lama's 'Middle Way Approach' that calls for 'genuine autonomy' for Tibetans within Tibet.

In May 2003, a second delegation of the Dalai Lama's envoys again travelled to China and afterwards issued a similar statement about the visit. After the second visit, two outstanding issues remained unresolved: China's demand for acknowledgment (from the Dalai Lama) of Taiwan as part of the PRC and determining whether any future dialogue would apply to all Tibetan regions or just the TAR. At the time of writing, Chinese rhetoric continues to claim that the Dalai Lama seeks only independence for his people rather than the 'genuine autonomy' he has called for, ever since his address to the European parliament in June 1988. There's a rumour that a third Tibetan delegation may visit Tibet in October 2004.

More than fifty years after China's occupation, Tibet remains under Chinese control and Tibetans are persecuted for the crime of owning a photograph of the Dalai Lama (since a policy reversal in May 1996). As a result of China's occupation, it is estimated that between 500,000 and 1.2 million Tibetans have lost their lives. Six thousand monasteries have been destroyed. Between 130,000 and 140,000 Tibetans live in exile in India, Nepal and a handful of Western nations, while an estimated 2500 Tibetans flee Tibet each year.

In the face of blatant human rights abuse in Tibet, Western leaders fall over themselves in their kowtowing to their Chinese counterparts. In their relationships with China, no word is more highly revered than trade.

THE BOY LAMA: AN AFTERWORD

In the wake of my second trip to India, I endeavour to conduct a somewhat circuitous correspondence with the Karmapa. Through two helpful third parties, he agrees to answer a couple of questions that I never had the opportunity to ask him in February.

A number of us await the correspondence from Gyuto with collective bated breath. My publisher says it's like awaiting a letter from God and I know exactly what she means.

When the replies reach me, finally, I do not know whether to be pleased or disappointed. They confirm what I already know.

While the Karmapa's is a story about courage and faith, it is also that of a classic quest for freedom. Hidden between the handful of other everyday questions, I wrote the following to the Karmapa:

'I have heard that when Your Holiness left Tibet, you believed that you were walking to freedom. What is your impression of this imagined freedom?'

The reply, in his own words, goes like this:

'I have gained an experience of myself. We all have a wish for a better situation than of the past. But then in the world of today, fulfilment of such wishes is difficult. Even if one's past situation was poor, it is necessary one have "*som-shey*", a conscious understanding of it.'[117]

Randwick, 24 June 2004

ENDNOTES

1   'Karmapa leaves Tibet', Tibet Information Network (TIN), 7/1/00

2   Isabel Hilton, 'Mishandling lamas', *The Guardian*, 10/1/00

3   Clemens Kuby, from his commentary in the film *Living Buddha*, Mind Films, 1996

4   Tsering Shakya, *Dragon in the Land of Snows*, p. xxii

5   Warren Smith, *Tibetan Nation*, p. 17

6   Nick Douglas and Meryl White, *Karmapa: the Black Hat Lama of Tibet*

7   Michele Martin, her own translation as it appeared in *Music in the Sky*

8   Kagyu Office's Karmapa website, www.kagyuoffice.com

9   Martin, p. 23

10 Martin, p. 24

11 Summary of World Broadcasts (SWB), 1949, No. 17, p. 21

12 Shakya, p. 19

13 Shakya, p. 25

14 Martin, p. 24

15 Martin, p. 24

16 Martin, p. 27

17 BBC Summary of World Broadcasts 1950, No. 77. p. 39

18 Shakya, p. 31

19 Dalai Lama, *Freedom in Exile*, pp. 63–64

20 Patrick French in his book *Tibet, Tibet*, eloquently illustrates this term – 'the mind's Tibet' – which was initially used by English poet, Sir Henry Newbolt, a schoolmate of Sir Francis Younghusband

21 Martin, p. 31

22 Dalai Lama, pp. 68–69

23 Smith, p. 321

24 Clemens Kuby

25 Martin, p. 36

26 Shakya, p. 92

27 *Daily Telegraph* (London), 28/4/01

28 Kagyu Thubten Chöling, *Karmapa, The Sacred Prophecy* p. 25

[29] Clemens Kuby

[30] Jamgon Kongtrul Rinpoche told Clemens Kuby that he believed the prediction letter produced by Tai Situ Rinpoche would lead the regents to the XVIIth Karmapa.

[31] conversation with Deepak Thakur, Delhi, 21/2/04

[32] Shakya, p. 119

[33] John F. Avedon, *In Exile from the Land of Snows*, p. 46

[34] Avedon, p. 70

[35] Dalai Lama, p. 108

[36] Kagyu Thubten Chöling, p. 79

[37] Mick Brown, *The Dance of 17 Lives: the Incredible True Life Story of Tibet's 17th Karmapa*

[38] Tibet Information Network News (TIN) Update, 7/1/00

[39] *Xinhua*, 27/1/99

[40] 'Buddhist teacher, 14, flees Chinese rule', *The New York Times*, 7/1/00

[41] Dexter Filkins, 'Lama's flight offers hope for Beijing accord', *The Los Angeles Times*, 8/1/00

[42] Isabel Hilton, 'Flight of the lama', *The New York Times*, 12/3/00

[43] Shakya, p. 189

[44] Dalai Lama, p. 162

[45] Agence France Presse, 26/8/03

[46] Martin, p. 55

[47] A *puja* is a ceremonial offering that could take the form of something material, such as flowers or food, or of something associated with speech or mind such as prayer. A *tsok*, or *tsog*, is also an offering that may or may not be given during a *puja*.

[48] Jamgon Kongtrol Labrang, 'EMA HO!', translated by Michele Martin

[49] Martin, p. 58

[50] Nehru's statement in the *Lok Sabha*, 27/4/59, as reproduced in *Tibet Disappears* by Chanakya Sen, p. 165

[51] Avedon, p. 66

[52] Tsering Shakya wrote that 'a highly placed source' had suggested this to him

[53] Shakya, p. 217

54 Paul Raffaele, *The Australian Magazine*, 6/4/02
55 Richard Casey, Australian Minister for External Affairs (1951–60), and Governor General (1965–69)
56 International Commission of Jurists, *The Question of Tibet and the Rule of Law*, 25/7/59
57 Dalai Lama, p. 136
58 Barbara Crossette, 'Buddhist leader, 14, flees Chinese rule in Tibet for India', *The New York Times*, 7/1/00
59 Pamela Constable, 'Young Buddhist leader flees Tibet for India', *The Washington Post*, 8/1/00
60 John Gittings, 'The boy who outwitted a superpower', *The Guardian*, 8/1/00
61 ' "Tired and very restless" Karmapa visits Dalai Lama', *Los Angeles Times*, 9/1/00
62 Martin, p. 112
63 Shakya, p. 267
64 'Boy lama allowed to stay in India', *The Daily Telegraph* (London), 12/1/00
65 *The New York Times*, 11/1/00
66 Arati R. Jerath, 'Fernandes lobbying for Karmapa – Tibetan guru', *The Indian Express*, 18/1/00
67 Arati R. Jerath, 'Fernandes Lobbying for Karmapa – Tibetan Guru', *The Indian Express*, 18/1/00
68 Media statement, 10/1/00
69 TIN translation of the Karmapa's speech at TIPA, 19/2/00
70 Shakya, p. 301
71 Smith, p. 365
72 *The Statesman*, 10/2/02
73 Nalandabodhi, www.nalandabodhi.org, 25/9/00
74 TIN, 29/2/00
75 He Long to the Dalai Lama, Delhi, January 1957, as quoted in *My Land, My People*
76 Shakya, p. 317
77 Shakya, p. 321
78 Melvyn C. Goldstein, and Cynthia M. Beall, *Nomads of Western Tibet, The Survival of a Way of Life*, University of California Press, Berkeley, California, 1990, p. 140

79 Goldstein and Beall, p. 142
80 Goldstein and Beall, p. 144
81 Summary of World Broadcasts (SWB) 1974, No. FE/4691/B11/15
82 SWB, 1974, No. FE/4780/B11/14
83 TIN, 5/1/01
84 *The Week Magazine*, 10/12/00
85 TIN, 5/1/01
86 Shakya, p. 371
87 Smith, p. 562
88 Ngawang Jigme Ngabo, 'Behind the Unrest in Tibet', *China Spring Digest*, Jan/Feb 1998, p. 26
89 Shakya, p. 392
90 Interview with Dekhung Gyaltsey Rinpoche, Sydney, 18/9/03
91 Voice of America, 1/2/00
92 Chinese Foreign Ministry Statement, 2/3/01
93 *Bangkok Post*, 1/2/01
94 *The Scotsman*, 1/2/01
95 *The Hindustan Times*, 6/2/01
96 1999 and 2000 Country Reports on Human Rights Practices released by the Bureau of Democracy, Human Rights and Labor, U.S. Department of State
97 Shakya, p. 431
98 Tashi Tsering, Tibet Journal, Vol IX, No. 3, Autumn 1984
99 Tashi Tsering
100 Kagyu Thubten Chöling, p. 46
101 Clemens Kuby
102 Agence France Presse, 21/2/01
103 Rahul Bedi, 'Tibet's boy lama tells the world of his leap to freedom', *The Daily Telegraph*, 28/4/02
104 Luke Harding, 'Tibetan leader at crossroads', *The Guardian*, 30/4/01
105 Jean West, 'The boy buddha', *The Herald* (Glasgow), 24/7/01
106 Angus McDonald, 'For high-ranking lama who fled to India, "sun of freedom rises"', *Seattle Post-Intelligencer/ Associated Press*, 1/5/01

107 *Time* (Asia), 29/4/02
108 Clemens Kuby
109 The Karmapa's speech is as reported by Jane Perkins, Dharamsala, 17/2/04
110 Jyoti Malhotra, 'Karmapa breaks his silence', *The Indian Express*, 27/2/04
111 *Xinhua*, May 1996
112 'Nomads killed in pasture fights', TIN, 21/6/99
113 Qi Jingfa, China's Vice-Minister for Agriculture, *Xinhua*, March 1998
114 Jiang Zemin, *China Daily*, 18/9/00
115 Li Dezhu, Minister of State Nationality Affairs Commission, quoted in Becquelin, Nicolas, *'Who Benefits? Regional disparities and the campaign to "develop the west"'*, China Rights Forum, No 2, 2002, p. 14
116 Lodi Gyari, media statement, 28/9/02
117 31/5/04, translation by Gonpo Tsering

BIBLIOGRAPHY

Avedon, John F., *In Exile from the Land of Snows*, Alfred A. Knopf, New York, 1984

Barnett, Robert, editor, with Akiner, Shirin, general editor, *Resistance and Reform in Tibet*, Indiana University Press, Bloomington and Indianapolis, 1994

Brown, Mick, *The Dance of 17 Lives: the Incredible True Story of Tibet's 17th Karmapa*, Bloomsbury, London, 2004

Butler, Alex, *Feminism, Nationalism and Exiled Tibetan Women*, kali for women, New Delhi, 2003

Coleman, Graham, editor, with the Orient Foundation, *A Handbook of Tibetan Culture*, Rider Books, London, 1993

Dalai Lama, XIVth, *Freedom in Exile: the Autobiography of His Holiness, the Dalai Lama of Tibet*, a John Curtis Book/ Hodder & Stoughton, London, 1990

Dalai Lama, XIVth, *My Land, My People: the Memoirs of His Holiness, the Dalai Lama of Tibet*, Potala Press, New York, 1962

David-Neel, Alexandra, *Magic and Mystery in Tibet*, Penguin, London, 1971

Douglas, Nick and White, Meryl, *Karmapa: the Black Hat Lama of Tibet*, Luzac & Company Ltd, London, 1976

Evans-Wetz, W. Y., *Tibet's Great Yogi: Milarepa*, Oxford, 1951

French, Patrick, *Tibet, Tibet: a Personal History of a Lost Land*, HarperCollins, London, 2003

Goldstein, Melvyn C. and Beall (photographs and text), Cynthia M., *Nomads of Western Tibet, the Survival of a Way of Life*, University of California Press, Berkeley, California, 1990

Hilton, Isabel, *The Search for the Panchen Lama*, Viking, London, 1999

Holmes, Ken, *His Holiness the 17th Gyalwa Karmapa, Urgyen Trinley Dorje*, Altea Publishing, Forres, 1995

International Commission of Jurists, *The Question of Tibet and the Rule of Law*, ICJ, Geneva, 1959

Jamgon Kongtrul Labrang, *EMA HO!, The Reincarnation of The Third Jamgon Kongtrul*, Pullahari, Nepal, 1998

Karko, Kate, *Namma: a Tibetan Love Story*, Sceptre, London, 2001

Kewley, Vanya, *Tibet: Behind the Ice Curtain*, Grafton Books, London, 1990

Kuby, Clemens, *Living Buddha*, Mind Films, 1996

Maheshwari, Anil, *The Buddha Cries! Karmapa Conundrum*, UBS Publishers' Distributors Ltd, New Delhi, 2000

Maraini, Fosco, *Secret Tibet*, The Harvill Press, London, 2000

Martin, Michele, *Music in the Sky: The Life, Art and Teachings of the 17th Karmapa*, Snow Lion Publications, Ithaca, 2003

Matthiessen, Peter, *The Snow Leopard*, Chatto & Windus Ltd, London, 1979

Norbu, Thupten Jigme (Takster Rinpoche), *Tibet is My Country*, Wisdom Publications, London 1986

Sen, Chanakya, *Tibet Disappears*, Asia Publishing House, New Delhi, 1960

Shakya, Tsering, *The Dragon in the Land of Snows: a History of Modern Tibet Since 1947*, Pimlico, London, 1999

Smith, Warren W. Jr., *Tibetan Nation: a History of Tibetan Nationalism and Sino-Tibetan Relations*, Westview Press, Boulder Colorado/HarperCollins Publishers India Pvt Ltd, New Delhi, 1997

Thinley, Karma, *The History of the Sixteen Karmapas of Tibet*, Prajna Press, Boulder, 1980

Thurman, Robert A. F., *Essential Tibetan Buddhism*, HarperSanFrancisco, 1996

Trungpa, Chögyam, *Born in Tibet*, George Allen & Unwin, London, 1966

Zangmo, Ani Karma Dechen, *Karmapa Khenno, A Sikkimese point of view*, 1994, Gangtok, Sikkim

ACKNOWLEDGMENTS

From the moment I first imagined writing a book on the Karmapa, Paul Bourke of the Australia Tibet Council has been a source of invaluable advice, information and encouragement. Kate Saunders has also assisted me generously from the outset and I am deeply grateful to both of them for their involvement. Others who have made a significant contribution to this book include Peter Gilmore, who answered scores of questions for me and opened his comprehensive Tibet library to me, and Tenzin Phuntsok Atisha of the Tibet Information Office, Canberra, for his advice and support. My thanks for their wisdom and insights also go to Alex Butler, Richard Boele, Sophie Cunningham, Dorji Dolma, Heike Fabig, Joyce Kornblatt and Sonam Ongmu.

From the Karmapa's retinue, I'd like to thank Lama Phuntsok and Gonpo Tsering. I am grateful to the efficient, friendly staff of the Tibetan government-in-exile's Department of Information and International Relations. Also in India, my thanks go to Jane Perkins, Monica Joyce, Geshe Palden Chodrak, Tashi Wangdi, Tai Situ Rinpoche, Tashi Tsering, Jamyang Dorjee, Dekhung Gyaltsey Rinpoche, Kalon Tripa Samdhong Rinpoche and, in particular, Deepak Thakur. Very heartfelt thanks go to the generous staff of the Norbulingka Insitute, who provided me with a writer's sanctuary and home away from home in the Himalayan foothills.

Thanks to Jane Palfreyman and Tony Peake, who believed in this book from the very outset, almost before I did myself. I am particularly grateful to Jo Butler for her rigorous editing and kind reassurances.

Finally, thank you to my support team: to Jane Gleeson-White and Katherine Bright-Holmes for always saying the right thing at the right time; to Ros Burrows for the wonderful care she gives Isla; to Jackie Naher for her unwavering faith in me; and to Paul Watchman, who stood by me through all this and, in particular, for his devoted fathering to our daughter during my two trips to India.

My final thanks go to His Holiness, the XVIIth Karmapa,

and to his sister Ngodup Palzom, for sharing their precious family stories with me.

The author and publisher wish to thank the following people and organisations for their assistance in allowing copyright material to be reproduced in the book: Isabel Hilton for her material from her article 'Mishandling lamas' from *The Guardian*; the Office of the XVIIth Karmapa for the use of part of the XVIth Karmapa's prediction letter and the poem 'I will not stay . . .'; Kate Saunders for material from her article 'A God in Exile' from the *Sunday Times Magazine*; the Tibet Information Network for the articles 'Karmapa leaves Tibet', 'Speech of the 17th Karmapa' and 'Anniversary of Karmapa's escape'; Michele Martin for the use of her translation from *Music in the Sky: The Life, Art & Teachings of the 17th Karmapa Ogyen Trinley Dorje*, Snow Lion Publications, 2003, www.snowlionpub.com; the Random House Group Limited for their permission to use the extract from *The Snow Leopard* by Peter Matthiessen, published by Chatto & Windus; *The Herald* (Glasgow, Scotland) for the use of Jean West's article 'The boy Buddha' © Newsquest Media Group; the Norbulingka Institute (www.norbulingka.org) for the use of the Tibetan images of animals throughout *Wrestling the Dragon*; Rokpa Trust/Samye Ling Monastery for the use of the Golden Rosary paintings used as section openers throughout *Wrestling the Dragon*; Jamgon Kongtrul Labrang for the use of the prediction letter as published in *EMA HO!, The Reincarnation of the Third Jamgon Kongtrul*, Pullahari, Nepal, 1998; Christopher Kremmer for material from his article 'Free spirited' from *The Sydney Morning Herald*; Barbara Crossette for material from her article 'Buddhist leader, 14, flees Chinese rule in Tibet for India' from *The New York Times*.